THE COMPLETE IDIOT'S GUIDE® TO

Solar Power for Your Home

by Dan Ramsey

ALPHA

A member of Penguin Group (USA) Inc.

This effort is dedicated to the Source of the sun and everything under it.

ALPHA BOOKS

Published by the Penguin Group

Penguin Group (USA) Inc., 375 Hudson Street, New York, New York 10014, U.S.A.

Penguin Group (Canada), 10 Alcorn Avenue, Toronto, Ontario, Canada M4V 3B2 (a division of Pearson Penguin Canada Inc.)

Penguin Books Ltd, 80 Strand, London WC2R 0RL, England

Penguin Ireland, 25 St Stephen's Green, Dublin 2, Ireland (a division of Penguin Books Ltd)

Penguin Group (Australia), 250 Camberwell Road, Camberwell, Victoria 3124, Australia (a division of Pearson Australia Group Pty Ltd)

Penguin Books India Pvt Ltd, 11 Community Centre, Panchsheel Park, New Delhi—110 017, India

Penguin Group (NZ), cnr Airborne and Rosedale Roads, Albany, Auckland 1310, New Zealand (a division of Pearson New Zealand Ltd)

Penguin Books (South Africa) (Pty) Ltd, 24 Sturdee Avenue, Rosebank, Johannesburg 2196, South Africa

Penguin Books Ltd, Registered Offices: 80 Strand, London WC2R 0RL, England

Copyright © 2003 by Dan Ramsey

International Standard Book Number: 0-02-864393-3
Library of Congress Catalog Card Number: 2002108500

07   06   10 9 8

Interpretation of the printing code: The rightmost number of the first series of numbers is the year of the book's printing; the rightmost number of the second series of numbers is the number of the book's printing. For example, a printing code of 03-1 shows that the first printing occurred in 2003.

Printed in the United States of America

Note: This publication contains the opinions and ideas of its author. It is intended to provide helpful and informative material on the subject matter covered. It is sold with the understanding that the author and publisher are not engaged in rendering professional services in the book. If the reader requires personal assistance or advice, a competent professional should be consulted.

The author and publisher specifically disclaim any responsibility for any liability, loss, or risk, personal or otherwise, which is incurred as a consequence, directly or indirectly, of the use and application of any of the contents of this book.

Most Alpha books are available at special quantity discounts for bulk purchases for sales promotions, premiums, fund-raising, or educational use. Special books, or book excerpts, can also be created to fit specific needs.

For details, write: Special Markets, Alpha Books, 375 Hudson Street, New York, NY 10014.

Publisher: *Marie Butler-Knight*
Product Manager: *Phil Kitchel*
Managing Editor: *Jennifer Chisholm*
Acquisitions Editor: *Mike Sanders*
Development Editor: *Lynn Northrup*
Production Editor: *Katherin Bidwell*
Copy Editor: *Susan Aufheimer*
Illustrator: *Chris Eliopoulos*
Cover/Book Designer: *Trina Wurst*
Indexer: *Heather McNeill*
Layout/Proofreading: *Megan Douglass, Becky Harmon*

Contents at a Glance

Contents

Foreword

Over the last two years, an energy meltdown has occurred in the western United States. On the heels of California's ill-conceived deregulation scheme, out-of-state utilities have cashed in on an energy scarcity opportunity, increasing prices for electricity and natural gas as much as sixfold. When electricity prices climb, the whole world wants to go solar. The era of oil and fossil fuels is coming to an end as we move through the early days of the third millennium. We sit on the cusp. Behind us (we hope) is the wanton devastation and destruction of natural habitat, while before us is the bountiful opportunity for a fruitful and fulfilling future. The world needs to come to its senses and eliminate its dependence upon fossil fuels.

The U.S. Congress' own Office of Technology Assessment estimates that all known oil reserves will have been depleted by 2037. Solar energy is the missing piece of the equation. Solar provides maximum power just when it's needed—in the middle of the summer afternoon, when air conditioning loads are heaviest and the huge bottleneck occurs in transmission lines. Prices keep declining. With the price of solar now approaching $3 to $4 per watt (after a 50 percent state rebate) on installed photovoltaics (solar electric modules), the payback period is only 5 to 10 years. That's a 10 to 20 percent return on investment—better than stocks, bonds, and long-term CDs, and you'll never have to pay another utility bill!

All around the world, there are signs that the stage is set for positive change. While the use of coal, oil, and nuclear power during the 1990s expanded by only slightly more than 1 percent each, annually, the use of photovoltaics has grown by 17 percent annually and wind-generated electricity by 26 percent.

Demystifying solar energy to the mainstream has always been a challenge since we opened the first Real Goods store in Willits, California, in 1978 and sold the first solar panel at retail in the country. In *The Complete Idiot's Guide to Solar Power for Your Home*, Dan Ramsey has triumphed in bringing photovoltaics down to earth and making solar power accessible to the average homeowner. This is a quick, easy, and compelling page-turner about everything you need to know from buying or building your solar home, to financing, retrofitting, installing, and maintaining your renewable energy system. Dan doesn't stop at solar electricity, but delves into solar water heating, space heating, wind and water power, and even solar landscaping. The book contains a wealth of information both for the do-it-yourselfer and for the plug-and-play homeowner who wants to hire a contractor to solarize his or her home. A complete novice will not feel technically overwhelmed, but inspired by the simplicity of the technology. The complete resource list at the back of the book alone is worth the price of admission.

Solar power is no longer the "pipe dream of environmentalists," as much as the utility companies would like to have us believe it. While there are still two billion people in the world without access to electricity (and another billion who have it less than 10 hours per day), there are now 500,000 homes worldwide (mostly in Third World villages) powered by photovoltaics. They know something the utilities don't—that power from the sun is the best power you can get. In this book Dan shows how it's accessible to all of us.

For those who aren't complacent with powering their own homes with solar, there is clearly a greater good to our yearnings for this new technology. Our species can't survive the continued loss of biodiversity, the decimation of forests, the shrinking of ocean fisheries, and the fouling of our atmosphere brought upon us by the "age of oil." We simply have to make things right. It is not too late to build a society that is environmentally sustainable; where water is safe to drink, air is safe to breathe, and communities, even countries, share resources equitably. Let us work toward a future where our great-grandchildren can look back and say, "Thank goodness they finally came to their senses …"

For the Earth,

John Schaeffer

Founder and President, Real Goods

Introduction

Houston, we have a problem!

We're running out of oil! The petroleum that fuels our daily lives is getting harder to find. And turning fossils into electricity is hazardous to our health.

Fortunately, we're not running out of options. We can cut back on the energy we use. And we can turn to the energy sources that have been there all along: the sun, wind, and water.

So why didn't we make this decision years ago? Economics. Fossils fueled the industrial age. We became dependent on cheap, available oil to keep things moving toward a brighter future. Well, the future is here—and the easy fuels are nearly depleted. Maybe soon, maybe *very* soon. Prices are going to shoot up, and there's going to be a mad scramble for the equipment that uses the sun and other renewable sources.

So what can you, a homeowner or renter, do *right now* to reduce the world's dependency on petroleum fuels? You can read this book!

No, I'm not a "tree hugger." I don't believe that the ecology equation excludes mankind's needs. I also don't believe ecology has been given a fair shake in our greed for more stuff. Moderation is the key to life. Give and take. Unfortunately, we've been blindly taking, and it's time to *at least* cut back.

That's what *The Complete Idiot's Guide to Solar Power for Your Home* is about: considering solar and other renewable energy resources to power our lives. It's also about becoming aware of the energy problem and finding some easy-to-implement solutions *right now*.

If you're like most folks, you don't know much about the sun except that you're not supposed to stare directly at it. Well, it's Earth's primary energy source and we're using it to grow food and do other things, but we're not giving it a fair chance to power our homes and lives. So this book is written to give you first an overview, then more and more specifics on how to put the sun to work for you.

You may have heard that solar power is expensive. Well, compared to here-today-gone-tomorrow fossil fuel, it is. However, solar technology has really brought prices down over the past few years. And governments have stepped up to offer rebates and incentives that make solar power much more economical. In fact, today's systems can pay back costs in just a few years—then furnish nearly free power for many more. Think of the investment as prepaid utility bills. There's even some great financing available for solar power systems.

These are the things you'll learn about as you read this book. It's your first investment in the solution. Even if you choose not to install a complete solar electric generation system in your home, this book will still be an excellent investment in knowing how to reduce oil dependency by cutting your energy costs. It shows you how you can save hundreds of dollars each year in energy bills.

How to Use This Book

The Complete Idiot's Guide to Solar Power for Your Home contains 26 chapters and two information-packed appendixes. Here's how it's laid out:

Part 1, "Saving Your Energy," shows you how to start right now saving energy costs. And it tells you about the technology, rebates, and financing available to those who go solar. You'll also get an overview of solar power installation in your existing home or a new one. You'll learn about design issues that can dramatically cut heating and cooling costs without a solar power system.

Part 2, "Solar Power," takes curious minds into the proven world of solar and other power resources. You'll learn how solar power is generated with photovoltaic (PV) cells and modules. And you'll find out how to store and distribute power. You'll also discover the most efficient application of solar energy: making hot water. You'll also learn about heating your home with passive solar energy. Need some more options? This part gives a glimpse at future power resources including fuel cells.

Part 3, "Solar Systems," is for plug-and-play folks. It covers the various types of solar power systems available today. These systems include all the components you need to go solar within days. You'll find complete systems to power your entire house, smaller systems to handle part but not all of the load, emergency systems for backup power, and even portable systems for travelers.

Part 4, "Getting It Done," guides you through buying, installing, and maintaining a solar power system—whether you'll build and install it yourself or hire a contractor to do some or all of it. Lots of specific information here.

Part 5, "Buying and Selling," takes you beyond installing and enjoying your solar power system. It shows you how to buy a solar home, what to look for, and what to ask. And someday you may sell your own solar home, so there's a chapter on getting top dollar by showing others the cost and ecological benefits. A full chapter explores the latest idea for solar power, selling your excess back to the local utility. Yes, you can do that—and make some money at it! The final chapter offers dozens of ideas on how you can take solar power and energy efficiency into other parts of your life.

You'll also find two comprehensive appendixes at the end of this book. A Solar Glossary clearly defines all those words and terms you may come across as you consider and shop for solar power. The Solar Resources appendix is your one stop for all the resources you'll need, including federal, state, and local government resources; solar equipment dealers and suppliers; energy-efficiency contractors; catalogs and magazines; and more.

Yes, there is a structure to this book. However, don't let it get in the way of enjoying the learning process. If you're curious about how PV cells work, turn to Chapter 9 right now. If you're interested in how you can use net metering to earn extra money from your system, step up to Chapter 25. If you think wind and water technology may be a good option, check out Chapter 12 first. This book is written for both front-to-back readers and browsers. Enjoy!

Extras

Throughout this book additional guides clarify new terms, offer additional information, or caution you about potential problems. They look like this:

Sun-Day School

These boxes offer clear definitions of words or terms used in selecting, installing, and using solar power equipment as well as in making your home more energy efficient.

Solar Eclipse

These cautions keep you from spending too much money or spending time in the hospital. Follow their advice so you can enjoy solar power.

Bright Idea

Check these boxes for hot tips that will save you time, money, and effort.

Sun Spots

These boxes give you some background on getting the most from your solar power system

Acknowledgments

It's amazing how many solar experts there are under the sun. I tapped into many of them while researching and writing this book for you. Here are the names of those who contributed their time and knowledge toward making this book informative and accurate. Thank you one and all!

First, a special thanks to my insider at the U.S. Dept. of Energy whose knowledge and patience I frequently tested: Paul Hesse. Paul is an excellent resource for all things solar. He's also a credit to the DOE and the government's attempt to inform us about energy options. Great job, Paul!

Thanks also to my insider at Gaiam Real Goods, Doug Pratt, a.k.a. Dr. Doug. He knows the solar industry, what's available, and where to get it. A great resource. He also served as one of this book's two technical advisors, reading to make sure that the info I give you is accurate. Thanks, Dr. Doug!

My other insider is Greg Dunbar. Greg is a licensed general contractor with lots of construction experience. Greg lives off-grid, away from utility lines, generating his own electricity. Greg knows … and fortunately, Greg shares! (Greg was also my technical reviewer for *The Complete Idiot's Guide to Building Your Own Home*; Alpha Books, 2002.)

Thanks to Kyra Epstein and Susan Bilo of the Million Solar Roofs Initiative for resources and updates on their program.

Many others contributed to this book as well. They are included in Appendix B. They contributed time and information toward making this book both informative and friendly. Thank you one and all.

Editorially, thanks to Mike Sanders at Alpha Books whose vision started the process. My appreciation also goes to Lynn Northrup, Susan Aufheimer, and Kathy Bidwell, whose sharpened pencils and pointed questions enhanced the value of this book. Thanks, too, to my agent, Sheree Bykofsky, and her staff. And thanks to Judy who, for 31 years, has been my editor and friend.

Special Thanks to the Technical Reviewer

The Complete Idiot's Guide to Solar Power for Your Home was reviewed by experts who double-checked the accuracy of what you'll learn here, to help us ensure that this book gives you everything you need to know about using solar power. Special thanks are extended to Greg Dunbar and Doug Pratt.

Greg has more than 20 years of construction and remodeling experience as a general contractor and subcontractor. Doug is senior technical writer for Gaiam Real Goods, a major resource for solar power and other renewable resource equipment.

Trademarks

All terms mentioned in this book that are known to be or are suspected of being trademarks or service marks have been appropriately capitalized. Alpha Books and Penguin Group (USA) Inc. cannot attest to the accuracy of this information. Use of a term in this book should not be regarded as affecting the validity of any trademark or service mark.

Part 1

Saving Your Energy

Puff. Puff. We're running out of energy!

Maybe not today, nor tomorrow, but soon the headlines will again read "Energy Crisis!" And maybe this will be the Big One. Maybe it will *really* happen and we'll need a cosigner to pay home utility bills. Or maybe we'll just float along for awhile, enjoying relatively cheap power. It could happen.

If so, what does "nonrenewable" energy source really mean? We know that it means that one of these days we're going to run out of cheap energy.

The solution is the sun. By figuring out what's really happening in the energy world—and energy technology—you can make some informed choices that will make everyone's life a little better. As we get older, we learn that nonrenewable energy doesn't last forever. It's time to take a closer look at our energy diet!

Chapter 1

Looking into the Sun

In This Chapter

◆ What's all the fuss about energy?

◆ Investigating our renewable energy sources

◆ How and why solar energy works

◆ How technology and attitudes are changing in favor of solar power

Life is good. Electricity keeps our food cold, warms it up, washes the dishes, and entertains us while we eat. It also runs our computer, washer, lights, and garage-door opener.

Then the electric bill comes. We pay it because it's a bargain! All this neat stuff working for us for just a few bucks a day. We wouldn't consider totally doing without the comforts, helpers, and gadgets that electricity powers in our lives. Nobody's ready to pull the plug.

But we all know in the back of our minds that the monthly electric bill isn't all we're paying. There's another bill—an energy-use bill that we pay every day in the form of spent resources that we can't get back, smog and health problems, taxes for energy regulations, and other concerns. These costs total into the billions of dollars. We get the *other* bill in increased health costs, higher consumer costs, and higher taxes. Unfortunately, some` of our long-term bills will be delivered to our children and their children. We don't know what the *total* bill will be.

So what can we do? We can look to alternative energy sources, especially those like the sun, that minimize long-term bills. Maybe we can't change the whole world, but we can change our little piece of it. We can consider solar power for our homes.

Finding the Energy

We've always needed *energy* to live. Energy has grown our food, baked our bread, and powered our bodies for thousands of years. It's always been that way, and it will probably always be so.

Lately, however, technology (applied science) has put increased demands on us to find additional sources of energy that can be put to work for us. We need *power* to light our homes, run our computers, move aircraft, turn wheels, and put satellites in orbit. We depend on power every day as we monitor hospital patients, watch television, refrigerate food, send e-mail, fight wars, and build structures. Technology can be good.

Unfortunately, technology requires lots of power. For the past century or so, we've been getting this power from fossil fuel, a limited resource. Even the experts don't know if we'll discover enough fossil fuels to keep us going at this pace for another 20 or another 200 years. We *do* know that eventually we will run out of this finite source of energy. And even if we had an unlimited supply of fossil fuels, using solar and other renewable energies is easier on our environment.

Sun-Day School

Energy is the ability to do work. **Power** is energy at work.

So, should we cut back on technology and all its benefits? Certainly we can trim down on our energy requirements (as I'll discuss in Chapter 2). We can weigh the costs and benefits to strike a balance. We can also use our noggins to find and use energy sources that don't have hidden costs nor steal from our children's future. We can use renewable energy sources.

Using Renewable Energy Sources

Renewable energy uses energy sources that are continually replenished by nature—the sun, wind, water, thermal heat, and plants. They've been here since the world began. Long before us.

Renewable energy technologies turn these fuels into usable forms of energy—electricity, heat, mechanical power, and chemicals. Let's take a closer look at our options.

Solar Energy

The sun, our star, has been around a long time. And, chances are, it will be around a lot longer. We're counting on it. Daily, we count on the sun to provide energy to us in the forms of light and heat. We've been doing so since mankind first breathed life. In fact, many civilizations through the ages have believed that the sun is the source of all life on Earth.

In the past 100 years, technology has been seeking a way to turn the sun's energy into electric power. We'll cover solar energy in the next section and throughout this book, so let's take a quick look at other renewable energy sources.

Sun Spots
Businesses can use solar energy, too. For example, the Rosebud Agency is a music artist management agency that represents soul, r&b, and gospel groups such as Booker T. and the MGs. Their San Francisco offices are 100 percent solar, a first in the music industry. In fact, Rosebud sells excess power to the local utility for distribution to other customers. In addition, the president drives a gas/electric hybrid car to work—on days he can't bicycle. Learn more at www.RosebudUS.com.

Wind Energy

The wind has been around forever as well, harnessed to move sailing ships and to pump water with windmills for hundreds of years. Today, wind turbines produce electricity in California, Texas, and many Great Plains states. Hawaii has them, too. Canada and Europe also use wind turbines.

Smaller turbines can produce 50 kilowatts of power; larger turbines can turn the wind energy into 1 to 2 megawatts of power. (A kilowatt [kW] is 1,000 watts of electrical power; a megawatt [MW] is 1,000 kilowatts of electrical power.) Large utility-scale projects with hundreds of turbines spread over acres are called wind farms. Though technology continually improves the efficiency of wind turbines, only about one eighth of 1 percent of all electricity generated in the United States comes from the wind, although this percentage is rising rapidly now. (We'll explore this in detail in Chapter 12.)

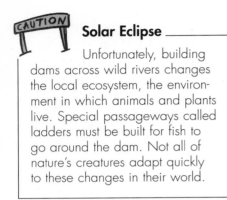

Solar Eclipse

Unfortunately, building dams across wild rivers changes the local ecosystem, the environment in which animals and plants live. Special passageways called ladders must be built for fish to go around the dam. Not all of nature's creatures adapt quickly to these changes in their world.

Hydro Energy

Less than 10 percent of U.S. energy needs are filled by hydro energy, mostly in western states. Large hydroelectric dams on the Columbia and Snake Rivers of the Pacific Northwest, and the Colorado River in the Southwest use the power of moving water. Water motion rotates turbines that generate the electricity.

Because energy is released without using up the water, hydro energy is a renewable resource. As long as clouds pick up water and deposit it at higher elevations to flow downhill, hydro energy will be an important source of electric power.

Bio Energy

Bio means "life," so bio energy is energy released from recently living things. It can be methane gas from decaying biomass at landfills, or biofuels such as ethanol alcohol made from corn and other plants. Home fireplaces burn wood (although not very efficiently), a renewable source of bio energy. Wood by-products are used to meet some industrial energy needs.

Bio energy is primarily used to replace or supplement other fuels because power from fossil fuel is cheaper. For example, ethanol is added to gasoline to reduce total emissions. Biomass is used with coal to lower emissions at coal power plants. These renewable energy sources will not soon replace coal and gasoline, but biomass and biofuels produce only about 1.6 percent of U.S. electrical energy.

Geothermal Energy

The center of Earth is cooking at 9,000° Fahrenheit. That's a lot of energy! Fortunately for us, some of that energy escapes to the surface in the form of steam and hot water that can be harnessed to produce electric power. Geothermal power plants need water of only 225° to 360° to produce electrical power.

You either live near a source of geothermal energy or you don't. All geothermal power plants in the United States are located in the western states of California, Nevada, Utah, and Hawaii. Together they produce *less than* one half of 1 percent of the electricity generated in the United States. Not much, but it all helps.

Other Energy Sources

Add them all up and you'll discover that the total energy produced in the United States using renewable resources is just 11.5 percent of the total—less than one eighth! But what about other energy sources? Nuclear power, on the downturn because of long-term environmental issues, produces 18.5 percent of our electricity. Petroleum and natural gas make another 18.2 percent. The subtotal is still less than half.

The majority of U.S. electric generation—51.9 percent—uses coal! In the process, fossil-fueled electric power plants released about 2.5 billion tons of carbon dioxide, 14 million tons of sulfur dioxide, 8.5 million tons of nitrous oxides, and a bunch of other stuff that isn't good for us.

We should also talk about the other uses we have of nonrenewable energy. Cars and trucks burn up a lot of gasoline and diesel fuels. In fact, we use about twice as much fossil fuels to run our cars than we do to power our homes. The result is that our energy resources can't keep up with demand and the U.S. market now imports more than half of its fossil fuel needs. Thirty years ago, we relied on importing a third of fossil fuels. Within 20 years, we'll need to import nearly two thirds. As a comparison, a hundred years ago the United States relied almost entirely on homegrown renewable energy resources.

So why should we consider renewable energy sources such as the sun? There are several compelling reasons:

- Fossil fuels are finite; the sun's energy is infinite.

- The sun offers many times more energy than we can ever use. At noon on a clear day at sea level, the sun delivers an average of 1,000 watts (1 kW) of energy per square meter!

- Costs of renewable energy will go down as more people use it.

- Solar energy doesn't pollute our environment (although the manufacturing of solar power equipment does slightly).

- Solar thermal energy can take care of our water and heating needs.

- Using solar energy will eliminate fuel imports and the associated economic and political problems.

Here Comes the Sun!

Think of the sun as the ultimate energy source. It's nuclear, but at a nice safe 93 million miles away. Plants and animals that eventually became fossil fuels were once nourished by the sun. The sun's heat powers Earth's winds and the clouds that transport water.

The first users of residential solar heating on this continent were the ancient Native Americans, who built homes in rock cliffs that faced south to collect and store solar thermal energy. During the 1980s, the federal government spent millions of dollars building houses with all-electric heating and air conditioning for the Navajo and Hopi in the Southwest. When the humongous electric bills came, many native Americans moved into ancestral cliff houses because they were more efficient at less cost. Eventually, the government and industry built the world's largest residential solar power system and residents moved back.

Solar energy works. Open the door of a car that's been sitting in the hot sun, and you will feel solar thermal energy. Or take a drink from a hose that's been laying in the sun.

The good news is that the lucky old sun with nothing to do but roll 'round heaven all day can satisfy Earth's energy needs many times over without depleting itself. The bad news is that solar energy today is used to produce just two tenths of 1 percent of our electricity. That's not very much!

The problem is not the availability of the sun. It's always there, of course, even when it's seemingly behind the clouds. The problem is that solar electricity is, in the short term, more expensive than other electricity. It's easier and cheaper to simply pay for the electricity conveniently delivered to you. Where does it come from? How did it get here? What are the longer term costs to our world? These are questions worth considering.

The sun radiates energy. If it were any closer than about 93 million miles, we would be cooked. If it were farther, we would freeze to death. About 10 percent of that radiated energy arrives at Earth in the form of sunlight. Fortunately, that's the form we need most here on Earth.

Sun Spots
How does a lighthouse get its light? At one time, whale oil was used as fuel, then fossil fuel, and eventually electricity. Until recently, the offshore lighthouse in New London, Connecticut, was served by a 6,000-foot underwater cable from a land utility pole. The Coast Guard recently replaced it with solar panels at a total cost of about $50,000, including removing the old equipment. The new system saves $15,000 a year in energy and maintenance costs, so it will soon be delivering free electricity to the important lighthouse.

How much sunlight a point on Earth receives depends on when it is, where it is, and what's in between. Any given point on Earth is slightly farther away from the sun during winter months and closer during summer months. Places closer to the equator get more sun than those farther north or farther south. Finally, clouds, smoke, and pollutants diffuse or reduce the solar radiation hitting a point on Earth.

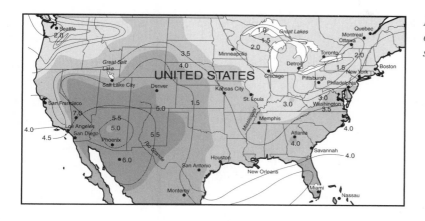

Map of the average number of hours each day the sun shines in the United States.

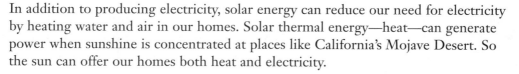

Map of the average number of hours each day the sun shines in Canada.

In addition to producing electricity, solar energy can reduce our need for electricity by heating water and air in our homes. Solar thermal energy—heat—can generate power when sunshine is concentrated at places like California's Mojave Desert. So the sun can offer our homes both heat and electricity.

Here are some ways we can use the sun's energy in our homes:

- ◆ Light rooms with sunlight
- ◆ Preheat water for showers, baths, and laundry
- ◆ Preheat air to maintain comfortable room temperatures
- ◆ Provide electricity to power appliances and tools

How can sunshine become electricity? I'll cover the "how" in detail in Chapter 9. But in a nutshell, modules or groups of silicon solar (called photovoltaic or PV) cells collect sunlight and convert it into electricity. The PV modules can be mounted on or near your home. In addition, solar energy can be used to warm air and water without the middleman, electricity. Fortunately, solar power systems are becoming increasingly efficient and cost-effective so that even renters can afford portable systems. The PV modules also last a long time. Many early units are still working after 30 years. A lifespan in excess of 20 years of constant use is expected and most modules are warranted for 10 to 25 years.

How sunlight can be used to make electricity.

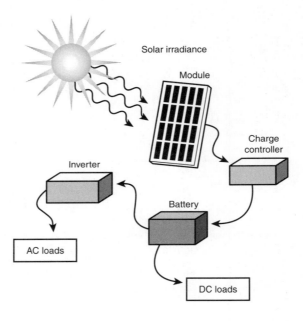

In addition, solar radiation can be collected and used to heat water using flat-plate panels mounted facing south on your home's roof. I'll give you the specifics in Chapter 10.

You can also design or redesign your home to have sunrooms and other air spaces that collect and distribute *passive* solar energy, thus cutting your power bill.

Sun-Day School

Solar energy is **passive,** delivered to your doorstep without a truck or power line. If it needs machinery, such as PV modules or pumps, in order to work in your home, it is active solar power.

Changing Technologies and Attitudes

Technology is making solar electricity less expensive each year. At the same time, those who have been pleading with us to consider solar energy are being heard. The federal and many state governments both use and encourage solar energy. Many push industry to share solar technology and lower equipment costs. Others offer rebates and tax incentives for investment in solar electric systems. And some have even required utility companies to buy electricity from users who have excess!

The purpose of this book is to inform you about the solar solution, your options, the economics, and the importance of solar power. Chapter 2 will guide you in figuring out how much power your home needs and uses. In future chapters you'll learn how to select, buy, and finance solar power for your home.

Meantime, don't stare at the sun!

The Least You Need to Know

- ◆ The sun provides free energy to Earth that can be used to power our lives.
- ◆ Nonrenewable fuels currently provide most of our electric and engine power—and nearly all of our pollutants.
- ◆ Homeowners and even renters can reduce energy costs with solar power.
- ◆ Solar power is becoming a cost-effective investment through applied technology.

Estimating Energy Needs

In This Chapter

◆ From amps to watts: understanding home energy

◆ Figuring your home energy consumption

◆ Calculating energy costs

◆ You *can* go solar!

Home energy sources include electricity (produced from oil, gas, coal, biomass, solar, wind, and others) as well as heating fuel. The average U.S. home pays about $1,300 a year in energy costs. That's more than a hundred bucks a month. In some parts of the country, winter bills for heating alone can be many hundreds of dollars. In other areas, summer air conditioning costs can match that. In colder climates, the monthly heating bill can be bigger than the mortgage. And some lucky folks live in moderate climates where heating and cooling demands are lower.

Where does it go? Those experts at the Department of Energy say that about 44 percent is used for heating and cooling; 33 percent for lighting, cooking, and appliances; about 14 percent for water heating; and the final 9 percent for refrigeration.

What's Home Energy?

Just like people, homes use energy in everyday tasks. People-energy is typically measured in calories consumed. A calorie is a measurement of heat energy. Homes count BTU (pronounced *bee-tee-you*), a British thermal unit, as a measurement of heat energy. One BTU equals 252 calories and will raise a pound of water 1° Fahrenheit. A barrel of fuel oil (42 U.S. gallons) offers 140,000 BTU of energy. To produce one million BTU of heat energy you'd need about 80 pounds of coal, 250 pounds of hardwood, 11 gallons of propane, 7 gallons of #2 fuel oil, or 293 kilowatt hours of electricity.

Those BTU can be used to develop heat for the house's air or to develop electricity to run appliances. And the appliances really don't care if the power originally came from oil, gas, sunlight, wind, or Uncle Bob on a treadmill.

Let's talk about electricity for a moment. Electricity is the flow of electrons through a wire similar to how water flows through a pipe. (This isn't exactly how it happens, but it's close enough for illustration purposes.)

To get water moving through a pipe, you open up a faucet where the water is under pressure to push it down the pipe to where there is less pressure. Electricity flows in the same manner. The difference in pressure between one prong on the electric plug and the other makes the electricity flow down one wire and to the electric appliance. That difference in pressure is measured in *volts*. The amount of electricity that actually flows is the current measured in *amperes* or *amps*. The resistance to flow that the wire (like the pipe) offers is measured in *ohms*.

Homes in the United States and Canada are wired for appliances that need voltage of 110V or 220V. The actual voltage delivered can fluctuate by about 10 percent (100V to 120V) and still cause no problems. Most appliances in the home are designed to use 110V of electricity. Things like electric clothes dryers, electric stoves and ovens, and some big shop tools need 220V to run.

Sun-Day School

A **volt** (V) is a unit of measure of the force given the electrons in an electric circuit. An **ampere** or **amp** (A) is a unit of measure of the flow of electrons. An **ohm** is a unit of measure of the resistance to the flow of an electric current. One volt produces one ampere of current against a resistance of one ohm.

Actually, the work is done by the electrical current, which is the flow of electrons in a wire, similar to the flow of water in a stream. (Power used by most home appliances is alternating current or AC. Solar power is direct current or DC. Batteries, too, use DC.) Current needed to run an alarm clock will be less than an amp, probably measured in milliamps (mA) or thousandths of an ampere. A refrigerator will need a few amps. A toaster, surprisingly, will need even more amps of current than a refrigerator. That's because the toaster runs current through high-resistance wire to develop heat that toasts your bagels.

Of course, the toaster may be in use for only a few minutes each day, the refrigerator compressor is on for a few hours, and the TV seemingly always. So what's a better way to measure an appliance's power needs than reading the amps?

Electric power is measured in watts. As you learned in Chapter 1, a kilowatt (kW) is a thousand watts of electrical power. A watt-hour (Wh) is a unit measure of energy, one watt of power over one hour of time. Power used over time is measured in kilowatt-hours (kWh), or one thousand watts used over one hour. Your electric power company charges you by the kilowatt-hour, so it will be an important measurement as you consider solar power.

Here's the formula: $V \times A = W$. That is, volts multiplied by amps equals watts. Power is the force times the flow. The amount of power used over a given time is the power in watts or kilowatts multiplied by the time in hours.

One more term: Load. A load is anything in an electrical circuit that, when the circuit is turned on, draws power from that circuit. A refrigerator is a load. A toaster, when toasting, is a load. A light, when switched on, is a load. So figuring out how much energy your home needs starts with totaling up all the loads as measured in watt-hours. That's called a load evaluation (an example form is shown in the following figure).

How does electricity get to you? Somewhere, there's an electrical power generating plant. It converts fuel, probably coal or oil, into electricity using turbines. High voltage power lines then distribute the power to stations, then substations, and then to transformers that deliver the electricity to your home as 220V.

So how do you get 110V electric service out of this? The power comes in on three wires; two have 110V each and the other is neutral. The main power panel in your house is wired to provide voltage between the neutral wire (ground) and one (110V) or both (220V) hot wires. The power panel then distributes the power to specific circuits wired when your home was built. The circuits might be wired for loads of 15A, 20A, 30A, or some other value. To protect the appliance(s), the electricity first goes through a circuit breaker that stops electricity flow if it exceeds the rating.

> **CAUTION**
>
> **Solar Eclipse**
>
> If you've never done so before, go find the main power panel for your home or apartment and carefully take a peak. You'll see where the main power line comes in and the circuit breakers with amp-ratings printed on them (15, 20, 30, etc.). Just don't touch anything except circuit breaker switches or you may get electrocuted and not be able to finish this book!

Where Does the Energy Go?

A load evaluation adds up all of the energy loads in your home to help you figure out what things cost—and where you can save money. In the following load evaluation form, there's a place to list each appliance in your home and calculate the average watt-hours it uses on the average day.

Appliance	Qty.	Volts	AC DC	P Y/N	Run Watts	Hours /Day	Days /Week	W-hours /Day	Percent of Total	Surge Watts	Ph-L Y/N
Espresso Maker (example)	1	117	AC	N	1350	0.20	7	270.0	6.8%	1350	N

Total Daily Average Watt-hrs

Simple load evaluation or analysis form for figuring a total of all electrical loads in your home.

The following table shows typical watt-hour loads for many household loads. Use it to complete your home's load evaluation form.

Use the manufacturer's specs if possible, but be careful of nameplate ratings that are the highest possible electrical draw for that appliance. Beware of appliances that have a "standby" mode and are really "on" 24 hours a day. If you can't find a rating, call us for advice (800-919-2400).

DESCRIPTION	WATTS
Refrigeration:	
4-yr.-old 22 cu. ft. auto defrost (approximate run time 7-9 hours per day)	500
New 22 cu. ft. auto defrost (approximate run time 7-8 hours per day)	200
12 cu. ft. Sun Frost refrigerator (approximate run time 6-9 hours per day)	58
4-yr.-old standard freezer (approximate run time 7-8 hours per day)	350
Dishwasher: cool dry	700
hot dry	1450
Trash compactor	1500
Can opener (electric)	100
Microwave (.5 cu. ft.)	900
Microwave (.8 to 1.5 cu. ft.)	1500
Exhaust hood	144
Coffeemaker	1200
Food processor	400
Toaster (2-slice)	1200
Coffee grinder	100
Blender	350
Food dehydrator	600
Mixer	120
Range, small burner	1250
Range, large burner	2100
Water Pumping:	
AC Jet Pump ($1/3$ hp), 300 gal per hour, 20' well depth, 30 psi	750

DESCRIPTION	WATTS
AC submersible pump ($1/2$ hp), 40' well depth, 30 psi	1000
DC pump for house pressure system (typical use is 1-2 hours per day)	60
DC submersible pump (typical use is 6 hours per day)	50
Shop:	
Worm drive 7 $1/4$" saw	1800
AC table saw, 10"	1800
AC grinder, $1/2$ hp	1080
Hand drill, $3/8$"	400
Hand drill, $1/2$"	600
Entertainment/Telephones:	
TV (27-inch color)	170
TV (19-inch color)	80
TV (12-inch black & white)	16
Video games (not incl. TV)	20
Satellite system, 12-ft dish/VCR	30
Laser disk/CD player	30
AC powered stereo (avg. volume)	55
AC stereo, home theater	500
DC powered stereo (avg. volume)	15
CB (receiving)	10
Cellular telephone (on standby)	5
Cordless telephone (on standby)	5
Electric piano	30
Guitar amplifier (avg. volume)	40
(Jimi Hendrix volume)	8500
General Household:	
Typical fluorescent light (60W equivalent)	15
Incandescent lights (as indicated on bulb)	
Electric clock	4
Clock radio	5
Electric blanket	400
Iron (electric)	1200

DESCRIPTION	WATTS
Clothes washer (vertical axis)	900
Clothes washer (horizontal axis)	250
Dryer (gas)	500
Dryer (electric)	5750
Vacuum cleaner, average	900
Central vacuum	1500
Furnace fan:	
$1/4$ hp	600
$1/3$ hp	700
$1/2$ hp	875
Garage door opener: $1/4$ hp	550
Alarm/security system	6
Air conditioner:	
1 ton or 10,000 BTU/hr	1500
Office/Den:	
Computer	55
17" color monitor	100
17" LCD "flat screen" monitor	45
Laptop computer	25
Ink jet printer	35
Dot matrix printer	200
Laser printer	900
Fax machine: (plain paper)	
standby	5
printing	50
Electric typewriter	200
Adding machine	8
Electric pencil sharpener	60
Hygiene:	
Hair dryer	1500
Waterpik	90
Whirlpool bath	750
Hair curler	750
Electric toothbrush: (charging stand)	6

List of typical loads for common household appliances.

(©Gaiam Real Goods)

For example, a 19-inch color television may require 70W for three hours of viewing a day. That's 210Wh (70 × 3). An 800W coffee maker that's on four hours daily has a load of 3.2 kWh. You get the picture.

What's average? It depends on how much you rely on electricity to heat your water, air, and food. Your daily average will probably be somewhere between 15 kWh and 20 kWh. Below 15 kWh is relatively efficient and above 20 kWh is wasteful. Your usage may vary.

Add up all the loads and you should have a good idea of how much energy it takes to keep your home comfortable. Next comes the reality. Pull out your latest electric bill. It will probably be shown in kilowatt-hours or kWh, and will include the service dates (from, to), number of billing days, the prior and current meter readings, and the difference or total usage. The electric bill will then multiply usage by your rate to come up with a subtotal.

As you compile your load evaluation form, there will be many head scratchers: appliances that seem to use up more power than you think they should. That's because they're on even when they say "off." What gives? Actually, these are called phantom loads. Examples include instant-on televisions in which power is on to keep the picture tube warmed up and ready to view. Electric clocks on appliances are also phantom loads, albeit low-amp loads. (Don't we already have enough clocks in the house?!) Appliances such as computer speaker systems and telephone answering systems that use a transformer box or wall wort are also phantom loads. Sure, they don't take much juice, but each one adds up. A little 4-watt phantom load can cost $5 or $10 a year in electricity. An instant-on TV can cost lots more. It all adds up.

What can you do about phantom loads? Unplug ones you really don't need. Easier, plug them into a power strip that has an on-off switch so you can turn off more than one. (I'll share lots more energy-efficient tips in Chapter 3.)

Besides electricity, your home uses lots of other energy. Depending on where you live (or where you're planning to live), the primary heat source may be electricity, fuel oil, natural gas, coal, wood, or, near state capitals, rhetoric. So pull out the utility bills for the last 12 months—or ask for a printout—and figure out how much you spent to heat water, air, and food.

Sun Spots

To keep folks from using more energy than what's considered normal, many electric utilities have a lower baseline rate and a higher rate for any usage above the baseline. Your bill may also include energy surcharges. What's important for estimating electric costs is the final charge divided by the kWh of power used to get a final kWh rate.

Bright Idea _____

Want to know how much power you've bought from your local utility over the last year? Ask them! Most can check their records (or let you do so online) to calculate your power usage. In fact, based on answers to usage questions, they can often tell you how much you spent on power for your refrigerator, oven, computer, television, dishwasher, and aquarium! To see a sample report, visit Pacific Gas & Electric's Energy Survey site at www.pge.com/energysurvey/.

How Much Does Home Energy Cost?

Which heating fuel is the most economical and efficient? The answer depends on the following:

♦ Cost of raw materials (crude oil, natural gas, sunlight, wind)

♦ Cost to process the material into useable power

♦ Cost to deliver the power to you

♦ Energy content of the fuel, measured in BTU

♦ Efficiency of the furnace or appliance

♦ Cost of maintaining the appliance

In many situations, the fuel resource used to develop electricity is already determined by local availability and costs. In the Pacific Northwest, hydroelectric power is cheapest because water is abundant. In the eastern United States the fuel is typically coal. In the Midwest, fuel oil and natural gas provide much of the heating fuel and most of the electricity. In California, it's a combination, but primarily natural gas.

Many home appliances use electricity. Heating appliances such as furnaces, stoves, and water heaters might use electricity or a less expensive heat source such as fuel oil or natural gas. The key here is what's least expensive.

Heating fuel prices fluctuate. A couple of years ago the Energy Information Administration figured out the national average residential fuel costs and divided it by the typical fuel appliance efficiency to come up with some interesting comparisons:

♦ Oil in a central heating system costs *$7.86* per million BTU.

♦ Natural gas in a central heating system costs *$8.25* per million BTU.

♦ Propane in a central heating system costs *$10.65* per million BTU.

♦ Electric resistance heat costs *$24.77* per million BTU.

That's right, electric heat costs more than three times as much as oil heat!

So, how much do electric appliances cost to run? Not that much—unless you add it all up. Consider the following examples (source: Pacific Gas & Electric):

- Electric baseboard or central air heater (2,000 sq. ft. home): $114.00 to $400.00 or more per month
- Natural or propane gas furnace heater (2,000 sq. ft. home): $41.00 to $200 or more per month
- Frost-free refrigerator (20 cu. ft.): $12.00 to $22.00 per month
- Water heater: electric, $20.00 to $70.00 per month; gas: $7.00 to $19.00 per month
- Window air conditioner: $.09 to $.28 per hour
- Central air conditioner: $.48 to $.66 per hour
- Laundry water: $.37 for electric water heater or $.10 for gas water heater per load
- Clothes washer: $.03 to $.23 per load
- Clothes dryer: electric, $.30 to $.60 per load; gas: $.10 to $.16 per load
- Electric oven: $.30 to $.60 per hour
- Gas oven: $.05 to $.11 per hour
- Microwave oven: $.01 to $.03 for 10 minutes
- Dishwasher: $.08 to $.09 per load
- Hair dryer: $.01 for 5 minutes
- Incandescent light bulb (100W): $.01 per hour
- Equivalent compact fluorescent light bulb (27W): $.01 for four hours
- Color television: $.01 to $.05 per hour
- Personal computer: $.01 to $.02 per hour

Considering a Solar Power System

You can save money by reducing the costs of heat and power your home needs. How? I'll cover that topic in Chapter 3. Every watt not used is a watt that doesn't have to be produced, distributed, or stored!

So how does the sun fit into all of this? The sun is an efficient source of solar energy that can be used to heat and/or power your home. There are two ways you can use solar energy to power your home.

First, you can encourage your local utility and state utility board to use more renewable energy sources, especially solar. You can become involved in the political and economic battle being fought over energy. Check Appendix B for more information.

Second, you can enlist as a soldier in the battle. You can install solar thermal and solar electric systems for your current home, next home, apartment, vacation cabin, recreation vehicle, business, or other energy-dependent residence.

Exactly how much will solar power systems cost you? Unfortunately, it's not quite that easy. Solar power systems are becoming a commodity that you can quickly size and buy at your local super-hardware store. Even so, there are incentives, rebates, buy backs, equipment life, depreciation, and many other factors that vary based on what you're doing and where you live. Be wary, though, as no program is safe from cuts while the legislature is in session.

Fortunately, this book is written to take you through each step of the process, offering the information you need to make wise decisions. Soon, you will have a rate per kWh for your solar power system that can be compared to costs for other power sources. You'll also know the hidden costs of other sources.

But before we get into all of that, let's see how you can save some money right now with the next chapter.

The Least You Need to Know

- Figuring out home energy costs will help you find smart ways of saving money.

- Your house is filled with loads that soak up energy, often more than you suspected.

- Electricity is sold to you by the kilowatt hour (kWh) so it will become the measurement for costing solar power systems.

- Solar thermal energy and electric power have few hidden long-term costs, unlike other power sources.

Chapter **3**

Energy Efficiency Now

In This Chapter

- ◆ How heat transfers in and around your house
- ◆ Get a free or low-cost energy audit
- ◆ Ways you can cut your energy costs *right now*
- ◆ Learn how you can cut the costs of your solar power system
- ◆ Build or retrofit an energy-efficient home

After reading Chapter 2, you have a pretty good idea of how much total energy your house or apartment uses and what it's used for.

This chapter offers some practical solutions for making your home more energy efficient. Included are ideas on how to reduce your home's dependency on costly energy. Once the fuel bill is cut and you're still living comfortably, you can begin investing in solar solutions. Every dollar of energy costs you save here can cut your solar investment by many dollars.

Understanding Heat Transfer

Here's how it works: heat energy seeks equilibrium. That is, heat on the outside of a cooler house wants to get in. Heat on the inside wants to go outdoors and play. If just nice dense walls stood in its way, heat transfer would be very slow. But most houses have doors and windows and lots of little air leaks to speed up the transfer.

Of course, that wouldn't be a problem if climate maintenance was free. Unfortunately, keeping a house cool in the heat and warm in a cold climate cost lots of bucks. Once purchased, that high-priced warm (or cool) air needs to stay where you put it. The trick is to minimize heat transfer through the house's walls, doors, and windows.

Auditing Your Energy

How efficiently is your home using the energy you buy for it? In human terms, what's its metabolic rate?

Good question. You can get a good answer with a *home energy audit*. You can do the audit yourself, hire a contractor to do some or all of it, or ask your energy provider(s) to do it for you. Let's take a closer look at your options.

Do It Yourself

You can easily conduct a home energy audit yourself. A simple walk-through can spot the more obvious energy losses, the ones that cost the most. Drafts or air leaks can suck up 5 to 30 percent of your home's energy, so that's a good place to start. On a very cold or very hot day, walk around the inside of your home feeling for temperature differences around windows, doors, fireplace dampers, attic hatches, and window air conditioners. Also check under sinks for gaps around pipes and around electrical outlets, especially on exterior walls. The solution is insulation, weatherstripping, and caulking.

Next, take a closer look at those windows and doors. Depending on how much energy you're losing through them, more energy-efficient windows may be a good investment. Before spending the money, though, consider hiring an expert who can give you exact costs and estimate how long it will take for energy savings to pay you back.

Sun-Day School

A **home energy audit** is an analysis of how things in your home use and lose energy. It checks not only appliances (users), but also doors and windows (losers). An audit helps you determine where costly energy is wasted.

A better way to find drafts is to do a pressurization test. To perform the test, close all exterior doors, windows, and fireplace flues. For safety, turn off all gas-burning appliances with pilot lights. Then turn on all exhaust fans, typically in the bathrooms and kitchen, to pull air out of the house. Finally, walk around inside the house perimeter with a burning incense stick or candle and watch the smoke or flame point *away* from drafts. Check closely around windows, doors, electric outlets, and fireplaces. The flame or smoke indicates how much of a draft there is by making the results of the draft visible. Remember to restart any gas appliances you turned off for the test.

Besides drafts, many homes lose energy through walls and ceilings. Insulation is installed in walls as they are built to keep expensive interior air inside the house. You can check your home's insulation in various ways. Easiest is to look at the building plans if you have them as they will indicate the R value of the home when built. An R value is a laboratory standard that defines a material's resistance to heat transfer. The higher the number, the more it will resist the transfer of heat through it. Otherwise, you may need to crawl up into the attic and below the house to see what insulation is exposed and try to read or estimate its R value.

You can sometimes check a wall's insulation by opening up an exterior electrical wall plug (make sure you turn it off at the main power panel first). Remove the cover and visually inspect the insulation for type, depth, and whether it has a plastic or paper vapor barrier intended to keep moisture away from the insulation.

Once you've checked your home's insulation, call your energy company or an insulation contractor to determine if it's adequate for the local climate. (You'll learn how to plan ahead and install the right insulation in your new or retrofitted home a little later in this chapter.)

The next part of your energy audit is to figure out how efficient your heating and/or cooling system is. If it is more than about 15 years old, chances are a new energy-efficient model is a good investment. Newer heating furnaces surpass 90 percent efficiency. Newer air conditioners and heat pumps, too, are designed to use less fuel. Also make sure that the ducts and pipes leading to and from these units are insulated and sealed as needed.

> **Sun Spots**
>
> About one third of escaping air in a home moves through floors, walls, and ceilings. Another third climbs out through plumbing, ducts, electric outlets, and vents. One sixth goes through the fireplace, if any. And the final sixth makes its escape through doors and windows.

At least 10 percent of your energy bills goes into lighting. Chapters 6 and 7 will show you how to enhance the natural light in your home. Meantime, you can cut energy costs now with just a few lighting tips:

◆ Buy bulbs by their lumens (light) and life expectancy rather than their wattage (60W, 75W, 100W).

◆ In bright rooms, remove some of the light bulbs.

◆ Replace incandescent bulbs with new compact fluorescent bulbs as they can last 10 times longer and use a quarter of the electricity.

Professional Energy Audits

House doctors and energy efficiency contractors have more tools and knowledge than you do. If you think your house is losing lots of the energy you buy it, consider investing in a professional audit to determine where the problems are. You can find house doctors and energy efficiency contractors in the telephone book's yellow pages under "Energy Conservation Services and Products" or a similar heading. Plan on spending up to $200 for a professional energy audit.

In addition, many public and private utility companies will do an energy audit on your home at little or no cost. To find out, drag out your utility bills and look for a customer service telephone number or Internet address. Utilities are listed in the phone book under "Electric Service and Utility Providers," "Gas Utility Companies," and similar headings.

What can these pros do that you can't? They have the knowledge and equipment to conduct a *blower door test* and a *thermographic scan* of your house. They also have the eyes and know-how to see things you may miss in your energy audit.

Sun-Day School

A **blower door test** uses a powerful fan installed in an exterior door frame to pull air out of the house and lower interior air pressure. It's like the pressurization test you can perform, except better. The auditor will probably use a smoke pencil or other equipment instead of incense or candles to find air leaks. Calibrated blower doors will actually tell the auditor how much air leakage the house has and indicate how effective air-sealing will be. A **thermographic scan** uses infrared light to detect places in your home where air and heat are leaking. In good weather, the auditor will do an exterior scan; in inclement weather the scan will probably be done on the interior of the home. Thermographic scans are quite accurate. They also cost $300 to $500 for the test.

Before the energy auditor arrives at your house, make a list of anything you recognize as an energy loss, such as an especially drafty room or door. In addition, make sure the auditor can easily access your furnace or other heat source as well as the main power panel and main gas shutoffs as appropriate. Have your energy bills nearby or get a printout of the last 12 months' bills from your utilities.

Where can you find a qualified energy auditor? Again, check the telephone book and your utility companies. In addition, try the National Association of Energy Service Companies (NAESCO) at 202-822-0950 or on the Internet at www.naesco.org.

Also, if you'll be financing your solar power system with an energy-efficient mortgage (read: lower interest rates!), you'll probably need a certified inspection by an accredited home energy rating system (HERS) inspector. Chapter 5 offers more specifics.

You've Been Audited, Now What?

Once your home has been audited for energy use and waste, what can you do about it? Solar power is an excellent resource. However, it requires an investment. And the less energy your home wastes, the smaller that investment will be. So there are many things you can do to your existing home or the one you're building to keep solar energy investment costs down.

First, prioritize. Where does your audit tell you that you're losing the most energy? Also factor in that some energy is more expensive than others. The question you're trying to answer is: Where can I most efficiently spend my money to cut energy costs?

Next, consider how much of the work you can do yourself and how much others should do. For example, following the instructions on the box, you can probably install window weatherstripping products. However, you may decide not to tackle installing new energy-efficient windows. Or you may have to hire an insulation contractor to drill holes in your home's walls and blow in insulation, but you might be able to install insulation in an open attic. Or you can buy and change out all of your light bulbs without assistance.

Finally, work by priority. Make a plan that gets you working on or paying for those projects with the highest return on your investment of time and money.

Payback, what business folks call the payback period, is as important to you as it is to businesses. Simply, payback is the time it takes for total savings to catch up with total costs. If a $1,000 investment in energy efficiency saves you $250 a year in energy costs, the payback is four years. After that, the savings continue while the costs don't. You profit. If the equipment lasts 20 years, you'll get 16 years of virtually free service (other than required maintenance).

Here are some projects that can pay you back relatively quickly and for little or no money:

 ◆ Wear a sweater inside during the winter or a light shirt or blouse during the summer to reduce heating and cooling needs.

 ◆ Close doors, windows, and heater vents in unoccupied rooms.

 ◆ Only use bathroom and kitchen fans as necessary because they pull conditioned air from your home.

- Caulk around plumbing and ducting, especially near the house's crawlspace and exterior.

- Install gaskets (available from hardware stores) under the cover plate on electrical outlets installed along outside walls.

- Caulk and weatherstrip doors and windows.

- Use solar awnings, shades, drapes, and other window coverings to keep excess heat from entering your home through south-or west-facing windows.

- If you have a fireplace, keep the flue damper or firebox doors tightly closed when not in use.

- Reset heat thermostats for greater efficiency.

- Replace an old thermostat with a new digital controller (cost: less than $100).

- Repair or replace leaky faucets, especially hot water faucets.

- Move a refrigerator away from a stove or other heat source.

- Keep the dryer's lint trap clean.

- Change out light bulbs for more efficient ones.

- Install storm windows and doors.

- Install ceiling fans as needed to circulate conditioned air.

- Clean or replacing dirty furnace filters every two to three months during use seasons.

- Insulate your hot water heater and related pipes to minimize energy loss.

- Lower the hot water heater temperature to 115°F.

- Take more showers than baths, as a five-minute shower takes half the water of a bath.

Bright Idea _____

At least twice a year, use the spigot near the bottom to drain a quart of water from your water heater. This removes sediment that impedes heat transfer.

- Maintain appliances and plumbing systems so energy isn't wasted.

- At least twice a year, vacuum the coils behind and under your refrigerator to keep it from working too hard; older refrigerators need to be cleaned more often.

- Replace worn out appliances with those that have higher energy-efficiency ratings.

The U.S. Department of Energy has an Energy Star program that rates and labels major appliances and other products for energy efficiency. An EnergyGuide is posted on new major appliances to show what the typical energy costs for the appliance are (see the following figure).

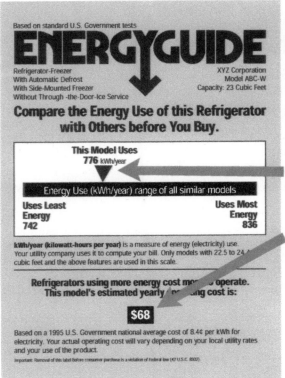

How to Read the EnergyGuide Label

The EnergyGuide label gives you two important pieces of information you can use for comparison of different brands and models when shopping for a new refrigerator:

• Estimated energy consumption on a scale showing a range for similar models

• Estimated yearly operating cost based on the national average cost of electricity.

An EnergyGuide on new appliances compares the typical energy used in a year based on averages.

In addition, here are some suggestions for projects with longer paybacks, and the chapters where you'll find more information:

◆ In moderate climates, consider an energy-efficient heat pump because it can save 30 to 40 percent in energy costs over a furnace and air conditioner (Chapter 7).

◆ Install a solar water heater (Chapter 10) to reduce water heating costs.

◆ Install a solar air heater (Chapter 11) to cut heating bills.

◆ Install a solar electric generating system (Chapter 9) to reduce the need for outside electricity.

◆ Consider installing wind, water, and other power-producing systems for your home (Chapters 12 and 13).

◆ Replace inefficient windows and doors (Chapter 7).

◆ Take advantage of any tax credits and rebates available to you (Chapter 4).

◆ If you're building a new home or refinancing your current one, consider an energy-efficient mortgage (Chapter 5).

Building and Retrofitting for Efficiency

Fortunately, you can, at little relative expense, design your house to minimize heat transfer. Experts know lots more about how to do this than our parents knew when they shopped for housing.

What you're looking for as you consider which building materials to buy is those materials with the highest R value. Of course, if some material has a specific R value, more is better. That is, 4 inches of fiberglass has an R-13 value. Six inches is rated at R-23. That's why 2" × 6" exterior walls are more energy efficient than 2" × 4" walls.

Local code and building practices will dictate the minimum R values you should have in your house. Obviously, you don't need the same value for a home in San Diego as you do for one in Minneapolis.

There's a point of diminishing returns, however. For example, it may cost more to increase the R value to its upper limits than the amount of energy it will save. Smart planning is important.

So here are some ideas to consider as you plan your house to be more energy efficient:

◆ Build your house with 2" × 6" exterior walls if you need a higher R value and pack it with thicker insulation.

◆ Use the most efficient insulation you can afford.

◆ Install low-emissivity (low-E) glass coated to reduce heat conductivity without reducing light.

◆ Insulate ceilings well, even higher than the local recommended R value.

◆ Ventilate the attic above well-insulated ceilings to allow trapped heat to escape.

◆ Install radiant barriers under the rafters to greatly limit heat infiltration during warm weather.

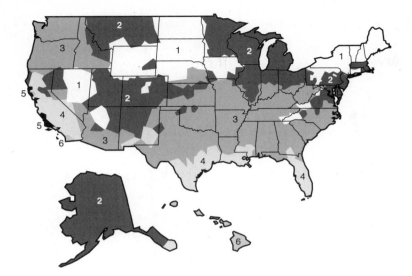

National insulation zones.

Insulation R values by zone.

| Zone | Gas | Heat pump | Fuel oil | Electric furnace | Ceiling | | Wall (A) | Floor | Crawl space (B) | Slab edge | Basement | |
					Attic	Cathederal					Interior	Exterior
1	✔	✔	✔		R-49	R-38	R-18	R-25	R-19	R-8	R-11	R-10
1				✔	R-49	R-60	R-28	R-25	R-19	R-8	R-19	R-15
2	✔	✔	✔		R-49	R-38	R-18	R-25	R-19	R-8	R-11	R-10
2				✔	R-49	R-38	R-22	R-25	R-19	R-8	R-19	R-15
3	✔	✔	✔	✔	R-49	R-38	R-18	R-25	R-19	R-8	R-11	R-10
4	✔	✔	✔		R-38	R-38	R-13	R-13	R-19	R-4	R-11	R-4
4				✔	R-49	R-38	R-18	R-25	R-19	R-8	R-11	R-10
5	✔				R-38	R-30	R-13	R-11	R-13	R-4	R-11	R-4
5		✔	✔		R-38	R-38	R-13	R-13	R-19	R-4	R-11	R-4
5				✔	R-49	R-38	R-18	R-25	R-19	R-8	R-11	R-10
6	✔				R-22	R-22	R-11	R-11	R-11	(C)	R-11	R-4
6		✔	✔		R-38	R-30	R-13	R-11	R-13	R-4	R-11	R-4
6				✔	R-49	R-38	R-18	R-25	R-19	R-8	R-11	R-10

(A) R-18, R-22, and R-28 exterior wall systems can be achieved by either cavity insulation or cavity insulation with insulating sheathing.
For 2 in x 4 in walls, use either 3-1/2-in thick R-15 or 3-1/2-in thick R-13 fiber glass insulation with insulating sheathing.
For 2 in x 6 in walls, use either 5-1/2-in thick R-21 or 6-1/4-in thick R-19 fiber glass insulation.

(B) Insulate crawl space walls only if the crawl space is dry all year, the floor above is not insulated, and all ventilation to the crawl space is blocked.
A vapor retarder (e.g., 4- or 6-mil polyethylene film) should be installed on the ground to reduce moisture migration into the crawl space.

(C) No slab edge insulation is recommended.

- Check walls as they are built to fill up any air leaks from the outside.

- Include a supplier-recommended moisture barrier in walls to keep them from sweating.

- Plan heat registers near the floor and the return vent near the ceiling because heat rises.

- Buy the most efficient model fireplace you can afford if you must have one in your home. Fireplaces are very inefficient heat sources.

- Buy a 92-plus percent efficient heating furnace rated in BTUs to match or exceed your house's needs.

- Make sure your thermostat is computerized and can be set to make multiple temperature changes during the day. Every degree you turn down your heat setting can save you about 2 percent of your fuel bill.

CAUTION

Solar Eclipse

A standard exterior door without a threshold and weatherstripping allows as much air to pass through as a 5-inch by 5-inch hole.

- Include double-glazed windows in your budget for long-term energy savings.

- Insulate any heating ducts that run through unheated basements or crawl spaces.

- Remember to use weatherstripping and apply caulking around exterior doors and windows.

What's next? There are folks out there who will help you buy and even give you tax incentives to purchase solar power for your home. Chapter 4 introduces you to them!

The Least You Need to Know

- An energy audit can save you money on your fuel bills today and cut the investment costs of solar power.

- Home energy can be deceptively inexpensive unless you also calculate related and environmental costs.

- There are many jobs you can do right now to cut energy costs in your home.

- You can plan an even more efficient home for your future using solar technology and energy efficiency.

Chapter 4

Cutting Solar Power Costs

In This Chapter

- The Million Solar Roofs Initiative
- Solar rebates
- Tax incentives for solar power
- Selling power to the utility company
- Your solar rights

Solar energy is a readily available power source. So why aren't all homes and power companies using it? Cost. The fact is, it's currently more expensive to produce electricity using a solar power system than it is with a non-renewable source. The problem certainly isn't availability as there's more sunlight than there is coal, oil, and gas in the world. The problem is mass production. Until more people decide to use solar energy, the cost of producing solar electric and thermal power systems will remain higher than for entrenched energy sources. When fossil fuel became less expensive than whale oil, the use of fossil fuel expanded and whale hunters found new jobs. It's an economic thing.

So when will the economics of solar energy make it cost less than fossil fuels? Soon.

This chapter tells you how you can cut the costs of solar power for your home with clout and incentives from various governments. By considering and using these opportunities you can not only reduce solar power costs for yourself, you can do so for others.

The Feds Step In

The U.S. Department of Energy (DOE) has been trying to encourage the use of solar energy by power companies, industry, and home builders for a couple of decades. Most of that support has been in the form of technical assistance. It funds programs that learn how to apply solar energy to meet power needs.

In 1997, the DOE announced the Million Solar Roofs Initiative or MSRI, a program intended to encourage the installation of solar energy systems on one million federal buildings by the year 2010. How? By coordinating the efforts of various federal, state, local, utility, financial, and industry groups toward that goal. The MSRI is intended to be a facilitator with clout. The federal government can coordinate such an extensive project more easily than any other single resource.

Of course, the DOE gets its funding and some of its direction from Congress, so it must satisfy the political side of the equation. People must use the program and keep pressure on Congress to keep it focused and funded. So far so good.

Sun-Day School

Greenhouse gases trap the heat of the sun in Earth's atmosphere, producing the greenhouse effect, increasing temperatures around the world. The two major greenhouse gases are water vapor and carbon dioxide. Other greenhouse gases include methane, ozone, chlorofluorocarbons, and nitrogen oxides.

The MSRI actually has a number of goals. It's trying to reduce *greenhouse gases* and other emissions by replacing fossil power with solar power. It figures that a million solar power systems will reduce carbon emissions into our atmosphere equivalent to the annual emissions from 850,000 cars.

The MSRI also wants to create about 70,000 additional high-tech jobs resulting from increased demand for photovoltaic, solar hot water, and related solar energy systems. And the MSRI is trying to encourage the growth of an industry—solar power—that can compete in the world market. Of course, all this means that if more folks buy solar energy systems, prices will come down. Supply and demand.

Again, the DOE is a facilitator between industry and consumers. MSRI system requirements are basic. A building's solar energy system must comply with the National Electrical Code (NEC) just as any new construction does. There are now NEC codes specifically for solar electrical systems. Equipment and appliances must also comply with Underwriters Laboratories (UL) and the Solar Rating and Certification Corporation (SRCC) standards.

Sun Spots

The U.S. federal government owns 500,000 buildings. Heating, cooling, and lighting them costs more than $3 billion a year. The Fed says it will install solar electric and solar thermal energy systems on 20,000 of those buildings (4 percent) by 2010. The General Services Administration has also set up easier procedures for federal agencies to get solar energy systems into their budgets. Even the Department of Defense is thinking solar, retrofitting Navy housing with solar hot water systems and adding solar space heating on an Army facility.

Photovoltaic (solar electricity) systems must be of a minimum size as well. Residential systems must produce at least 0.5 kW, school and church systems must be a minimum of 1 kW, and commercial system must be a minimum of 2 kW.

Solar thermal water heating systems for residences must have a collector area of at least 20 square feet and residential swimming pool systems must be at least 100 square feet in size. Commercial domestic systems need to have at least 40 square feet of collectors, and commercial swimming pool heating systems need to be at least 400 square feet in size. We'll cover solar thermal water heating systems in greater detail in Chapter 10.

Finally, solar thermal space heating systems (discussed in Chapter 11) need to have a collector area of at least 100 square feet to qualify for the MSRI program.

Want to know more about the MSRI and what it's up to? It's online at www.millionsolarroofs.com. The site, sponsored by the Department of Energy, can direct you to MSRI partners in your area as well as announce grants and other financial opportunities. The site also has an extensive library of information on solar power topics.

Bright Idea

The NEC code for photovoltaic power systems is reprinted in the latest edition of *Solar Living Sourcebook* (see Appendix B for details). It also includes extensive information on current solar living products.

Rebates

A rebate is money given back. Many manufacturers use rebates to get folks to try their products. Federal, state, and local governments try to get people to buy and install solar power by using rebates. The money may be paid to the consumer, the installer, the retailer, or the manufacturer. Ultimately, the consumer benefits through lower initial costs—as long as the consumer *knows* about the rebate.

One form of rebate is known as a buy down. Someone, typically a government program, pays part of the initial cost of a solar power system. Typically, the buy down amount is established by the state legislature for a specified period. The buy down amounts are based on the system's generating capacity, measured in watts or kilowatts. In some programs, rebates are given on a first-come, first-served basis. Those who apply earliest get the higher rebate.

Can you qualify for a state buy down? How? Good questions! The best place to start asking these questions is your state's energy department. Appendix B offers specific contact information. In addition, you can contact the National Association of State Energy Officials at 703-299-8800 or online at www.naseo.org. Its website includes a map on which you can click to find out about your state's energy office. From there you can find out what solar energy rebates and resources are available.

Here's another great resource: The North Carolina Solar Center and the Interstate Renewable Energy Council developed and maintain the Database of State Incentives for Renewable Energy (DSIRE). You can get a copy of it by contacting the North Carolina Solar Center, North Carolina State University, Box 7401, Raleigh, NC, 27695-7401, 919-515-5778. It's also online at www.dsireusa.org. It tells you, state by state, what resources and opportunities are available to those considering renewable resources.

For example, New York incentives for renewable energy include financial incentives; investment and awareness programs; and rules, regulations, and policies. More specifically, financial incentives to New York State residents include information on the following:

- Green Building Tax Credit Program
- Solar Electric Generating Tax Credit
- Solar and Wind Energy Systems Exemption
- Renewable R&D Grant Program
- Energy $mart Loan Program
- Residential Photovoltaics Program
- Long Island Solar Pioneer Program

That's just some of the programs in *one* state. Most states have something going to encourage people to install solar power for their homes.

Local governments, too, try to encourage renewable energy resources. For example, Los Angeles recently announced a limited-time rebate offer in addition to what the State of California was offering. The combined deal cut the purchase price of PV systems by about half! L.A. also offered an additional rebate on solar equipment manufactured in that city to encourage local industry.

Sun Spots

A residential solar hot water system may cost from $1,800 to $3,500, depending on climate, and whether it is built into a new home (less expensive) or adding on to an existing one (more expensive). A solar electric (PV) system is more difficult to estimate due to local solar conditions, costs, rebates, and incentives. A residential PV system recently installed in Sacramento, California, for example, cost about $7,000 per kWh. The cost of power from that system was about $0.24 per kWh. Rebates and incentives can lower that cost by *half*.

Tax Incentives

As of early 2002, there are no federal income tax incentives for homeowners to encourage them to buy renewable energy equipment. However, rebates from an electric utility for residential solar power systems and appliances are exempt from federal income tax.

Consider this: There is a 10 percent energy credit available to businesses that incur certain expenses for solar or geothermal energy property placed in service during the tax year. If you own or plan to own a home-based business, get the instructions for IRS Form 3468 and talk with a tax advisor about how the energy credit may lower your federal tax obligation.

Specifically, line 2 of Form 3468 offers an energy credit of 10 percent of energy property placed in service during a specific tax year. Energy property is equipment that uses solar energy to generate electricity, to heat or cool a structure, or to provide solar process heat. It also includes geothermal energy property. Additional requirements are included in "Instructions for Form 3468" available from the IRS at 1-800-829-1040 or online at www.irs.gov.

CAUTION

Solar Eclipse

What about a solar tax credit for individuals? About 20 years ago, the U.S. federal government offered a 50 percent tax credit for solar installations. Unfortunately, some unscrupulous people used it to build and sell shoddy solar water heating systems door to door at inflated prices. An individual income tax solar credit may return someday, but it will need some image repair and better guidelines.

Businesses can also take advantage of a five-year accelerated depreciation on solar and other business equipment. Talk with your business accountant for more information.

What about state income tax? Of course that depends on which state you're living in and what the current tax laws say. For example, in California, individual taxpayers who purchase certain approved solar or wind energy systems are allowed a credit for installation costs. They must file Form 3508, "Solar Energy System Credit."

Another good question to ask is: Will the money I spend on improving my home with a solar power system increase my property taxes? The definitive answer is: Maybe yes and maybe no. Some states, counties, and cities have a moratorium on taxing solar property enhancements. Others don't. Some say they will exempt any solar improvements made before a specified date. Others will not begin taxing the improvement until a certain date.

How can you learn what rebates and tax incentives are available to you? The resources listed in this chapter and in Appendix B are the best place to start. In addition, talk with local solar equipment suppliers and contractors whose job it is to know about rebates and incentives that help them sell more.

Selling Your Excess Power

The 1978 federal PURPA (Public Utility Regulatory Policy Act) says that if individuals and businesses generate excess renewable-generated power and want to sell it, the local utility *must* buy it at "avoided" or wholesale cost. In addition, as of January 2002, 32 states and the District of Columbia have state *net metering* programs that allow you to sell electricity to utilities. Three more states have net metering programs with specific, but not all, utilities in the state.

Sun-Day School

Net metering allows your electricity meter to spin forward when electricity flows from the utility into your home, and backward when your power system delivers unused power to the utility. However, you must make sure your system is a qualified facility (see Chapter 25) and your local utility allows net metering.

Fortunately, many states have passed laws to force utilities to make it easier. Some states even allow you to sell electricity to the utility at the peak-usage rate and buy from it at the low-usage rate. Chapter 25 offers more specifics on the program. This can dramatically decrease the long-term costs of your solar power system, so find out now whether net metering is available to you. Besides state energy offices, a solar power system retailer (see Chapter 19) or solar power contractor (see Chapter 20) can offer localized advice.

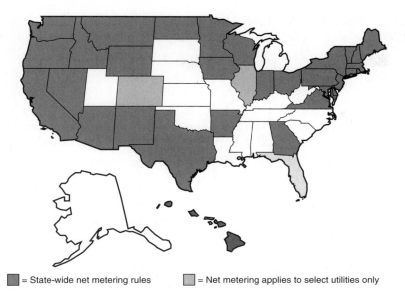

Map of U.S. states with net metering rules.

■ = State-wide net metering rules   □ = Net metering applies to select utilities only

Your Right to Light

You have rights! As a property owner, you *may* have the right to unobstructed, direct sunlight. No one can build or block your property's solar access. I say "may" because not all communities give you that right. It comes under zoning laws. Several communities in the United States have specific solar access planning guidelines and ordinances. The ordinances are specific. Their intent is to encourage the use of solar energy systems.

For example, San Jose, California, defines solar access by the amount of shade a dwelling has at solar noon on December 21, the shortest day of the year. It says that solar shading from a structure or vegetation can't be more than 20 percent of a south-facing wall or 10 percent of a south-facing window. That's specific!

Many states have enacted laws to protect landowners' rights to sunlight. For example, California Civil Code Section 801.5 follows:

> (a) The right of receiving sunlight as specified in subdivision 18 of Section 801 shall be referred to as a solar easement. "Solar easement" means the right of receiving sunlight across real property of another for any solar energy system.
>
> As used in this section, "solar energy system" means either of the following:
>
> 1. Any solar collector or other solar energy device whose primary purpose is to provide for the collection, storage, and distribution of solar energy for space heating, space cooling, electric generation, or water heating.

2. Any structural design feature of a building, whose primary purpose is to provide for the collection, storage, and distribution of solar energy for electricity generation, space heating or cooling, or for water heating.

(b) Any instrument creating a solar easement shall include, at a minimum, all of the following:

1. A description of the dimensions of the easement expressed in measurable terms, such as vertical or horizontal angles measured in degrees, or the hours of the day on specified dates during which direct sunlight to a specified surface of a solar collector, device, or structural design feature may not be obstructed, or a combination of these descriptions.

2. The restrictions placed upon vegetation, structures, and other objects that would impair or obstruct the passage of sunlight through the easement.

3. The terms or conditions, if any, under which the easement may be revised or terminated.

Check with local governments to learn what your solar access rights—and obligations—are. They may give you the right to have trees removed that block your home's solar access. In addition, it may mean that you can't build a two-story house that will block someone else's solar access. You'll learn more about this topic in Chapter 8.

Meantime, let's move on to Chapter 5, which offers dozens of ideas and resources for financing your solar home.

The Least You Need to Know

◆ The Million Solar Roofs Initiative is a federal program aimed at bringing solar resources together to bring down costs.

◆ State and local rebates and buy downs reduce the out-of-pocket costs of solar energy systems.

◆ Federal and state tax incentives can further reduce solar power costs.

◆ You may be able to generate extra solar electricity and sell it back to the utility company.

◆ Your property may be subject to solar access zoning laws that can impact the cost of your system.

Chapter 5

Financing Your Solar Home

In This Chapter

- ◆ Finding the money to pay for your solar home
- ◆ Why your home needs an energy rating
- ◆ All about federal solar financing programs
- ◆ State financing resources
- ◆ Getting your utility or system vendor to finance

Solar power can be expensive. Depending on whether you're seeking solar electricity, hot water, hot air, or all of the above, a solar power system for your home can cost up to $50,000. Add a swimming pool heater and the price goes up.

Fortunately, the previous chapters have introduced you to solar power systems and got you thinking about what you want. You then learned about programs, rebates, buy downs, tax credits, and other incentives that can cut the cost of solar power by more than half. And you've learned that some folks are able to actually sell electricity back to the utility company, further lowering costs.

Even before you decide exactly what kind of solar power system you will install in your home and start getting bids, you need to know what funds are available. So the next step is to find out what financing is available to stretch your investment over a longer period. That's what this chapter is all about. There is a surprising amount of money out there waiting for smart solar investors!

About Financing

Maybe you don't need to finance your solar power system. Maybe you have the cash on hand from winning the lottery or something. Even so, consider financing solar equipment and installation. The interest rates are typically very low, so you can invest that money somewhere else for a greater return.

You can finance purchases with a consumer loan, a supplier loan, or a first or second mortgage. Which makes the most sense? Consumer loans don't require collateral, except your promise to pay them back, so their interest is usually the highest. Examples include credit cards and finance company loans. Interest on the loan will range from about 12 to 24 percent.

Alternately, whoever sells you the solar equipment or system may offer financing, using the equipment as collateral. Interest is typically lower, ranging from 8 to 14 percent. In some cases, suppliers offer manufacturer rebates or buy downs that will lower the interest rate, much like car manufacturers sometimes offer below-cost financing. Their "loss" is rolled up in the final purchase price.

Sun-Day School

A **mortgage** is a document in which the borrower (mortgagor) gives the lender (mortgagee) rights to property as security for the repayment of the loan. A **first mortgage** offers a lender first rights to take money from the proceeds of selling a defaulted property. A **second mortgage** offers second rights after the first rights have been satisfied. The mortgage lien is removed once the debt is repaid.

The lowest rates are available to homeowners who are building a new home or retrofitting an old one with solar equipment. The reason is that, if you default, the lender can collect against the value of the house and not just against the equipment. Without rebates, *first* and *second mortgage* rates currently run between 6 and 12 percent interest.

Another advantage to financing solar power systems with a *mortgage* is that mortgage interest is deductible against federal and most state income taxes. For example, if you're in a 30 percent tax bracket, $1,000 in interest paid earns a tax credit of $300; it's like actually paying just $700 in interest. For more information, contact the Internal Revenue Service at 1-800-829-1040 or online at www.irs.gov.

Where can you apply for a consumer loan or a first or second mortgage? If you currently have a mortgage or consumer loan, contact that company first. It can help start your education. If you are buying a new home, your lender can include the costs of solar planning and solar equipment in the first mortgage. If you already have a first mortgage on an existing home, you can either refinance the mortgage for an amount large enough to cover the system or apply for a second mortgage. A second mortgage makes sense if the interest rates on your first mortgage are lower than you could get by refinancing (including new loan costs). Or your first mortgage may be held by a private party (contract) not willing to invest in improvements.

If you decide to get a new first or second mortgage, you can get a conventional loan or a special loan through conventional lenders (banks, savings and loans). Special loans include those that offer rebates, buy downs, and lower rates for energy-efficient projects. Many mortgage lenders can help you get one of these special loans, but you should make yourself an informed consumer so you know you're getting the best deal. The forthcoming section on energy-efficient financing will guide you through the maze.

Home Energy Rating

Before getting knee-deep in mortgages and acronyms, consider that you will probably need a home energy rating. Most energy-efficient financing programs we'll discuss in this chapter will encourage you to have your current home (or building plans) reviewed and rated by a certified professional energy rater.

The energy rater's job is to inspect the energy-related features of a home, such as insulation levels, window efficiency, heating and cooling systems, and air leakage. The resulting report will include the home's energy rating and an estimate of annual energy use and costs. The report may also recommend energy-efficient improvements, their costs, the potential savings, and expected payback time for improvements.

To get the best financing package possible, the lender wants to know that the improvements are cost-effective and will save you more money than what's borrowed to install them. This works to your advantage because it typically helps you qualify for a higher loan amount—or lower interest rate—than a lender can give you without the potential savings.

Who pays for the home energy inspection and rating? Ultimately, the homeowner, though it may be rolled into the lender's loan costs. Check Appendix B to find out more about the Home Energy Rating System (HERS) and certified inspectors in your area. Also, your lender may have a favorite.

Sun Spots
A typical Home Energy Rating System (HERS) report will include estimated annual energy uses and cost by system (space heating, space cooling, water heating, other energy uses) for the current home both with and without energy-efficient improvements. It then uses a one- to five-star rating system that compares before and after improvements. For example, a two-star rating means that energy costs in the current home are 200 to 300 percent higher than an ideal or reference home.

Energy-Efficient Financing

There are two primary types of energy-efficient mortgages (EEMs): new and existing home. Which you choose, obviously, depends on whether you're building a new energy-efficient home or you're investing in a house that's already built to which you'll add solar. Most lenders described here will be most happy to help you with either type, though you may find that some are easier to work with on new-home mortgages and others are more experienced with mortgages for retrofits.

As you take a look at these resources, keep in mind that nothing is safe from change while Congress is in session. That is, today's program may become tomorrow's history. New programs get funded, meaning the money for older programs gets reallocated. Limits change. Even so, many of these programs have been around for a few years with minor changes, so we're safe discussing them. Talk with your lender(s) about the latest wrinkles in these programs.

Fannie Mae

Fannie Mae is the newer name for the Federal National Mortgage Association. Everyone referred to FNMA as "Fannie Mae" so long that it's now the name. Fannie Mae is a private, shareholder-owned corporation, set up by Congress to keep money flowing in the mortgage market. It doesn't actually lend money directly to home buyers. Instead, it purchases mortgages from lenders to ensure that funds are available.

Fannie Mae encourages lenders to offer EEMs by providing guidelines and incentives. Fannie Mae buys conventional mortgages as well, up to $240,000 on new homes. They also buy residential energy efficiency improvement loans (REEIL, for you acronym fans) up to $15,000 for retrofitting older homes. The REEIL mortgages are at interest rates *below* current market rates, making them very attractive to homeowners. The mortgage must fund energy-efficient upgrades such as solar electricity (PV), solar water, and solar space heating systems. Even conventional mortgages for new home construction are at market rates and often very attractive. Adjustable and fixed interest rates are available as well as balloon payments at the end of a specified period.

Technically, money borrowed through Fannie Mae for energy-efficient improvements is a loan rather than a mortgage. This is because the money is secured by your good credit and not by the equipment itself. Also, the loan is limited to 10 years.

Who offers Fannie Mae EEMs? Conventional mortgage lenders. Work through your bank, savings and loan, mortgage company, or mortgage broker. For the latest information on Fannie Mae mortgages and loans call 1-800-732-6643 or visit online at www. fanniemae.com.

> **CAUTION**
>
> ### Solar Eclipse
>
> Can you get a Fannie Mae mortgage for constructing or retrofitting an off-grid house? Theoretically, yes. However, some lenders may not want to write a loan for a house that isn't connected to an electric utility. Before you start spending money, make sure area lenders are willing to finance your solar home.

Freddie Mac

Not to be outdone, the Federal Home Mortgage Loan Corporation (FHMLC) likes to be called Freddie Mac, though it hasn't officially changed its name—yet. Freddie Mac also buys conforming mortgages from lenders, packages them as securities, and sells them as guaranteed investments to insurance companies and pension funds. It's in what's called the secondary mortgage market.

Freddie Mac's programs are similar to Fannie Mae's except that it is more interested in long-term EEMs than in short-term loans. The current mortgage limit is $240,000 with up to 10 percent of the loan available for solar PV and thermal systems. Loan terms are 15, 20, and 30 years, as are most conventional mortgage loans. Interest rates are very attractive with fixed mortgages at market rates and variable mortgages at the prime rate plus 2 percent. First mortgages can be written for up to 95 percent of the property's value.

Freddie Mac mortgages, too, are available through traditional mortgage lenders. For additional information call 1-800-FREDDIE (373-3343) or visit the website at www. freddiemac.com.

Farmer Mac

Building or retrofitting a country home? The U.S. Department of Agriculture (USDA) has money to lend both rural homeowners and rural utility services. It is especially interested in helping new and existing rural utilities use solar electricity and solar thermal energy. Why? Because Congress told them to.

USDA's division called the Farmers Home Administration or FmHA is referred to as Farmer Mac. (Isn't it cute?) It guarantees and insures rural housing mortgage loans, encouraging those that use solar energy. For additional information and specific loan requirements, contact the USDA at 202-720-4323 or visit online at www.usda.gov.

Department of Energy (DOE)

The Department of Energy doesn't actually lend money to develop solar energy systems. However, it does fund programs like the State Weatherization Assistance Program that helps states fund weatherization projects for low-income Americans. The program can also install solar hot water systems. For additional information, call 1-800-363-3732.

As you've learned in other chapters, the DOE funds various solar research and information projects that benefit consumers. One of the most popular is the National Database of State Incentives for Renewable Energy (DSIRE), which was covered in Chapter 4.

Department of Housing and Urban Development (HUD)

HUD's function is to develop communities of opportunity, funding affordable housing for low- and moderate-income families. Within that charter it encourages the purchase and retrofitting of energy-efficient homes. Specifically, HUD loans can include solar power (PV), thermal space, and water heating projects. Depending on the loan type, the loan value can actually exceed the property's value.

HUD has a variety of on-going programs to encourage energy-efficient home ownership. They include the Community Development Block Grant Program, the HOME Investment Partnership Program, HOPE VI that replaces old housing with new, and, the most famous, the *Federal Housing Administration* (FHA) Program.

FHA EEM mortgages can be written for new and existing one- to four-unit properties that have a home energy rating. The improvements can be funded up to 5 percent of the property value with a limit of $8,000. The EEM can be used in conjunction with other FHA loans such as the 203(b).

Sun-Day School

The **Federal Housing Administration** is a HUD division that insures home loans to make them more attractive investments and thus keep interest rates down. Many Americans have purchased their first (and subsequent) homes using FHA-insured mortgages. There are a variety of programs including the popular Energy Efficient Mortgage Program that recognizes solar and other renewable energy sources.

Another resource is Title I Property Improvement Mortgage Insurance that helps homeowners get a second mortgage of up to $25,000 for solar improvements. There's also a Mortgage Increase for Solar Systems Program that allows mortgages 20 percent larger than other FHA-insured loans *if* it funds solar heating and electricity systems.

There are other FHA-insured financing opportunities as well. Your lender may or may not be up on the latest programs and requirements, so check area telephone books for your local HUD office or visit it online at www.hud.gov.

Department of Veterans Affairs (VA)

Like the FHA, the Department of Veterans Affairs doesn't actually lend money on homes. It guarantees that the purchaser will pay the loan off. The purchasers have to be qualified veterans of the U.S. armed services.

VA loans are guaranteed first mortgages of up to 100 percent of the home's value plus loan costs. Interest rates are fixed and are very attractive because the VA is guaranteeing the loan. The loan is actually made by a conventional lender that follows VA guidelines.

VA loans can fund to build a new home, buy an existing house, or retrofit a house with solar or other energy systems. VA-guaranteed loans can also fund the purchase of a lot and manufactured home.

For additional information on VA loans for energy-efficient and solar homes, call 1-800-848-4904 or visit the website at www.va.gov/vas/loan.

Environmental Protection Agency (EPA)

Even the Environmental Protection Agency is getting into the solar home mortgage business. Its stated mission is to protect human health and safeguard the natural environment, so encouraging solar homes fits right in.

Here's how they do it. The EPA manages the Energy Star Financing Program, working with lenders to finance new homes that are Energy Star-rated. To qualify as an Energy Star home, the structure must be 30 percent more energy efficient than the typical home, called a Model. Some of these homes utilize solar electric and solar thermal systems to qualify.

The benefits to buyers go beyond the home's higher efficiency. The Energy Star lender can give you a larger mortgage than one you could otherwise qualify for. Interest rates are attractively low. And the EPA will pay up to about half of the lender's closing costs for you.

Unfortunately, not all lenders can offer Energy Star financing. Currently, there are only a few national and regional lenders authorized to package these loans. In addition, not all builders are qualified to construct Energy Star homes. Fortunately, interest in these homes is growing and more builders and lenders are getting certified.

For additional information on EPA Energy Star financing, call toll-free 1-888-STAR-YES (782-7937) or visit the website at www.energystar.gov.

You may also hear about a program called E Seal. Set up by the Edison Electric Institute, E Seal is a certification program for energy-efficient homes and their builders. It also manages a program called E Seal Mortgage. For additional information, call 202-508-5557 or visit its website at www.eei.org/esg/e_seal/.

State Energy Financing

Many states are pioneers in helping residents finance solar homes. Others are followers. Fortunately, 35 states now offer some form of financial assistance to those who are buying or retrofitting solar power homes.

What does your state or territory do to help finance solar homes? The first place to check is with the National Association of State Energy Officials at 703-299-8800 or online at www.naseo.org. It's a central clearinghouse for information on requirements and financing for solar and other energy resources.

Bright Idea

For more information about solar financing, contact EREC, the Energy Efficiency and Renewable Energy Clearing-house, at 1-800-363-3732 or online at www.eren.doe.gov.

In addition, RESNET (Residential Energy Services Network) is a national network of mortgage companies, real estate brokerages, builders, appraisers, utilities, and other energy and housing professionals. Its aim is to improve the energy efficiency of the nation's housing. It offers state-by-state directories of conventional EEM lenders and energy raters. Contact RESNET at 760-806-3448 or online at www.natresnet.org.

Utility Financing

Here's another important financial resource: your local utility. Most public utilities and many private ones are encouraging energy efficiency by coordinating all the resources. They offer information and advice, develop lender packages, certify and recommend builders, identify and certify energy system inspectors, and related tasks.

The first place to look for utility information is on your monthly utility bill. There will be a customer service telephone number or website address for general information. That's a start. You can ask about energy efficiency programs, resources, and funding. Some (those mandated by legislature to do so) will be cooperative and helpful. Other utilities (private and commercial) may not. The best ones will direct you to an on-staff energy counselor who can talk you through the process and help you find the right financial package.

Solar Vendors

The more you can afford, the more that solar power system vendors can sell. So it is in their best interest to know about the best financial packages available to energy projects. In some cases, the manufacturer or distributor of solar equipment will finance packages at attractive interest rates. This may be your best resource if you're buying a solar water heating system that doesn't require a mortgage on your home.

Which vendors offer or know of financing? Most. Again, a good place to start is in Appendix B. Also check your telephone book yellow pages under "Solar Products— Dealers and Services" as well as "Building General Contractors." Ads and a few telephone calls will help you identify solar power system vendors who offer financial packages.

Will you be building a new solar home or retrofitting one? Chapter 6 offers valuable information and tips for those considering a new home, and Chapter 7 is for retrofitters.

The Least You Need to Know

- The federal government sponsors numerous cost-effective financial packages to encourage solar homes.

- State governments and local utilities, too, can help you find the money to invest in energy efficiency.

- Various home energy rating systems are in use to help measure savings from solar and other renewable energy sources.

- The best source of funding smaller solar power systems is often the contractor or vendor who sells you the equipment.

Building Your Solar Home

In This Chapter

◆ Finding out about local building codes

◆ An overview of the construction process

◆ The basics of solar design

◆ Orienting your solar home for peak energy efficiency

◆ Finding the right architect, contractor, and suppliers

Congratulations! The lender has okayed your new construction permit and you're ready to build (or have a contractor build) an energy-efficient solar home. Now what?

Not so fast. We haven't gotten into the specifics of designing and selecting solar power and heat components. That will come in Parts 2 and 3. Meantime, you're probably eager to see how it's all going to be built.

This chapter offers an overview of the solar home construction process including an introduction to passive and active designs. For more specifics on construction, read my book, *The Complete Idiot's Guide to Building Your Own Home* (Alpha Books, 2002) which covers all aspects of the process. End of commercial.

Building Codes

Not every community is ready for those who want to build solar homes. It's not that the communities are unfriendly, it's that they may say "no" to something they've never seen. Fortunately, more communities are learning about solar options and are actually encouraging solar homes, doing their best to help builders and owners.

So what can you do to make sure that your community will allow your solar home?

◆ Contact your local building department early to discuss your plans for a solar home and ask for relevant ordinances and codes.

◆ Study local building codes and construction guidelines.

◆ Ask about local contractors who have experience constructing solar homes.

◆ Check with your homeowner or neighborhood association to see if there are any restrictions or support for solar homes.

Beginning the Construction Process

Building a home can take from 3 to 12 months, depending on complexity and who is building it. However, the work starts even earlier as the building site is selected and the home's plans are developed.

Designing your home can be frustrating fun. It's frustrating because you probably have a budget limited by what the lender says you can afford. It's fun because this is *your* home with *your* design ideas.

Besides the solar elements, which we'll get to later in this chapter, there are livability questions:

◆ How many bedrooms?

◆ How many baths?

◆ Special use rooms (office, family room, entertainment room)?

◆ Storage and recreation requirements (RV parking, swimming pool)?

◆ Single, double, or triple garage?

◆ What town and neighborhood?

◆ Which lot or parcel?

- ◆ Available services (electric, water, sewer, cable) to the building site?

- ◆ Preferred architectural style?

- ◆ Solar orientation (which way is the sun)?

- ◆ Typical lot costs including utility hookup fees?

Bright Idea

Buy a notebook and start your own Home Book with ideas, resources, costs, and designs so you can begin the building process.

As you will see, passive solar laws are simple to understand but more complex to implement. You'll need a qualified solar architect to help you design the most efficient passive solar home for your climate and building site. Chapter 11 offers a good overview of designing a passive solar home, one where the home itself is the collector.

Home construction has become an efficient process over the past 100 years. Even so, there is room within the process for variations such as including passive and active solar components. Unfortunately, not all building contractors are familiar with them so you will need to find one who understands solar power. If a solar building contractor isn't readily available where you are building, make sure that you hire an architect who will draw up specific plans that can't be misinterpreted. Appendix B offers some resources for finding qualified solar contractors.

It's also best if the building inspector on your project is knowledgeable about solar power systems. The best way to hire the right team is to contact your local building authority (county, city) and discuss your plans with a senior inspector or other official. She or he may recommend a local contractor who has solar experience. A specific inspector may also be recommended, at least for the solar components of the job.

The conventional residential construction process includes the following 20 steps, in roughly the order they'd be accomplished:

- ◆ Preconstruction preparation

- ◆ Excavation

- ◆ Pest control

- ◆ Concrete

- ◆ Waterproofing

- ◆ Framing

- ◆ Roofing

- ◆ Plumbing

- Electrical
- HVAC (heating, ventilation, air conditioning)
- Siding and/or masonry
- Barriers (doors and windows)
- Insulation
- Drywall
- Trim
- Painting
- Cabinetry
- Flooring and tile
- Gutters and downspouts
- Landscaping and driveways

Solar construction is incorporated into these steps, primarily in the preconstruction preparation, plumbing, electrical, HVAC, and landscaping stages. Depending on your solar design, it may also impact excavation, framing, roofing, insulation, and other steps. Otherwise, your solar home is constructed in the same manner as conventional homes.

Solar Design

In Chapter 1, I introduced the terms active and passive in regard to solar design. An active solar home is a house that collects thermal heat in water or air, then distributes that heat using pumps or fans. A passive solar home is a house that uses a room, floor, or another part of the building as a solar collector. The room's air or walls (or both) collect thermal heat from the sun and store it for use in other parts of the home *without* pumps or fans.

How can a passive solar power system distribute thermal energy without pumps or fans, you ask? You've probably noticed that heat moves from warmer materials to cooler ones until there is no longer a temperature difference between the two. In fact, the wind is the movement of air warmed by the sun. A passive solar building distributes heat throughout the living space through *conduction*, *convection*, and *radiation*. These are the laws. You can't break any of these laws, but you can take advantage of them as you design and build your own home.

Another law is that opaque objects absorb solar radiation. Darker objects absorb more than lighter colors. This was clarified for me at an outdoor auto show a few years ago where two classic cars of the same model, one black and one white, sat in the sun. The light car was cool to the touch while the black car was very hot to touch. That's why solar collectors are dark in color, to capture the greatest amount of solar radiation. And that's why everyone in the South seems to drive a white car.

The difference between a passive solar home and a conventional home is design. A passive solar home incorporates a collector, absorber, thermal mass, distribution, and control that best take advantage of the local climate.

Sun-Day School

Conduction is the way heat moves through materials. An electric stove burner heats up a skillet. **Convection** is the way heat circulates through liquids and gases. Warm air rises to the ceiling. **Radiant** heat moves through the air from warmer objects to cooler ones. A sun-heated floor warms the air around it.

There are three types of design techniques:

- **Direct gain** is the simplest passive design technique. Sunlight enters the house through south-facing windows with special glazing or glass. The sunlight then strikes dark masonry floors and/or walls that absorb and store solar heat. At night, as the room cools, the heat stored in thermal mass radiates into the room. Because water stores twice as much heat as masonry, specially designed walls can be filled with water for greater solar heating efficiency.

- **Indirect gain** stores its solar thermal energy between the south-facing windows and the living space in a special solar heat-absorbing wall called a Trombe wall (named after Felix Trombe, one of its inventors). The wall then radiates thermal energy into the living space. The main difference between direct-gain and indirect-gain designs is the distance between the glass and the thermal mass. Indirect-gain components are closer to each other.

- **Isolated gain** is another popular passive solar design. A sunspace, also known as a solar room or solarium, uses solar energy to warm the air in a room. It works in much the same way as a greenhouse, except that a sunroom requires more ventilation control so people inside don't get too hot or cold.

Orienting Your Solar Home

As you can see, designing your home to take advantage of the sun's energy can save you thousands of dollars in energy costs over the years. That's why it's vital that you make sure your home is not only designed but oriented or placed on the building lot to take full advantage of solar radiation.

The most productive hours of sunlight are from about 9:00 A.M to 3:00 P.M., called solar noon. For much of the year, your site will probably receive solar radiation before and after these times, but it will contain less energy. The least sunlight will be at solar noon on the shortest day of the year, December 21. The most will be six months later or approximately June 21.

Orientation is important in designing a solar passive home, but it is most critical for one that will use PV to develop solar electricity. And it's especially important if the PV modules are installed in a fixed position without a tracking system. I'll cover the specifics of selecting, orienting, and mounting PVs in Chapter 9. Generally, a house that is slightly longer in the east-west dimension will be warmer in the winter and cooler in the summer.

The best solar orientation is facing the widest part of the house to the south.

(©Gaiam Real Goods)

For now, know that there are resources and tools to help you orient your house for optimum solar reception. The Solar Pathfinder (931-593-3552; www.solarpathfinder.com), for example, is a small plastic dome and tripod that helps track solar travel over a specific site. In addition, Appendix B and Chapter 9 include numerous products and free Internet sites to help you orient your home.

Energy-Efficient Design

As you learned in Chapter 3, you can save on the cost of solar equipment and design by first making your home design as energy efficient as possible.

What does that mean? Here's what most energy-efficient home designs have in common:

- A well-constructed and tightly sealed thermal envelope
- Energy-efficient doors, windows, and appliances
- Properly sized, high-efficiency heating and cooling systems
- Controlled ventilation

Let's take a closer look at each of these components of building an energy-efficient home.

Thermal Envelope

A thermal envelope is everything about the house that shields the living space from the outdoors. It includes the wall and roof assemblies, insulation, vapor retarders, windows, and weatherstripping.

Today's wall and roof assemblies are designed to keep interior air in and exterior air out. For example, structural insulated panels (SIPs) of plywood or oriented-strand board are glued to foam board that serves as an insulation barrier.

An energy-efficient house has much higher insulation R-values than required by most local building codes. An R-value is the ability of a material to resist heat transfer. The lower the value, the faster the heat loss. For example, a typical house might have insulation of R-11 in the exterior walls, R-19 in the ceiling, and no insulation in the floors and foundation walls. An energy-efficient home will have wall insulation of R-20 to R-30, and ceiling and floor insulation of R-50 to R-70.

Solar Eclipse

It makes little sense to save money on winter heating just to spend it on summer cooling. A passive solar home design must provide summer comfort as well, primarily by using intelligent window placement, which can be supplemented by awnings, shutters, and trellises.

In addition, an energy-efficient home will have vapor retarders that minimize the condensation of water vapor on exterior walls. In colder climates, warm indoor air condenses inside exterior walls. In humid climates, warm outdoor air condenses on the outside surfaces of exterior walls. Condensation leads to inefficient heat loss as well as mildew and other problems. An efficient thermal envelope minimizes heat loss and mildew with vapor retarders.

Doors, Windows, and Appliances

Typical homes lose more than 25 percent of their heat through windows and surrounding window framing. That's a lot of expensive heat lost to inefficiency. South-facing windows should have a high solar heat gain coefficient (SHGC) to allow winter sun and heat into the house. North-, east-, and west-facing windows should have low SHGC to reduce loss. Your home's designer, contractor, and materials supplier can help you select the most energy-efficient windows and doors for long-term value.

Modern appliances are much more energy efficient than those of a decade ago. Those with the Energy Star label exceed the federal government's minimum efficiency by a large percentage. Energy-efficient appliances may cost more to purchase. However, they then cost less to operate, meaning they eventually cost less than inefficient appliances.

The highest gains in energy efficiency are found in buying efficient models of those appliances that use the most energy. That means getting energy-efficient water heaters, clothes washers and dryers, dishwashers, and refrigerators.

Heating and Cooling

With energy-efficient insulation and a well-designed thermal envelope, your home will need much less heating and cooling. In fact, smart designing can save you thousands of dollars by requiring a system only half the size needed by a nonefficient home.

To keep from over-buying a system that costs more to purchase and operate than you really need, make sure your home designer gets the latest information on energy-efficient HVAC systems.

> **Sun Spots**
>
> Heat pumps, a combined heater and air conditioner, are much more efficient to operate than separate furnaces and air conditioning systems. Heat pumps work too hard in very hot and very cold climates, so they aren't as efficient as in moderate climates.

Controlled Ventilation

An energy-efficient house must be tightly sealed, but it also needs some controlled air flow or ventilation for the health of the house and the people inside. There will always be ways for air to escape. Unfortunately, with the outgoing air goes expensive heat and cooling.

Airtight homes use energy recovery ventilators (ERV) that salvage as much as 70 percent of the energy from the stale exhaust air. A heat exchanger inside the ERV pulls the heat or cool from the air for recycling. Other systems are also used to make sure that stale air is removed from the house, but many systems don't recycle the energy.

Is a controlled ventilation system right for your new home? Much depends on the local climate and how much it costs to keep the home comfortable. If the loss is of minimal value, it may not be worth the expense of engineering and equipment to try to capture and reuse the energy. Your utility supplier and architect can give you more specifics.

Contractors and Suppliers

Hiring the right contractor and supplier is always important when building a house. It's especially important when you're building a nonstandard home such as a solar home.

A building contractor usually doesn't pound nails or rough-in plumbing. He or she is the construction manager, making sure that everyone is doing the job according to the approved building plans. In most cases, your building contractor will …

- Supervise all aspects of the work done at the building site.

- Hire, supervise, pay, and fire subcontractors as needed to get the job done.

- Buy all materials and supplies needed in construction.

- Make sure that the site is inspected and approved by the local building department.

- Coordinate getting building permits and any variances.

- Make sure that all subcontractors are legal and have the needed insurance (like worker's compensation insurance).

For this effort, the general contractor (GC) typically gets 15 to 20 percent of the total value of the project. Alternately, the GC could be hired to manage the project for a specified hourly rate. Or a lump sum may be agreed upon.

What does it take to be a licensed general contractor? Contractors are licensed based on knowledge, experience, and other assets. For example, in California, a licensed general contractor must …

- Be 18 years of age or older.

- Prove at least four full years of experience as a journeyman, foreman, supervisor, or contractor in the appropriate classification.

- Pass a written test.

- Have a specific amount of operating capital (currently more than $2,500).

- Register a contractor's bond or cash deposit ($7,500).

- Pay the examination fee ($250) and licensing fee ($150) plus a biannual renewal fee ($300).

In most states, there is more than one type of general contractor. There's a general engineering contractor who requires specialized engineering knowledge and skills. And there's a general building contractor for constructing houses and other shelters.

In addition, there are various specialty contractors or subcontractors for specific trades (electrical contractor, carpentry contractor, etc.). The one you're most interested in is the solar contractor. Most states certify solar contractors, which means they have to pass a special test and show that they have solar construction experience.

How do you hire the *best* contractor? It's just like buying anything else. You first find out what's available, then get the cost, and finally compare to get the best value. Of course, you're not buying toothpaste here. You're buying a building partner and there's lots more money involved.

Start the process early by asking building inspectors, solar equipment suppliers, and solar home owners about local contractors. Keep notes in your Home Book, that notebook you've set aside for writing down ideas, resources, costs, and designs as you begin the construction process. You want to know who's qualified, who's available, and who's recommended by people with more building experience than you.

Once you've developed or selected a specific home design and plans, you ask qualified contractors to bid on construction. You'll probably have to supply a set of detailed plans to any contractor from which you want a detailed bid.

Solar Eclipse _____

Keep in mind that the lowest cost isn't necessarily the best value. The lowest bidder may not have solar experience. Or the bidder may not be fully licensed and insured. There are often reasons besides efficiency that allow a contractor to bid low. Some reasons are legitimate while others aren't. It can save you thousands of dollars and days of frustration if you can pick the best *value* in a building contractor.

Again, check out my book, *The Complete Idiot's Guide to Building Your Own Home*, for lots more information and guidelines on selecting a qualified contractor—and for being your own building contractor.

What if you've decided to retrofit your current or next home with solar power rather than build a new home? That's the topic of the next chapter. And if you'd rather buy a solar home already built or retrofitted, skip ahead to Chapter 23.

The Least You Need to Know

- Find out early how cooperative your local building department will be toward solar homes.

- The standard construction process can easily be modified to fit the requirements of solar home construction.

- Your solar home can take advantage of passive and active solar designing to save money.

◆ Make sure that your home's design and orientation fit the solar opportunities and limitations of your building lot.

◆ Make sure that your solar home is as energy efficient as possible to keep your investment in solar power equipment as low as possible.

◆ Find an architect and a building contractor with solar construction experience to ensure that the home is planned and built for efficiency.

Retrofitting Your Home for Solar Power

In This Chapter

◆ Understanding your home's solar climate

◆ Determining how your home's orientation enhances or limits sunlight

◆ What to consider when planning your solar power system

◆ What will it cost?

◆ Trading in energy-guzzling appliances and upgrading insulation

Solar power is the future. But what do you do if your home was built in the past? How can you retrofit your current home to take advantage of solar energy?

This chapter offers dozens of ideas on replacing home energy components (retrofitting) with solar power, heating, cooling, appliances, and more. It shows you how to make the most of what you have as well as the best that's available today.

Solar Climate

You already have a home, cabin, RV, or other structure, and you want to put solar power to work. Good for you! Let's see what you have to work with. First, let's take a closer look at the local climate, then figure out what your current home has going for it, solar-wise.

Weather is what happens today. Climate is what happens over many, many days. For example, a home near Phoenix, Arizona, may be getting a cold rain today, but the local climate is hot and dry. A home atop a nearby mountain may get more snow in winter and sunshine in the summer than a similar home in town. The hilltop home then has a microclimate; that is, the climate immediately surrounding the home.

Sunlight, weather patterns, and microclimates affect the performance of solar power and thermal energy systems. The more direct sunlight a system receives, for example, the more electricity or heat it produces. In contrast, clouds, fog, frost, rain, and falling snow reduce the amount of solar energy that can be captured. Water and trees can make a solar energy system work more effectively or less effectively, depending on where they are located.

So the first step in retrofitting your home is to figure out how much solar energy is available to it. The amount of sunlight (solar radiation) reaching a specific site depends on the latitude, time of day, and time of year.

Think about this: Locations nearer the equator get more sunlight through the year than places at higher latitudes. In the United States, for example, the southern states receive more solar radiation than the northern states. But two cities at the same latitude can get differing amounts of sunlight through the year. Seattle, Washington, for example, doesn't get the same amount of sunlight as Minot, North Dakota, even though they are at about the same latitude. And Minot gets much colder weather.

Sun Spots
Earth's equator isn't directly under the sun. Earth is actually tilted 23.5 degrees relative to the sun. This tilting results in *longer* days in the Northern Hemisphere (north of the equator) from the spring or vernal equinox to the fall or autumnal equinox. At the same time, the Southern Hemisphere has *shorter* days. An equinox is the time when both the day and night are 12 hours long. Spring equinox occurs each year about March 23 and fall equinox about September 22.

There are many factors besides proximity to the equator. Clouds scatter and absorb solar radiation, creating diffuse sunlight with less energy than direct sunlight. Smog can have the same effect. The flat land around Minot doesn't stop cold weather from Canada from crossing the border without permission. Seattle, however, is protected by the Olympic Mountain Range and tempered by the waters of Puget Sound.

A solar radiation map, shown in Chapter 1, will give you an approximation of the amount of sunlight your location gets. Of course, microclimates and local obstructions will impact this.

Because Earth is round, the sun strikes its surface at different angles ranging from 0° (just above the horizon) to 90° (directly overhead). When the sun's rays are vertical, Earth's surface gets all the energy possible. The more slanted the sun's rays are, the longer they travel through the atmosphere, becoming more scattered and diffuse. That's why mornings and evenings are cooler than midday.

The polar regions of Earth never get a high sun, and because Earth is tilted slightly, the poles get no sun at all during part of the year.

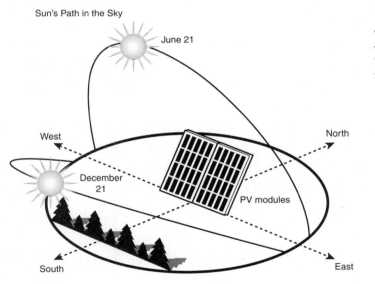

The sun's noontime height above the horizon changes seasonally, an important fact when you're orienting PV modules.

The United States is in the middle latitudes (between the North Pole and the equator) so it receives more solar energy in the summer because the days are longer *and* because the sun is nearly overhead.

That's a review of solar energy for those who slept through science class in high school. Of course, there's lots more to the topic. But it does remind you of the basics so you can better understand how the location, orientation, and climate at your homesite impacts the job of retrofitting for solar energy.

Your Current Home

So, let's take a look at where you live. Hey, nice place!

Chances are, you're not going to be able to turn your house to take more advantage of the sun—unless you're living in an RV. Where it is, it is. Fortunately, the solar power and thermal energy systems you're going to install can be oriented or turned to take advantage of the greatest amount of solar radiation. In fact, PV modules can be installed on motorized frames that actually follow or track the sun's relative movement through the sky to gather the greatest solar energy. Pretty nifty!

In Chapter 6, I briefly discussed some tools to help you determine how much solar energy your home is capable of receiving. The previous solar radiation map is a starting point, but you want to know how your home's orientation, altitude, and surroundings enhance or limit the sunlight. This is especially important because you will want to size, price, buy, and install a system that is the optimum size for your existing home. You don't want to get it in place and then find out that it's too small to do the job. Nor do you want to buy a system that's wasteful.

In addition to solar radiation, your homesite needs enough space to take advantage of that sunlight. Depending on where on your site the sunlight is best, you need to have enough room to mount solar power or thermal modules. (Final selection and mounting will be covered in Chapters 9 and 10.)

For example, a solar power system for generating electricity to serve a standard house may be about 500 square feet in size. That's about 20 feet by 25 feet. Depending on the PV module's efficiency, it would produce from 1.5 kW to 6.2 kW. That's quite a range, illustrating that the module's efficiency (percent of sunlight converted to electricity) is vital to sizing. It's also important to price because, as you can imagine, higher-efficiency modules cost more to buy.

Here's another consideration when retrofitting your home's roof for solar power: weight. Will your home's roof safely support the solar panels and equipment needed to gather and distribute solar power? In most cases, yes. However, your building permit for the system may require that an engineering company assess the load-bearing capacity of your home's roof and make structural recommendations, particularly with older homes that may have been built before standardized building codes.

CAUTION

Solar Eclipse

System weight is a consideration if you're going to install certain types of solar thermal hot water systems on the roof. "Batch-type" solar collectors store 20 to 50 gallons of water in the rooftop collector. Solar power systems add weight to the roof's load, so consider mounting some or all of the system on a special frame above the ground or against a south-facing wall.

Planning Your Solar Power System

Several factors will influence the size of the PV system you select. For starters, consider how much of your present electricity needs your PV system should supply.

Chapter 2 gave you a total for what power your home currently uses. If you want to meet 50 percent of your electricity needs with a PV system, you'll choose a system sized to produce and store about half of your usual electricity demand.

Also consider what federal, state, and utility buy-down programs will do to help you (see Chapter 4). They may have a minimum or maximum size of system that they'll help you buy. For example, a buy down may be limited to 125 percent of the power you purchased from your utility last year. If you used 6,000 kWh last year, they may not offer a rebate on a system that delivers more than 7,500 kWh a year. Why? Because they don't want to encourage you to use *more* energy than before. (And they may not want you to become a utility generator that competes with existing utility companies!)

Here's an important question in planning your retrofit (or new) solar power system: Does it come with batteries? Batteries store electric power. A battery system can give your home electricity when the sun isn't out (when you need lights the most). A battery system can also serve as a backup resource in areas where power outages are frequent. If your house has utility power, batteries are optional. If you don't have utility power, then you *should* have batteries.

Chapter 14 offers a more comprehensive look at battery systems. For now, consider whether you want to include a storage system in your solar plans. Remote locations, poor utility line maintenance, or mangled deregulation schemes would all be very good reasons to consider battery backup to your utility power.

Remember that retrofitting your home for solar power systems may require a local building permit. That topic and process are covered in Chapter 6 as well as in my book, *The Complete Idiot's Guide to Building Your Own Home* (Alpha Books, 2002).

Pricing Your Solar Power System

So, how much will it cost to install a solar power or thermal system? The cost of a PV system depends on the system's size and components, but also scales somewhat with the system size or rating and the amount of energy produced. Batteries add $3,000 to $5,000 to the cost of any system, so only buy 'em if you need 'em.

As you can see, there are numerous requirements, variables, incentives, and efficiency factors. To get a rough idea, here are some ballpark numbers:

◆ A small single-PV panel system with built-in *inverter* that produces about 100 watts of power may cost around $900 installed or about $9 per watt.

◆ A medium-sized system of 2 kW (2,000 watts) may cost $13,000 to $20,000 installed, or $6.50 to $10.00 per watt.

◆ A larger residential system of 5 kW may cost $30,000 to $40,000 installed, or $6.00 to $8.00 per watt.

Before you call 911 for resuscitation, know that these estimates don't include deductions for any rebates or other incentives. Also, remember that once the system has returned your initial investment in savings, it is working virtually for free. And solar power systems can keep on paying you back for 25 years or more!

Sun-Day School

An **inverter** converts direct current (DC) from a battery to alternating current (AC) for use by home appliances and lights.

And before you get too excited about solar costs, you might price a utility line extension for new construction. Utility companies give very little in the way of free footage anymore, and most line extensions will cost in excess of $1 per inch. If you have to extend more than 300 to 400 yards, solar may actually cost you less initially than hooking up to the local utility.

The real point of this exercise in estimating costs is not to put you on blood pressure medicine. It's to help you know what factors are most important as you retrofit your home for solar.

Fortunately, solar thermal systems for heating hot water are more economical to install than solar power systems. And they save the power used to heat the water. However, the costs are a little tougher to calculate and investment incentives are not always available. Even so, solar water heating systems are less expensive and can give you a faster return on your investment.

Replacing Appliances

Major appliances take a lot of electricity to operate, especially electric water heaters, electric dryers, and refrigerators. Fortunately, technology has produced some very efficient appliances over the past 10 years.

As you learned in Chapter 1, the most expensive heat source is electricity. Electric radiant heat, for example, typically costs more than three times the price of oil heat.

So Chapter 3 suggested that you retrofit your home with lower cost heating. However, HVAC isn't the only way that heat is made in your home. Water heaters, stoves, and ovens are often powered by electricity. If you're using costly electricity for heat in your home, consider replacing these heating appliances with less costly energy sources, especially those from renewable sources.

Aside from HVAC systems, the refrigerator is probably the largest power user in your home. Today's typical refrigerator uses less than 650 kWh of power each year. It's probably not cost-effective to scrap an older, but operating refrigerator for a new energy-efficient unit. However, if your fridge is nearing the end of its lifespan (10 to 20 years is typical), compare energy ratings and you may find that power savings may help you buy a new one sooner. A super-efficient model will cost about twice the price of a standard refrigerator, but will save you money in the long term.

Bright Idea

How efficient can a refrigerator get? The best can run on less than 1 kWh a day! The most energy-efficient models can cut that usage by more than half. Of course, they're more expensive to purchase than name-brand units, but the energy savings offsets the initial expense. You can find them through some large appliance retailers and the catalogs listed in Appendix B.

Heat exchangers can be installed in existing homes to recover half or more of otherwise wasted heat from HVAC systems. Tied in to your heating system controls, they can dramatically reduce heating costs. Gas furnaces range in efficiency from 78 to 96 percent.

To find out what other energy-efficient appliances are available, get a copy of the latest catalogs from Real Goods (www.realgoods.com) or check the other resources in Appendix B. There are even solar clothes dryers on the market!

Upgrading Insulation and Weatherstripping

Chapter 3 offered numerous ideas on making your existing home more energy efficient. The less energy your home uses, the less your solar power system will cost. So it makes sense to take care of insulation and weatherstripping in your home before retrofitting it with a solar power system.

Your home energy audit probably suggested where you can insulate and weatherstrip your home for greatest gain. Easier-to-reach spaces like attics and under the floor typically are the best places to start upgrading insulation. Even installing a radiant barrier under the floor can dramatically reduce energy loss.

You may opt to have a contractor upgrade the insulation in the walls of your existing home. For most homes, the contractor drills strategic holes in the exterior walls and blows (with a reverse vacuum) insulation into wall cavities. Your local utility can recommend and may even give you a rebate for upgrading your home's insulation and energy efficiency.

There's still more that you can do to your new or existing home to reduce the cost of your solar power system. You can landscape for optimum solar energy, covered in the next chapter.

The Least You Need to Know

- ◆ Solar climate is the amount of sunlight your homesite receives over a long period of time.

- ◆ Solar radiation at your home can be greater or lesser than other homes in your area, depending on microclimates.

- ◆ Replacing major appliances with more energy-efficient models is an investment in reducing long-term power costs.

- ◆ You can retrofit your existing home with solar power equipment and energy-efficient appliances to cut long-term power costs.

Chapter 8

Solar Landscaping

In This Chapter

◆ Smart landscaping can save energy dollars

◆ The environmental benefits of trees and plants

◆ How local climate and microclimate impact your landscaping

◆ Options for shading and wind protection

◆ Designing a solar-friendly yard

◆ Selecting the right trees and shrubs

Whether you're building a new solar home or retrofitting the one you have, smart solar landscaping can dramatically cut your summer and winter energy costs. That means you can save money on utility bills *and* reduce your investment in solar power equipment.

In addition, smart landscaping can protect your home from winter and summer sun, reduce the need to water lawn and plants, and help control noise and even air pollution. That's a tall order, yes, but solar landscaping is up to it. You'll find out how in this chapter.

Saving Money with Landscaping

Want to save $100 to $250 a year in energy costs? Simply plant three trees. Placed in the right spot, these trees can provide sufficient shade to reduce your utility bill.

Actually, carefully positioned trees can save up to 25 percent of a household's energy consumption for heating and cooling. The experts say that, on average, a well-designed landscape can save you enough in energy costs to pay back your initial investment in less than eight years. For example, an 8-foot deciduous (leaf-shedding) tree costs about as much as a large window awning for shade in the summer, yet still admits some winter sunshine into your home.

Summer

You may have noticed the coolness of parks and wooded areas compared to the temperature of nearby city streets. Because cool air settles near the ground, air temperatures directly under trees can be as much as 25°F cooler than air temperatures above nearby blacktop. The process is called *evapotranspiration* (a word you may hear on *Jeopardy!*). One study found summer daytime air temperatures to be 3° to 6° cooler in tree-shaded neighborhoods than in treeless areas.

Sun-Day School

Evapotranspiration— the process by which a plant actively moves and releases water vapor—from trees can reduce surrounding air temperatures as much as 9°F.

In fact, a well-planned landscape can reduce an unshaded home's summer air-conditioning costs by 15 to 50 percent. So smart solar landscaping can pay off in summer utility savings.

Winter

Ever heard of wind chill? If the outside temperature is 10°F and the wind speed is 20 miles per hour, the wind chill is –24°F, meaning that the temperature actually feels as cold as –24°F. That's a fact. Another useful fact is that trees, fences, or geographical features can be used as windbreaks to shield your house from the wind.

One Midwest study found that windbreaks to the north, west, and east of houses cut fuel consumption by an average of 40 percent. Houses with windbreaks placed only on the windward side (the side from which the wind is coming) averaged 25 percent less fuel consumption than similar but unprotected homes. If you live in a windy climate, your well-planned landscape can reduce your winter heating bills by approximately one third. That's good news!

Trees Clean the Air, Too

In addition to the obvious benefits of improving the appearance of your home (and adding to its resale value), planting lots of trees and other growing things around your home offers numerous environmental benefits. Trees and vegetation control erosion, protect water supplies, provide food and habitat for wildlife, and clean the air by absorbing carbon dioxide and releasing oxygen.

Sun Spots

The National Academy of Sciences estimates that urban America has 100 million spaces where trees could be planted. It goes on to say that filling these spaces with trees and lightening the color of dark, urban surfaces would result in annual energy savings of *50 billion kWh*—25 percent of the 200 billion kWh needed every year by air conditioners in the United States. Further, these trees would reduce electric power plant emissions of carbon dioxide by *35 million tons* annually and save users of utility-supplied electricity *at least $3.5 billion each year.*

Replacing a turf lawn with natural grasses and ground cover can benefit the environment as well by reducing the need for gas-powered mowers and trimmers. For example, some grasses, such as buffalo grass and fescue, grow to only a certain height—about 6 inches. They are also water thrifty.

Considering the Climate

As introduced in the previous chapter, weather is what happens today and climate is what happens over many, many days. The United States and Canada can be divided into four climatic regions: cool, temperate, hot-arid, and hot-humid. Your home's best solar landscape strategy depends on which region you live in. That means what you do to enhance solar efficiency for a home in Atlanta (hot-humid) is different from what you would do in Minneapolis (cool) or San Diego (temperate). Let's take a look at recommendations for each climate.

For a cool climate …

- Use dense windbreaks to protect the home from cold winter winds.

- Allow the winter sun to reach south-facing windows.

- Shade south and west windows and walls from the direct summer sun, if summer overheating is a problem.

For a temperate climate …

- ◆ Maximize warming effects of the sun in the winter.
- ◆ Maximize shade during the summer.
- ◆ Deflect winter winds away from buildings.
- ◆ Funnel summer breezes toward the home.

For a hot-arid climate …

- ◆ Provide shade to cool roofs, walls, and windows.
- ◆ Allow summer winds to access naturally cooled homes.
- ◆ Block or deflect winds away from air-conditioned homes.

For a hot-humid climate …

- ◆ Channel summer breezes toward the home.
- ◆ Maximize summer shade with trees that still allow penetration of low-angle winter sun.
- ◆ Avoid locating planting beds close to the home if they require frequent watering.

In addition, there is the climate immediately surrounding your home, its microclimate. If your home is located on a sunny southern slope, it may have a warm microclimate, even if you live in a cool region. Or, even though you live in a hot-humid region, your home may be situated in a comfortable microclimate because of abundant shade and dry breezes. Nearby bodies of water may increase your site's humidity or decrease its air temperature.

Your home's microclimate may be more sunny, shady, windy, calm, rainy, snowy, moist, or dry than average local conditions. These factors all help determine what plants may or may not grow in your microclimate.

Designing for Solar Advantage

So how can you best plan landscaping to take advantage of solar opportunities? First, make sure your home is oriented and designed to admit low-angle winter sun, reject overhead summer sun, and minimize the cooling effect of winter winds.

Design and orient your new house to maximize a homesite's natural advantages and lessen its disadvantages. Notice the homesite's exposure to sun, wind, and water. Also note the location and proximity of nearby buildings, fences, water bodies, trees, and pavement—and their possible climatic effects. Buildings provide shade and windbreak. Fences and walls block or channel the wind. Water bodies moderate temperature but increase humidity and produce glare. Trees provide shade, windbreaks, or wind channels. Pavement reflects or absorbs heat, depending on whether its color is light or dark.

If your home is already built, inventory its comfort and energy problems as covered in Chapter 7.

For both new and existing homes, use shading, wind protection, and other landscaping ideas to make your homesite more energy efficient and solar friendly.

> **Bright Idea**
>
> When building a new home here in the Northern Hemisphere, align the home's long axis in an east-west direction. The home's longest wall with the most window area should face south or southeast. The home's north-facing and west-facing walls should have fewer windows because these walls generally face winter's prevailing winds. Fewer west windows means less unwanted heat gain on summer afternoons as well.

Shading

Solar heat passing through windows and the roof is the major reason for air conditioner use. Fortunately, shading is the most cost-effective way to reduce solar heat gain and cut air-conditioning costs.

Using shade effectively requires you to know the size, shape, and location of the moving shadow that your shading device casts. Remember that homes in cool regions may never overheat and may not require shading.

You can select trees with appropriate sizes, densities, and shapes for almost any shading application. To block solar heat in the summer but let much of it in during the winter, use deciduous trees. To provide continuous shade or to block heavy winds, use evergreen trees or shrubs.

Plant deciduous trees with high, spreading crowns (leaves and branches) to the south of your home for maximum summertime roof shading. Plant trees with crowns lower to the ground to the west for shade from the lower afternoon sun. Don't plant trees that will block south-facing walls from winter solar energy. Popular deciduous trees include oaks, elms, and maples. Ask your local nursery about specific varieties that grow best in your climate.

A 6 to 8-foot deciduous tree planted near your home can begin shading windows the first year. Depending on the species and the home, the tree will shade the roof in 5 to 10 years. (Be sure to find out how large the tree will grow before positioning it in your yard; there's more about selecting the right trees and plants later in this chapter.)

There are many related ways of keeping our homes cooler in summer and warmer in winter with smart landscaping. Here are a few:

◆ If you have an air conditioner, planting a tree to shade the unit can increase its efficiency by as much as 10 percent.

◆ Trees, shrubs, and groundcover plants can also shade the ground and pavement around the home. This reduces heat radiation and cools the air before it reaches your home's walls and windows.

◆ Use a large bush or row of shrubs to shade a patio or driveway.

◆ Plant a hedge to shade a sidewalk.

◆ Keep in mind that fewer west windows means less unwanted heat gain on summer afternoons.

Solar Eclipse

Can you dig it? Make sure you know where any underground wires, cables, and pipes are before digging so you can avoid them. Call your local utility services to find out. Some areas have a single telephone number you can call to check on all underground hazards. Check inside the front of your local telephone book.

◆ Vines can shade walls during their first growing season. A lattice or trellis with climbing vines, or a planter box with trailing vines, shades the home's perimeter while admitting cooling breezes to the shaded area. Or try using a trellis for climbing vines to shade a patio area.

◆ Shrubs planted close to the house will fill in rapidly and begin shading walls and windows within a few years. However, avoid allowing dense foliage to grow immediately next to a home where wetness or continual humidity is a problem.

Well-landscaped homes in wet areas allow winds to flow around the home, keeping the home and its surrounding soil reasonably dry.

Wind Protection

Wind can reduce your home's energy efficiency as well. Properly selected and placed landscaping can provide excellent wind protection and cut energy costs. In addition, these benefits will increase as the trees and shrubs mature.

The best windbreaks block wind close to the ground by using trees and shrubs that have low crowns. Evergreen trees and shrubs planted to the north and northwest of the home are the most common type of windbreak. Trees, bushes, and shrubs are often planted together to block or impede wind from ground level to the treetops. Or, evergreen trees combined with a wall, fence, or earth berm (natural or man-made walls or raised areas of soil) can deflect or lift the wind over the home.

A windbreak will reduce wind speed for up to 30 times the windbreak's height. A 20-foot windbreak, for example, can reduce the wind's speed for up to 600 feet. However, for maximum protection, plant your windbreak at a distance from your home of two to five times the mature height of the trees. That's 40 to 100 feet away from the house for a tree that will mature to about 20 feet in height. Of course, you don't have much control over windbreaks on a small residential lot.

If snow tends to drift in your area, plant low shrubs on the windward side of your windbreak. The shrubs will trap snow before it blows next to your home, increasing heat loss.

In addition to more distant windbreaks, planting shrubs, bushes, and vines next to your house creates dead air spaces that insulate your home in both winter and summer. Plant so there will be at least one foot of space between full-grown plants and your home's wall.

CAUTION

Solar Eclipse

Be careful not to plant evergreens too close to your home's south side if you are counting on warmth from the winter sun!

Summer winds, especially at night, can have a cooling effect if used for home ventilation. However, if winds are hot and your home is air conditioned all summer, you may want to keep summer winds from circulating near your home.

Planning Your Landscape

Before you start landscaping for energy efficiency, first develop a plan. The components of your plan could include deciduous trees and plants, coniferous trees and plants, earth berms, walls, fences, sheds, and garages. Here's how to create a landscape plan before you plant around your existing home or before you begin construction on a new house.

Use paper and colored pencils to begin designing your landscape. First, sketch a simple, scaled drawing of your yard. Locate its buildings, walks, driveways, and utilities (sewer, electric, gas, cable, and telephone lines). Note the location of all paved surfaces—streets, driveways, patios, or sidewalks—near your home. Then identify potential uses for different areas of your yard: vegetable gardens, flower beds, patios, and play areas.

Draw arrows to show sun angles and prevailing winds for both summer and winter. As you sketch, circle the areas of your yard needing shade or wind protection.

Indicate with arrows how you want views to be preserved or screened. Mark routes of noise pollution you wish to block. Also, highlight areas where landscaping height or width may be restricted, such as under utility lines or along sidewalks.

Notice yard areas that suffer from poor drainage and standing water. Some trees and shrubs will not grow well in poorly drained areas; others will. Note existing trees and shrubs. If they provide valued shade or windbreak, plan for their replacement when they become old or sick.

Perhaps you want more defined property boundaries or less traffic noise. Consider a "living fence" of dense trees, bushes, or shrubs. Depending on its location and application, this hedge can be customized to be tall, short, wide, narrow, open, or dense. Privet is a species of shrub that grows in most parts of the United States and can serve as a living fence.

Areas of lawn not used as picnic or play areas can be converted to planting beds or *xeriscaped* areas. Converting a traditional lawn to alternative, water-conserving grasses or other forms of xeriscaping saves energy and reduces water consumption.

Sun-Day School

Xeriscaping is a landscaping technique that uses vegetation that is drought resistant and able to survive on rainfall and groundwater once established.

Maybe you live in an urban area where yards are small and neighbors close. Your neighbor's yard may be the best place for trees to shade your south-facing windows. Your yard may be the best location for their windbreak. Bringing your neighbors into your plans could benefit everyone involved.

The more you identify your goals and familiarize yourself with your yard's features—current and proposed—the better your chances for success with your landscaping projects.

Selecting Trees and Shrubs

Trees and shrubs come in all shapes and sizes. How you select your trees and shrubs and how you plant them will directly affect your home's comfort and energy efficiency.

Trees and shrubs have a life span of many years and can become more attractive and functional with age. But poor planning of landscape improvements often creates trouble. Ensure proper plant placement and minimal maintenance *before* you plant!

Shapes

Tree shapes are very diverse. The density of a tree's leaves or needles is important to consider. Dense evergreens, like spruces, make great windbreaks for winter winds. If you're looking just to impede summer winds, choose a tree or shrub with more open branches and leaves. Such trees are also good for filtering morning sun from the east, while denser trees are better for blocking harsh afternoon summer sun.

Growth

Should you plant slow-growing or fast-growing tree species? Although a slow-growing tree may require many years of growth before it shades your roof, it will generally live longer than a fast-growing tree. Also, because slow-growing trees often have deeper roots and stronger branches, they are less prone to breakage by windstorms or heavy snow loads. And they can be more drought resistant than fast-growing trees.

Consider growth rate, strength, and brittleness when locating trees near walkways or structures. Ask whether the mature tree's root system is likely to damage sidewalks, foundations, or sewer lines. The smaller your yard, the more important it is to select a tree with manageable roots.

Buying

Landscape professionals can help you choose and locate new trees, shrubs, or ground cover. Share your drawings and tentative ideas with your local nursery or landscape contractor. As long as you have defined intended uses and spaces in which planting is actually possible, a competent nursery or landscape specialist will be able to help you make decisions. They know the local climate and what trees and shrubs will flourish in your yard.

When planting trees, shrubs, hedges, or bushes, find out how large the mature specimen will grow. In all cases, determine spacing by the *mature* sizes. For those plants close to your house, plan for at least 1 foot (30 centimeters) of extra clearance between the full-grown shrub and the wall of the home. This will prevent heavy pruning or damage to home siding in the future.

Bright Idea

After considering the placement of your trees and consulting landscaping and nursery professionals, go back to your drawings or plans and add the new information on species, shape, and mature-size spacing. This provides a final, prepurchase review to make sure that all elements will work well together—in the short *and* long term.

When you are ready to purchase your trees and shrubs, avoid buying damaged specimens. Thoroughly inspect the trunk, limbs, leaves, and roots to make sure the plant was handled carefully during growing, digging, and shipping. Reject plant stock with signs of insects or disease such as cocoons, egg masses, cankers, or lesions.

After you purchase the plants, be sure to keep tiny roots damp and shaded at all times. The plants will not survive if these roots inside the root ball are allowed to dry before planting.

Contact your county extension agents, public libraries, local nurseries, landscape architects, landscape contractors, and state and local energy offices for additional information on regionally appropriate plants and their maintenance requirements.

You've gone a long way in this section on saving your energy. Next, we get more specific about selecting the best solar equipment and systems to reduce your home's energy costs.

The Least You Need to Know

- Well-placed trees can save you up to 25 percent of your home's heating and cooling bill.

- Smart solar landscaping can reduce a home's air-conditioning costs by up to 50 percent.

- Plant landscaping that works with your local climate and microclimate, not against it.

- Plant trees for solar shade as well as wind protection.

- For efficiency, plan your solar landscaping on paper and talk with local nurseries to make sure selected plants meet your goals.

Part 2

Solar Power

Wow! Solar power really *is* an option! That's good news. And there's more good news. Solar electric generation is just one of many smart options. There's passive solar, solar water heating, solar space heating, wind power, hydropower, and even fuel cells.

Technology is applied science. And technology has really been applied over the past two decades to energy options. There are smart controllers that manage home energy. There are PV modules that actually track the sun across the sky absorbing as much light as possible. There are batteries that last longer than a Honda.

So let's take a peek at what technology has been busy doing lately to warm and light our homes with power from the sun.

Chapter 9

Solar Electric Generation

In This Chapter

- Turning sunlight into electricity
- Components in a typical solar power system
- Selecting components for your system
- Installing solar power systems

Buying a solar power system is like paying years of utility bills in advance. Of course, once it's paid off it begins paying you back. That's the good part.

The not-so-good part is that you have to learn about photovoltaics, crystalline silicon, lead-acid batteries, and other scientific stuff. Fortunately, I'll explain all of this and more in this chapter, so let's get started!

Understanding Solar Electricity

Photovoltaic (PV) technology converts sunlight into electricity. However, it *doesn't* use the sun's heat to do so. Then how does the magic happen?

PV produces electricity directly from the electrons freed by the interaction of sunlight and the semiconductor materials in the PV cells. How does *that* work?

Let's begin at the beginning. The basic building block of PV technology is the solar cell. *Solar* or *PV cells* are wired together to produce a PV module, the smallest PV component sold commercially. PV modules range in power from about 10 watts to 300 watts.

Sun-Day School

A **solar** or **PV cell** is the smallest semiconductor element within a PV module to perform the immediate conversion of light into electrical energy. Output is direct current or DC.

PV modules produce direct current or DC. Your home uses alternating current or AC. What to do? You can either use only DC loads or you can convert it. An inverter is a special piece of equipment that changes DC electricity into AC. If you don't need the PV electricity right then, you can either store it or ship it off to someone who needs it. Let's consider these options one at a time.

Direct current (DC) solar power system.

Direct-Current (DC) System

PV modules

Charge controller

Grounding circuit

Electric load (DC)

Grounding circuit

Battery

Alternating current (AC) solar power system.

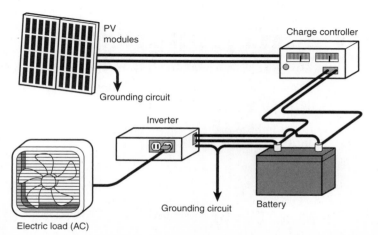

Alternating-Current (AC) System

PV modules

Charge controller

Grounding circuit

Inverter

Electric load (AC)

Grounding circuit

Battery

Batteries Not Included

Batteries can be installed in your solar power system to store PV electricity until needed. These batteries serve the same function as the one in your car. Car batteries store electricity developed by the engine and alternator until needed to start the car or run the CD player, for example. Solar batteries hang on to the PV electricity until needed to operate lights or appliances in your home. But once the batteries are completely full, you need to turn off any more incoming power, or your batteries will be damaged. You probably figured out that solar batteries are DC just like the one in your car. That means the batteries are installed in a solar power system *after* the PV modules and *before* the inverter. That makes sense. Batteries in your solar power system can make sure you have power even when the sun isn't out—or it's hiding, or you need more power at the moment than your PV modules are delivering.

Should you include batteries in your solar power system? The answer depends on what you want your system to do. If you have local power outages, a battery system can power your life until the utility company delivers again. If your home is off-grid—not connected to the local utility grid—you'll want batteries to power lights for reading and other activities at night when your solar power system is sleeping. If you'll be selling power back to the local utility, a battery array may pay for itself. However, remember that there's an ecological issue, because solar batteries are lead-acid batteries, and the manufacturing and use of lead-acid batteries isn't good for nature. Even so, it may be better than the alternative of relying on fossil fuels because you have no way of storing solar power.

> **Bright Idea**
>
> Need batteries for your solar power system? Buy the best deep-cycle batteries you can afford. Industrial deep-cycle batteries can cost $200 each, but have a life expectancy of 15 to 20 years. Compare this with golf-cart batteries that last three to five years and cost about $80 each.

Net Metering

So what's this about shipping power to other folks? If your solar power system is connected to the utility grid and you have an agreement with the power company to do so, your system can send electricity to the grid for use by others. It's called net metering.

Laws in more than 30 states now require utilities to allow net metering with *approved* residential customers, meaning that your solar electric generating system complies with the utility's requirements and you've signed an agreement. Chapter 25 offers more specifics and how-tos on net metering.

One major advantage of net metering is that the utility must pay you the *retail* rather than the *wholesale* price for your power. That means your solar power system can actually produce a little income to offset costs. No, you won't get rich—the power company will make sure of that. But it can help you make a decision to invest in solar power.

Want another financial incentive? In some areas, you can sell your solar power to the utility during peak hours at one rate, then buy it back during off-peak hours at a lower rate. Contact your state's utility department (see Appendix B for more specific details). Additional financial incentives for solar power, such as tax credits and rebates, are covered in Chapter 4.

Here's how to calculate electricity bill savings for a PV system. First, determine the system's size in kilowatts (kW). Next, using the map, select the energy production factor for your location. Then plug these numbers in to the following equation:

Annual PV System Energy = (PV kW) × (kWh ÷ kW-year)

Annual Energy Bill Savings = (kWh per year) × (Residential Rate)/100

For example, a 2-kW system in Denver, Colorado, at a residential energy rate of $0.07 per kWh will save about $266 a year. Here's the math:

1,900 kWh per kW-year × $0.07 per kWh × 2 kW = $266 per year

That's about $22.17 a month in savings.

System Components

There's a lot going on in the world of PV. Let's take a look at the technologies, the applications, and the issues so you can make an informed choice when selecting your system.

Sun Spots

The San Francisco Airport has installed UNI-SOLAR PV laminates on one of their support buildings to test the product. It's a flexible, nonreflective, thin-film amorphous silicon cell that is manufactured and installed in the roofing material itself. It works just like other PV cell materials, yet is part of the building. It's manufactured and sold by Bekaert ECD Solar Systems, and is expected to be available for residential application within the next couple of years.

Most PV cells today are made from crystalline silicon (c-Si) using a variety of production methods. The raw material, sand, is impure, so manufacturing processes must remove these impurities and defects. The result is called solar-grade silicon feedstock.

To make the silicon even better at gathering and converting sunlight, it is doped. That is, boron or phosphorus is added to tweak the frequencies of light that the silicon responds to. Alternately, a coating can be applied.

Thin-film photovoltaic cells use layers of semiconductor materials only a few micrometers thick. The layers are attached to an inexpensive backing such as glass, flexible plastic, or stainless steel. Complete PV modules can also be encased in a shell to protect cells and to enhance production.

How efficient are solar cells? Aha! That's the question you'll be asking suppliers as you trade cost for efficiency. The more expensive modules offer a higher efficiency factor than less expensive modules. As a ballpark, most systems will range between 5 to 15 percent efficiency. That is, 5 to 15 percent of the energy they receive from sunlight will be turned into electricity.

That's the simple explanation of how PV modules are manufactured. There's *lots* more to this technology, including high-efficiency multijunction devices, and Group III and V technologies. You can get a headache just thinking about it. Fortunately, you don't have to know everything about solar technology to put it to work for you. You just have to know how to select and pay for it. And there are lots of people offering to help.

There are many ways that PV technology is applied to making electricity from sunlight. Concentrating PV collectors, for example, use lenses and mirrors to focus the sunlight on to solar cells. Building-integrated PV systems are made with dual purposes such as to collect sunlight *and* serve as roofing or other building materials. Standalone systems are made to, er, stand alone. That is, they supply power to remote sites where no other electric service is available such as microwave towers on mountain tops.

> **Sun Spots**
>
> The National Center for Photovoltaics stays up nights figuring new ways to harness the sun for electric power. It creates, develops, and deploys PV and related technologies using lots of scientists and engineers working in an impressive laboratory. Find out what it's currently up to at National Center for Photovoltaics, National Renewable Energy Laboratory, 1617 Cole Blvd., Golden, CO 80401; or on its website at www.nrel.gov/ncpv.

Selecting Your Solar Power System

What are the components of a solar power system? PV power generation systems are made up of interconnecting components, each with a specific job to do. One of the major strengths of PV systems is modularity. As your need grows, individual components can be replaced or added to provide increased capacity.

Selecting System Components

System components typically include the solar array, optional battery bank and charge controller, inverter, and distribution parts.

The solar array consists of one or more PV modules that convert sunlight into electric energy. The modules are connected in series and/or parallel to provide the voltage and current levels needed by the system. The array is usually mounted on a metal structure and tilted to face the sun.

The optional battery bank contains one or more deep-cycle batteries. The batteries store the power produced by the solar array and discharge it as needed. The charge controller makes sure that the batteries are recharged by the solar array, and prevents overcharging.

The inverter converts DC power from the solar arrays into AC needed by most appliances and household loads. A home that uses only DC lights and appliances, such as an off-grid house or RV, doesn't need an inverter.

Sun-Day School

An **intertie** system is one that links an independent power producer, such as your solar power system, with a public power system so that they can draw from each other.

What else? That depends. Additional equipment may include an array combiner box, cabling, fuses, switches, circuit breakers, and a meter. If an *intertie* or net-metering system is installed, it will require a meter that can travel in both directions. For greatest solar efficiency, the PV modules can be mounted with motors to actually track the sun across the sky.

Sizing Your System

As you can imagine, the size of your solar power system depends on your electrical needs. Chapter 2 showed you how to calculate your home's current energy needs. Chapter 3 offered numerous suggestions for reducing dependency on electricity so your home doesn't need a large solar power system. In addition, you've decided how much of your energy needs you want or need to have supplied by a PV system. You may be aiming for 50 percent, 75 percent, or all of your power from solar.

For instance, maybe last year your house and its occupants used 6,000 kWh of electricity, but an energy audit and energy-efficient measures cut that need by 25 percent. You estimate that your home's energy needs are now about 4,500 kWh of electricity a year. Further, you've decided to install a system that can cut that in half—and have room for future expansion. You want to take advantage of rebates and tax incentives as well as net metering. So what size system do you need?

Fortunately, solar power systems are becoming more and more friendly. That is, once you know the size of the system you need you can begin shopping based on size and equipment.

For example, one solar equipment supplier offers an intertie system, including battery backup, designed to produce 2.3 kWh per day for about $9,000. (Costs are reduced by rebates, as discussed in Chapter 4.) The system includes four PV modules, power panel, fuse system, interconnect cables, lightning protector, roof or ground mounting frame, and four 12v batteries. It's designed to accept up to 36 additional PV modules for future expansion.

The power panel is more than half the cost because it combines the inverter with automatic controls. The controls manage the power generated by the solar modules, supplementing it with power from the utility company as needed. It has numerous safety features that not only protect your home and appliances, but also protect any public utility workers who think they turned off the power to lines on which they're working. In fact, your agreement with the local utility will require that you install an intertie system with these safety features.

Sun Spots

A good quality solar module will include 36 cells on a panel that's about 26 by 56 inches and about 2 inches thick. It will produce 120 watts of power and weigh about 26 pounds. Warranties range up to 25 years. Cost per module before rebates, is under $700 a unit. Cheaper units of the same size produce about one third the wattage for about one third the price. The warranty is about 10 years, so they are actually more expensive than better quality modules.

A bigger intertie system with 20 PV modules and battery backup will run about $20,000 (less rebates) and give you an average of 11.6 kWh per day. Need even more? A 40-module system will deliver 23 kWh per day for a price tag of around $35,000, less rebates. Each system uses about the same model power panel so you're paying mostly for additional PV modules and batteries.

Direct intertie systems are also available, without battery backup systems. They allow you to sell excess solar power to the utility as it is produced. System prices range from about $7,500 for a 4.3 kWh per day system to nearly $19,000 for a 13.3 kWh per day system. I'll cover solar power systems for homes, RVs, supplemental power, and emergency power more fully in Part 3.

Keep in mind that rebates, tax credits, and other discounts can cut these prices in half, depending on the system size and where you live. Installation charges are additional, but typically are eligible for rebate money as well.

Of course, if you're your own utility company, supplying power to your residence alone, off-grid, your system doesn't need to be as complex. Full standalone systems are available or you can get suppliers to design one for your needs. Besides an inverter/power panel, PV modules, batteries, cables, a build-your-own system should include the following:

- PV combiner box
- DC ground fault protection
- Lightning protector
- Safety and overcurrent protection

Installing Your Solar Power System

Should you attempt to install your own solar power system? Actually, you may not have a choice: No. You're installing an electrical system that, in many areas, requires a building permit and an electrical inspection and certificate. A local electrical contractor, hopefully one with solar power system experience, will need to install the system.

For a system as described in this chapter, figure on the cost of labor to be about $1,500 to $2,000. Most of the work will be installing the power panel. If you're handy, you may be able to cut costs by helping with the installation of PV modules and running or trenching cable.

How are PV modules mounted? Of course, you want them oriented so they receive the greatest amount of solar radiation throughout the year. The permanent angle is equal to your home's latitude in degrees. For example, a home in Boulder, Colorado, at 40° latitude would mount modules on a permanent frame set at an angle of 40° to level.

CAUTION

Solar Eclipse

Think of electricity as being alive—with teeth! Make sure it's fast asleep (off) before attempting to work on electrical circuits. Don't take someone's word for it that the circuit is off. Check for yourself. Make sure the *correct* circuit breakers are off, then test the circuit with a voltmeter or other circuit tester (available for a few dollars at most hardware stores) before working on electrical systems.

The PV module mounts can be fixed or tracking. Fixed mounts are much easier and cheaper to build and install. Tracking mounts can be manually or mechanically moved. If your modules are installed where they can easily be adjusted seasonally, the mounts can be tipped up 15° for winter (lower sun) or down 15° for summer (higher sun). At a home in Boulder, for example, the mounting would be tipped to 55° in winter and down to 25° in summer.

Smart tracking systems can actually follow the sun as it travels from east to west across the sky each day. These systems require sensors, controllers, and motors—and more money. However, they can recoup their cost in increased efficiency.

Solar technology is improving every month and costs are slowly coming down as more people buy them. So even if you don't buy a system today, keep watching the marketplace. It's getting better.

Chapter 20 offers tips on selecting a solar power system installation contractor and Chapter 21 shows you how to do it yourself. For more information on residential electrical systems and how they fit into the home construction process, read *The Complete Idiot's Guide to Building Your Own Home* (Alpha Books, 2002), especially Chapter 22.

You now know how electricity is generated from sunlight and how you can harness it to power your home. Next, let's look at how you can take a big energy load off your solar power system by using the sun to heat water.

The Least You Need to Know

- ◆ Photovoltaic technology converts sunlight into electricity that can replace fossil fuel power.

- ◆ In most states, you can utilize net metering (or selling excess solar power to utilities) with an intertie system.

- ◆ System components typically include the solar array, optional battery bank and charge controller, inverter, and distribution parts.

- ◆ Solar power systems can be set up for expansion as power demands increase or PV module prices go down.

- ◆ Whether you can install your own solar power system depends on local building codes and permits.

Chapter 10

Solar Water Heating

In This Chapter

- ◆ Finding ways of reducing wasted hot water
- ◆ How solar water heaters work
- ◆ Tips for keeping swimming pool heating costs down
- ◆ Considering a solar-heated pool

Being in "hot water" isn't such a bad thing. In fact, if you're trying to wake up, wash dishes, clean clothes, or bathe a pet, it's a good thing!

It must be good because everyone uses it. Lots of hot water gets used every year by the average (if there is such a thing) family. In this chapter you'll find out how to cut costs and to select a solar water heating system that fits your needs and your budget.

Cutting Hot Water Costs

Water heating is the third-largest energy expense in your home. It typically adds up to about 14 percent of your utility bill. That's a lot of money going down the drain!

Here are the numbers: A family of four, each showering for five minutes a day, uses 700 gallons of water a week! Here's the breakdown for a typical U.S. home: Showers use up 37 percent of the home's hot water, washing clothes takes 26 percent, the dishwasher uses 14 percent, the bathroom flushes 12 percent, and sinks drain the final 11 percent for food prep and drinking water.

Before turning to solar water heating options, there are four ways to cut your water heating bills:

◆ Use less hot water.

◆ Turn down the thermostat on your water heater.

◆ Insulate your water heater.

◆ Install a more efficient water heater.

More specifically, here's how you can both save on water and cut the costs of an installed solar water system:

◆ Repair leaky faucets as soon as discovered.

◆ Insulate your water storage tanks and pipes (don't cover the thermostat).

Insulating your home's water heater can save on energy costs and your solar investment.

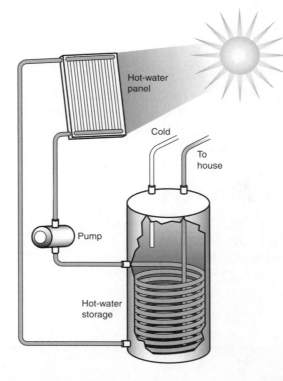

◆ Install nonaerating, low-flow faucets and showerheads for greater efficiency.

◆ Consider buying and installing a new, more energy-efficient water heater if your water heater is more than seven years old.

◆ Compare EnergyGuide labels for the most efficient model when buying a new water heater.

◆ Lower the thermostat on your water heater to about 115°F.

◆ Drain a quart of water from your water tank every three months to remove sediment that reduces efficiency.

◆ Take more showers than baths (the typical shower takes about half the water of a bath).

Solar Water Heaters

Solar water heaters have been around more than 100 years. They were the first application of modern solar technology. More than 1,500,000 homes and businesses have invested in solar water heating systems in the United States and throughout the world—and most feel that it was a good investment. In fact, a solar water heating system can be the most cost-effective solar investment you can make to meet your home's energy needs. Fortunately, solar technology has made solar water heating systems even more efficient while making them easier and less expensive to build and install.

If your home has an unshaded, south-facing location, such as a roof, you can install a solar water heating system for $1,500 to $3,000 in initial investment. Think of the money as prepaying for hot water.

In addition to gaining long-term financial rewards, solar water heaters don't produce harmful greenhouse gasses. In fact, over a 20-year period, it's estimated that a single residential solar water heater can avoid 50 tons of carbon dioxide emissions. That's a lot!

What should you look for in a solar water heating system? First, watch for systems certified by the Solar Rating and Certification Program (SRCC) or the Florida Solar Energy Center (FSEC).

What are your solar options? The first option is to replace your existing water heater with one that uses less fossil-fuel energy. Over the past 20 years, technology has come up with some great ideas you may not be aware of. Let's take a look at some of the best.

If you're using electricity to heat water, heat pump water heaters are three to five times more efficient than conventional resistive heaters. How is that possible? Heat pump water heaters use a compressor and refrigerant fluid to transfer heat. Yes, they are still powered by electricity, but they use less electricity so your solar power system will cost less.

Indirect water heaters use the home's heating system boiler to help keep water hot. It helps, but isn't as efficient as installing a solar water heater.

A demand water heater makes more sense. A standard water heater holds 30 to 80 gallons of water and attempts to keep it hot at all times—for showers and dishes, when you're sleeping, when you're away for a week—always. A demand water heater, on the other hand, produces hot water on demand. Hot water reaches the showerhead just as quickly with these heaters, with no standby waste. Unfortunately, these systems operate only on natural gas or propane, meaning that the pilot light must always be burning, a waste.

Okay, let's get to the really good stuff: solar water heaters. The sun is continually giving us energy to use, if we harness it. How can we turn solar thermal energy into hot water? By running cold water where it can be heated by the sun. That makes sense. You can rig up some pipe on your roof and run water through it to get hot water. Or you can sit a large tank of cold water in a sunny spot and let it get warm.

One of the problems with these ideas is temperature control. You certainly don't want shower water coming out of the tap at 180°F—or at 60°F. You want water delivered at a consistent temperature. Optimum delivery temperature is 120°F. I'll cover this topic after discussing how to get solar hot water in the first place.

As suggested, there are two types of solar water heating systems: *flat plate collectors* (pipes) and *batch collectors* (tanks). Flat plate collectors circulate a fluid through black metal piping or plates, insulated underneath and covered on top with special glass to gather and distribute the sun's heat efficiently. Batch collectors are simply insulated tanks painted black to better absorb the sun's thermal energy. Hot water from these sources can be directly piped to the plumbing system or, better, used to preheat water for an efficient water heater.

Sun-Day School

A **flat plate collector** is a rectangular box with a transparent cover, typically installed on a building's roof to collect solar thermal energy. Small tubes run through the box and carry either water or an antifreeze solution. If water, it goes directly to the water system. If another fluid, it goes through a heat exchanger to heat water. A **batch collector** (also known as a breadbox collector) uses a glass-insulated tank, painted black on the outside, to hold water. The tank absorbs and traps the sun's thermal energy to heat water inside. Mounted on the roof or on the ground, it is plumbed into the house's water system. How many collectors you need depends on your hot water usage.

There are other technologies being applied, but they all work on the same principles—solar thermal energy is captured and used to directly or indirectly heat water for the home. In addition to flat plate and batch collectors, there are evacuated tube, concentrating, transpired, and other types of collectors. They all have the same input (solar energy) and output (hot water).

What's it going to cost to install a solar hot water system—and when will it pay back? Of course, that depends on the system you install, how much hot water you use, and how energy efficient your home is otherwise. Here's a starting point: A 50-gallon passive batch-type heater used to preheat water for your conventional water heater will cost about $1,500 plus installation. If you figure $500 for installation, your total is about $2,000. If the system can save you $300 a year in water heating costs, the unit pays for itself in seven years. After that it's virtually free (minor maintenance, eventual replacement). Smaller systems can be installed for $1,300.

Let's talk about controllers. Of course, you won't need to add an output temperature controller if you're preheating water for a conventional water heater. It has its own controls to regulate temperature before it arrives at the fixture. You will want a controller going into the conventional tank to limit the input temperature range. You don't want boiling water in your tank!

Control typically means a sensor to measure the temperature of preheated water, followed by a mixer that blends in cooler water as needed to keep water below a specific set-point. This automatic temperature control is called a "tempering valve." Most have adjustable set-points between 120°F and 160°F.

Bright Idea

Want to try out an inexpensive solar hot water heater for an outdoor shower? For less than $20 you can get a low-tech Super Solar Shower (available from resources listed in Appendix B) that will heat 5 gallons of water from 60° to 108°F in about three hours in the sun on a 70°F day.

As you will learn when shopping for a solar water heating system, there are many types. To help guide you, here are the more popular ones:

◆ **Direct systems** pump water from a storage tank through one or more collectors and back to a tank; the pump is regulated by an electric controller, an appliance timer, or a PV panel.

◆ **Indirect systems** circulate a fluid through a heat exchanger that transfers the heat from the fluid to the water.

Solar Eclipse

If you live in a hard-freeze zone (where it gets below freezing and stays there for more than a day or two), you need a freeze-proof solar collector, or you need to mothball your system for the winter. If needed, make sure you get this feature in your solar water heating system.

◆ **Thermosiphons** use a tank mounted above collectors; as the collector heats the water it rises to the storage tank and heavier cold water drains down to the collector.

◆ **Draindown systems** are a variation needed for collectors in cold climates; they automatically drain water out of a system before it can freeze.

◆ **Swimming pool systems** heat and circulate water for swimming pools, our next topic.

Making Your Swimming Pool More Efficient

Swimming pools offer a great way to exercise and beat the summer heat. However, installing and maintaining a pool can get expensive. Fortunately, the sun can provide the heat needed to keep your pool warm enough for a nice swim.

Before investing in a solar water heating system for your pool, however, make sure that your pool is efficiently filtering and circulating the water it has. Inefficiency costs money! In fact, installing a smaller, higher-efficiency pump and running less each day can save up to 75 percent in energy costs.

Which pump you choose depends on the size of your swimming pool, how much it is used, and local weather conditions. One study shows that a three-quarter-horsepower or smaller pump is generally sufficient for most residential pools. At the same time, install a larger filter and make sure that pipes are as short and straight as possible. A large cartridge-type filter is more efficient than the cheaper diatomaceous earth types. In addition, cartridges require about half as much power to push the water through.

What about circulation? You can save some bucks by simply cutting back on the amount of time the circulation pumps run. Many are set to run 6 to 12 hours a day. However, about one to three hours a day is typically all that's needed to keep water fresh. Cutting back may mean that the pool filter doesn't collect as much debris, but you can skim it off as needed or keep the pool covered. You'll save some money!

What's next? Most of a pool's heat loss occurs at the surface where the heated water evaporates or radiates away. A pool cover offers an effective way of keeping heat (and water) in a pool by reducing surface evaporation. A pool cover can reduce water loss by one third to one half! And each gallon of 80° water that evaporates removes about 8,000 BTU from the pool. In addition, reducing water loss also reduces the amount of chemical water treatment required.

The best way to reduce evaporation and even take advantage of the sun's radiation is to add a solar or bubble cover to your swimming pool. Dark covers hold more heat in than clear or light-colored solar covers. A solar cover can pay for itself in energy savings within the first year, yet they have a life of three to five years.

One more energy-conservation tip for your pool: Install a windbreak. A fence or plants around a pool can reduce evaporation by 300 percent or more! That's money evaporating. An effective windbreak must be high and close enough to the pool to block wind from moving across the water's surface, but it can't block sunlight. See Chapter 8 for more on effective solar landscaping.

Heating Your Pool with Solar Energy

Let's say you've made your swimming pool operate more efficiently. Now you can size and install a solar water heating system for your pool, knowing what it needs. Actually, you'll consider two things: solar pool heaters and collectors.

A solar pool heater can be a good investment, especially when installing a new pool or replacing an older heating system. Such heating systems are one of the most cost-effective applications of solar energy. It's relatively easy to integrate a solar water heater into an existing system. The pool's water is pumped through the filter, then through solar energy collectors before going back into the pool. The sun heats the water.

Solar domestic water heater systems raise a small amount of water to a temperature of about 140°F. Solar pool heaters are different in that they raise the temperature of lots of water to about 80°F. So a solar-heated pool may require a slightly larger pump than a conventionally heated pool.

Bright Idea

A solar pool can not only cut operating costs, but also extend the swimming season for many months each year!

A basic solar heating system for an in-ground swimming pool will cost about $600 for an 10 by 16-foot pool (160 square feet). Add an extra solar panel (about $250 each) for each additional 80 square feet. The guideline is that the solar collectors should be half the size of the pool's surface.

Pool water too hot? Solar collectors can also be used to cool a pool in hot climates or during peak summer months by circulating the water through collectors at night.

Speaking of collectors, solar pool collectors normally don't need glazing (glass) or insulation because they operate during warmer months when solar radiation and ambient temperatures are higher, and we don't need very hot output. This means that the collectors are simpler and less expensive than those for the home's hot water system.

Most pool collectors are of plastic or rubber treated with a UV light inhibitor to extend the panels' life. They also weigh less than standard collectors and thus can be mounted more easily.

Sun Spots

Solar pools can save lots of money. One application is the International Swim Center in Santa Clara, California. Heaters using solar energy heat three large pools—a 50-meter racing pool, a 25-yard diving pool (17 feet deep!), and a 25-yard training pool. Nearly 13,000 square feet of flat-plate collectors heat 1.2 million gallons of water, 60 percent of the heat needed for the municipal pool. And it's been cutting heating costs since 1979!

How big should the pool's solar heat collectors be? Much depends on the local climate, the other equipment and heat sources used, and how much of the heat you want to come from solar energy. A good rule of thumb is that the collector surface area should be about half that of the pool it serves. Figure a 10 by 12-foot collector for a 12 by 20-foot pool. If local solar conditions aren't ideal, bump that size up to 75 percent of the pool's surface; in the example, that's 10 by 18-foot for collectors.

Solar collectors should be installed as close to the pool as possible so heat isn't lost in long pipes. If the pool is primarily used in the summer months, tilt the collectors at the angle of the latitude minus about 15°. That's 25° of angle for Boulder, Colorado, located at 40° latitude. If it's a year-round pool, build frames that you can manually adjust seasonally. Alternatively, invest in motorized frames.

Okay. We've used that lucky ol' sun to generate electricity and heat your home's water. What's next? Chapter 11 offers you dozens of ways to heat the air in your home with "free" solar energy.

The Least You Need to Know

◆ The average house spends more on heating water than on any other energy use.

◆ Solar thermal energy can be used to reduce or eliminate your home's need for fossil-powered hot water.

◆ A wide variety of commercially available solar water heaters offers a relatively quick return on your investment.

◆ You can dramatically cut the costs of owning a swimming pool by using solar energy to keep it comfortable.

◆ Additional energy-efficient steps can save you even more money on your pool's heating bill.

11

Solar Space Heating

In This Chapter

◆ How passive solar energy can heat and cool your home

◆ Working with the sun instead of against it

◆ Planning a sunspace that enhances your heating system

◆ How to store solar energy in your home

◆ How to distribute and control your home's solar heat

◆ Cooling with solar energy

Cats have the right idea. If solar thermal energy is radiating through a window somewhere in the house, a cat will find it and lay down for a snooze in the sun. Cats know that the best warmth is that from the sun. Of course, on a hot day, they find a shaded spot that takes advantage of the sun-warmed air without lying directly in the hot sunlight. Cats can teach us something about solar space heating.

This chapter offers numerous ideas on how to build a new home or retrofit your existing home to take advantage of solar space heating. It combines what a cat already knows with what humans have learned about harnessing solar thermal energy.

Passive Solar Basics

You probably live in a passive solar home right now and don't even know it. Passive solar homes use a room or another part of the structure as a solar thermal energy collector, and in fact, your home's windows, walls, and floors collect, store, and distribute solar energy every day. Everything under the sun does! However, your home may not be very efficient at using the sun's energy. It may be too hot on one side of the house and too cold on another. Or one room may get toasty while another is chilly. That's because the typical home isn't designed to use solar energy to its advantage.

Drive down the street of any subdivision and you'll notice that the homes are oriented to the street, not necessarily the sun. Most look like a humongous cookie cutter passed by, stamping out houses in an orderly fashion. They were designed for the efficiency of the contractor and the utilities, not the people who will live in them. Sure, they may have energy-efficient appliances in the kitchen. Otherwise, they were built to sell, not to be lived in with any great degree of energy efficiency.

The reason for this knock-em-out architecture is economics. By placing houses in neat rows, roads are shorter, utilities don't have to go as far, and construction crews don't have to look at each home as a new jigsaw puzzle. The home is either Plan A or Plan B, a mirrored version of Plan A.

What's the solution? Think like the sun. Consider the sun, local climate, and other conditions at the building site before building. If you've already built, consider how you can take best advantage of the sun without rotating your home on its foundation.

So what does the sun think? It thinks and acts based on natural laws. For those who slept through science class (and for those of us who barely remember being in school), here's a quick review of natural laws that the sun and heat follow:

◆ Heat moves from warmer materials to cooler ones until there is no longer a temperature difference between the two. A passive solar building takes advantage of this law to distribute heat by conduction, convection, and radiation.

◆ Conduction is the way heat moves through materials, traveling from molecule to molecule—and from object to object.

◆ Convection is the way heat circulates through liquids and gases. Lighter, warmer fluid rises, and cooler, denser fluid sinks. These "fluids" include air. For instance, warm air rises because it is lighter than colder air, which sinks. This is why warmer air accumulates in the attic while the basement stays cool. Passive solar homes can use the law of air convection to carry solar heat from a south wall into the building's interior.

◆ Finally, class, radiant heat moves through the air from warmer objects to cooler ones. There are two kinds of radiation used in passive solar design: solar radiation and infrared radiation. When radiation hits an object, it is either absorbed, reflected, or transmitted, depending on the object. Opaque objects absorb most of the radiation that hits them, darker colors more than lighter ones. Infrared radiation happens when warmer objects get close to colder ones, such as your standing on a cold floor.

Okay. Those are the laws. How can you make them work to your benefit and save you some money on heating your home?

Working with the Sun

Sunlight is relatively easy to put to work. In a basic design, sunlight passes through glass and warms the sunspace using a principle called *isolated gain*. The glass is either vertical (such as a window) or sloped at an angle (such as a sunroom's roof).

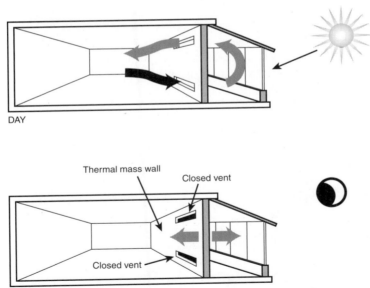

A sunroom uses isolated gain to heat the home day and night.

As cats know, it's not always easy to find a sunny spot that isn't too hot. The key is to moderate temperature swings and the best way to do it is with massive materials such as masonry or water. Throughout the day the mass collects solar thermal energy, then at night or during cloudy weather this thermal mass releases the heat it holds to warm the sunspace. Well-insulated windows and walls help retain the warm air. Controls such as operable windows, vents, and fans keep the sunspace from overheating. Fans and vents help circulate the warm air to the rest of the house.

Sunspaces can serve three main functions:

◆ Auxiliary heat

◆ Warmth for growing indoor plants

◆ Warmth for living

The design of your sunspace depends on how you plan to use it as well as how the design fits into your new or existing home. Fortunately, there are many useful resources for planning and installing the best solar space heating system for your home and needs.

Sun-Day School

Isolated gain uses a sunroom or other isolated area to develop and distribute solar energy. **Direct gain** is the heat a structure gains directly from solar radiation. Sunlight enters the house through a collector such as south-facing windows. The sunlight then shines on masonry floors and/or walls that absorb and store the solar heat. At night, the room's air cools and the heat stored in the thermal mass is released into the room.

Thermal mass in the interior absorbs the sunlight and radiates the heat at night.

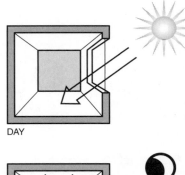

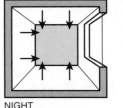

If its main purpose is to provide heat, you can maximize *direct gain* by using sloped glass, few plants, little thermal mass, and well-insulated end walls. If you live where winters are sunny, carefully sized thermal mass can prevent extreme overheating during the day. Most sunspaces are multifunctional rooms.

If your sunroom is to serve primarily as a greenhouse, remember that plants need lots of light, fresh air, water, and protection from extreme temperatures. Also consider that a sunspace dedicated to the well-being of plants may not be the most comfortable environment for people. And greenhouses will not have excess solar energy to heat the rest of the house.

The third and most popular use of sunspaces is for living. They are sunrooms. They are year-round living areas, so they are designed with minimum glare and only moderate humidity. Carefully sized thermal mass can stabilize temperature extremes and improve the room's comfort level. If thermal mass is installed as a wall or floor, remember not to cover the mass with rugs, pictures, or plants. Let the mass do its job unobstructed.

You might think that designing a sunspace would be easy. It's not. For greatest efficiency, the sunspace, glazing (clear sheet material such as glass or plastic specially treated to allow sunlight to pass into sunspaces or solar collectors, trapping heat inside), insulation, and thermal mass must all be planned in balance. They must also match the local climate and seasonal changes. You certainly don't want a sunroom that's too hot or cold to use except for a few weeks each year.

Fortunately, architects, engineers, and designers have lots of experience—and tools—for the job. Computer software is now available for designing passive solar projects like sunspaces. Your solar architect will use this software. If you're a computer-literate do-it-yourselfer, check the resources listed in Appendix B, including passive solar design software.

> **Sun Spots**
>
> Why include a sunspace in your new or existing home? A well-designed sunspace can provide up to 60 percent of a home's winter heating requirements. In addition, it can offer overnight warmth, summer cooling, and a great place to stretch out and read a book by natural light.

Orienting Your Solar Space

In the Northern Hemisphere, the sun tracks along the southern sky. That means an effective sunspace must face south. Due solar south is ideal, but 30 degrees east or west of due south is okay.

If retrofitting your home, consider how the sunspace will look on the south side of your house. If the south side of your house faces the street, you'll want to design it so it protects your home's privacy while looking like it wasn't an add-on.

The sun gets pretty low in the winter sky. You don't want trees or plants over 10 feet tall within about 15 feet of a solar window because they will block solar gain. Early morning or late afternoon shade is okay. The most productive solar hours are typically the six between 10 A.M. to 3 P.M., so trees that don't block the sun's rays to your sunspace during these hours are usually fine. Find your location's solar noon—the moment of the day that divides the daylight hours for that day exactly in half. It's the midpoint between sunrise and sunset.

If possible, locate the sunspace so that the house walls serve as one or both end walls of sunspace. This reduces heat loss. Also make sure that the sunspace is adjacent to rooms most occupied during the day, such as the kitchen, family living areas, or playrooms.

What about the glass or solar glazing? Although sloped glazing collects more heat in the winter, many designers prefer vertical glazing or a combination of vertical and sloped. There's a good reason. Sloped glazing loses more heat at night and can cause overheating in warmer weather. Vertical glazing allows maximum heat gain in winter, when the sun's angle is low, and less gain as the sun rises toward its summer zenith. In addition, vertical glazing is easier to install and less apt to leak, making it a smarter choice for the do-it-yourselfer and a solar retrofit.

Choose the best solar glazing for your home according to your needs and your budget. Glass is more popular because people are familiar with that material. However, newer plastic glazings can be cheaper, stronger, lighter, and easier to install. In addition, some of the latest plastic glazings are actually more efficient than glass at transmitting solar energy while cutting heat loss. The downside is that plastic glazing scratches more easily than glass and is harder to seal.

Solar Eclipse

Clear glass transmits 80 to 90 percent of incoming solar radiation, absorbing or reflecting only 10 to 20 percent. The solar energy is then passed into the room as infrared radiation (sounds kinda atomic, doesn't it?). When buying windows, make sure the glass or glazing has high absorption and transmission qualities. Your solar equipment vendor can give you more specifics.

Better solar glazing has low-emissivity or low-E coatings. These are thin, almost-invisible metal or metal oxide films that reduce radiant heat loss and gain while dramatically improving a window's insulation value. For example, double-glazed low-E windows are about as energy efficient as triple-glazed windows using regular glass. But they cost and weigh less.

Special double-glazed windows can also benefit from filling the space between the panels with something other than air. Argon, sulphur hexafluoride, carbon dioxide, and other gasses increase the insulating value.

Technology continually enhances solar glazing, so ask your supplier or contractor about the latest and greatest. Just remember that it needs to be not only effective, but cost-effective.

Storing Solar Heat

I've mentioned thermal mass, but haven't gotten too specific. Let's get down to it. Water is the most efficient thermal mass because it holds the most heat per unit of volume. Homeowners and solar designers have used everything from plastic jugs to 55-gallon drums to hold water as thermal mass. More efficient are sealed columns filled with water and chemicals to minimize mildew. They use the *indirect gain* method.

Though they store only about half as much heat as water, masonry masses can serve other purposes (floor, walls), so are popular thermal masses. The most effective are of solid brick, concrete, or stone, 4- to 6-inches thick, the right thickness for a wall. To enhance the storage of thermal energy, surfaces should be painted black or dark blue. Even a deep red color has an absorption over the required 70 percent.

Sun-Day School

An **indirect gain** passive solar home stores thermal energy between the south-facing windows and the living spaces. The most common is a Trombe wall directly behind the window glazing. It collects the heat and passes it into the room.

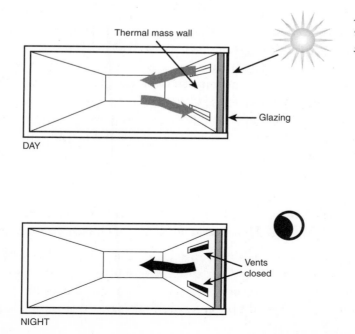

A thermal mass or Trombe wall collects and distributes solar heat.

Thermal mass wall

Glazing

DAY

Vents closed

NIGHT

First question: Where should the thermal mass be? In the sunspace's floor and/or the north, east, and west walls. It will collect and store both direct heat from the sun as well as heat from the air in the room.

Second question: How much thermal mass is needed? If the mass is masonry, for every square foot of south-facing glazing, figure about 3 square feet of 4-inch-thick masonry. For a water mass, figure about 3 gallons for each square foot of glazing. For example, a 100-square-foot south-facing glazing, plan on 300 square feet of 4-inch masonry or a water mass wall containing 300 gallons. These are just guidelines, so get a solar architect to give you the specifics for your home and location.

Once you've paid good money to trap solar heat in a sunspace and its thermal mass, you don't want to let it get away easily. That means insulating the heck out of the sunspace. Insulate the space's roof, floor, and walls to keep the energy in. Also plan for window coverings and other movable insulation to trap the warm air in the sunspace after sol has set or on days when he can't be seen.

Distributing and Controlling Solar Heat

There are a couple of ways of distributing warm air from your sunspace to other parts of the house. It can enter the heating system's duct work for distribution, or it can move passively. Warm air rises. By designing doors, windows, hallways, and room vents to take advantage of this fact, the air warmed in the sunspace will travel on its own through the house. A strategically placed ceiling fan or two can help push it along.

Also consider a thermosiphon. In a thermosiphon, warm air rises in the sunspace and passes into the adjoining space through an opening. Cool air from the adjoining space is drawn into the sunspace to be heated. How big of an opening is needed in a wall to take advantage of thermosiphoning? The minimum for a single opening should be about 8 square feet for every 100 square feet of glass area. So a 12-foot long solar glazing wall that's 8 feet tall should have an opening that's at least 2 feet by 4 feet. Less total opening space is needed if one opening is high and one is low. In that case, the same wall needs only two openings of at least 2½ square feet each if they are 8 feet apart. That's a rule of thumb, easily confirmed or contradicted by passive solar design software measuring your home's conditions.

Maybe you've done your job *too* well and it's getting hot in your sunspace. How can you tell? Plants and people are wilting! The aquarium is boiling! The cat left the room!

Overheating can kill plants and make the sunspace unlivable. To control overheating, you can install operable vents at the top of the sunspace where temperatures are the highest and at the bottom where they are the lowest. Vents can be opened and closed manually as needed or by thermostatically controlled motors.

If it's impossible to get the warm air circulating through the house on its own (passive), install fans with thermostatic controls to get things moving. Alternately, you can install climate controls on movable window shades.

Cooling with the Sun

You can get more than heat from the sun. You can also cool your house with it. Actually, the movement of solar-heated air will cool parts of your home. Many passive solar designs include natural ventilation for cooling. Casement or other operable windows for solar gain can also be fitted with vertical panels, called wing walls, on the windward side of the house. These panels can accelerate the natural breeze in the interior to keep the air cooler.

Another passive solar cooling device is the thermal chimney. It works like a fireplace's chimney to vent hot air from the house out through the roof. A solar architect can show you how it actually works and how to control it without losing too much energy.

What's next on our solar journey? Chapter 12 offers some proven ways of supplementing your home's solar power system with two more natural resources: wind and water.

The Least You Need to Know

- ◆ Using the natural laws of solar energy can save you thousands of dollars in future utility bills—and keep you as comfortable as a cat.

- ◆ Direct gain uses energy directly from the sun, indirect gain uses thermal mass in the living space, and isolated gain uses a separate air space to store thermal energy.

- ◆ Solar glazing is specially designed to take advantage of solar thermal energy and transfer it to your living space with minimum loss.

- ◆ Sunrooms can use convection to distribute solar heat without fans.

- ◆ Solar energy can also be used to cool your home by encouraging natural ventilation and air flow.

Chapter 12

Wind and Water Power

In This Chapter

- ◆ Finding enough wind to make electricity
- ◆ How to select a wind turbine system
- ◆ Using water to generate electricity
- ◆ Picking an efficient hydropower system
- ◆ Figuring the economics of wind and water power

Solar energy isn't the only renewable resource you can use to generate electricity. Wind and water flow can also do the trick.

This chapter offers you some renewable energy options if you live where you can take advantage of them. City dwellers on small lots typically can't capture the wind or enough water to make it worthwhile. However, country folk—and those who want to join them—can use technology to build productive power systems to supplement solar power.

Harnessing the Wind

In some locations, the wind can be a nuisance—unless it's harnessed to produce electricity. Then at least it's a profitable nuisance. If you're living on a larger parcel of land (more than an acre), as about a quarter of Americans are, you might be able to turn the wind into power. For many rural home locations, wind power is an excellent and cost-effective—and renewable—power source.

Technology has advanced wind power systems so that locations with little natural air movement can generate at least some of the electricity a home needs. And it can be cost-effective. Depending on your wind resource, a small wind energy system can lower your electricity bill by 50 to 90 percent. Combine this with a solar power system, and you may never have to pay a utility bill again—as long as the sun shines and the wind blows.

How much wind is necessary? Not much. Wind is a renewable resource just like the sun and the flow of water. Because of changes in terrain over a large parcel of land, you may be able to find a point on your property where the wind moves sufficiently rapidly to install a cost-effective generation system. If you're looking for a new home-site, you can put wind on your list of desired features.

To answer the question of how much wind, a wind turbine power system can be effective with an average annual wind speed as low as 10 miles per hour. Actually, some of the newest systems can operate with even less, though the cost per kWh is relatively high.

Bright Idea

You can view the *Wind Energy Resource Atlas of the United States* on the National Wind Technology Center website at www.nrel.gov/wind/. The Department of Energy (DOE) sponsors the Windpowering America website at www.eren. doe.gov/windpoweringamerica/ as well. If you don't have access to the Internet, contact the DOE (see Appendix B).

To measure local wind conditions, visit a science or weather equipment store for wind speed equipment. Most electronic weather stations can measure wind speed and direction. Alternately, wind socks are available that indicate speed by how full they become with wind.

The U.S. Department of Energy and other agencies have produced wind resource maps that show the estimated yearly electricity production available from a small wind turbine. The maps are based on the average wind speed, but you'll want a location that gives you consistent wind speeds if possible. Otherwise, you'll want a battery system for storing generated power. (You may anyway.)

The highest average wind speeds are usually found along the seacoasts, on ridge lines, and on the Great Plains. If you don't know local wind conditions, but live near an airport, ask the airport manager for the info. Even the smallest airports track local wind speeds and direction for pilots. However, airport winds are typically about 20 percent greater than the surrounding area. That's because the measurement is made 20 to 30 feet above the ground, where wind speeds are greater than at ground level, and because airports are flat with little obstruction to slow winds down as trees and buildings do.

A wind turbine looks like a cross between a weathervane and a small airplane. That's because it is. The weathervane part rotates to turn the propeller into the wind. The prop then spins as the wind passes over the aerodynamic blades. An airplane pulls itself through the air (an analogy) using engine power. A wind turbine gathers the wind's power and turns it into electricity.

The best location on your property for a wind turbine is away from anything that will slow the wind down and near anything that will speed it up. That makes sense. Trees and buildings will absorb, deflect, and ruffle up much of the wind's energy. Your turbine needs to be 30 feet higher than any obstruction within a 200-foot radius, or it's going to get beat up, die young, and suffer low output. Hills can channel the wind to make wind speed at the ridge higher than the surrounding valleys.

As you learned from the earlier airport wind calculation, the higher the turbine, the greater the wind's velocity. There's a practical as well as economic limit because the poles on which they are mounted get more expensive with every foot of height.

Selecting a Wind Power System

Wind turbines are the primary (read: most expensive) component of a wind power system. They are the working end. Most wind turbines are horizontal upwind machines with two or three blades. The amount of power a turbine can produce depends on the diameter of the blades or rotor. That's called the sweep area, and it means the quantity of wind that the turbine intercepts.

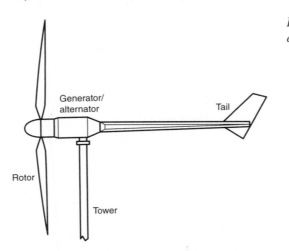

Basic parts of a small wind electric system.

Generator/alternator

Tail

Rotor

Tower

Right behind the rotor is the alternator or generator. It converts the rotor's rotation into electricity. Behind that is the body and the tail similar to an airplane's tail designed to keep the turbine pointed into the wind. Finally, the tower holds everything off the ground where the wind is best.

The tower is typically at least 30-feet-plus-the-sweep-radius high. It should be even higher if there are obstructions within 300 feet that would slow down the wind. Towers can go to 100 feet or higher. They cost more than shorter towers but can increase power output sufficiently to make it a worthwhile investment. There's 40 percent more wind at 100 feet than at ground level. Taller towers are the cheapest way to increase output.

Turbine towers are either freestanding or guyed (uses wire or cable supports). Most home wind power systems use guyed towers because they are less expensive and easier to install and maintain. But how the heck can you get a 30- to 100-foot tower up? Most towers are designed for simple tilt-up, tilt-down installation. You assemble everything safely at ground level, and then raise the tower. Tilt-down towers can be installed by one or two persons following manufacturer's instructions. They are also handier when it's time for maintenance. Of course, that means you need a flat space around the tower that's greater than the tower's height.

As with other renewable energy systems, you'll need more than the generating equipment. You also need wiring and maybe batteries to store electricity. Fortunately, they are the same as those needed for solar and water power systems. That means you can tie your wind turbine's output into your renewable energy electrical system to keep costs down. Of course, make sure that the system is sized to accept the additional power.

Solar Eclipse

Don't install a wind turbine on any building people plan to sleep in. Wind turbines transmit a varied and incredible variety of noises down their towers, and roofs make great amplifier membranes. Roof mounts are available, but they are only recommended for outbuildings.

How much will a wind turbine power system cost? A small system, called a micro turbine, can be purchased and self-installed for about $1,000. It can put out about 400 watts of power at 28 mph wind speeds. It's intended more for remote locations, especially where portability is important, such as for campers. Large turbine systems can run up to $30,000 installed. Yikes! Fortunately, in Chapter 4, you learned how to dramatically cut the cost of energy investment with rebates and tax incentives. They usually apply to all renewable energy systems, not just to solar power systems. And you can probably sell excess electricity through net metering, as described in Chapters 9 and 25.

For example, one popular wind turbine system with a 7-foot rotor diameter has a rating of 900 watts with a 28 mph wind. It can handle winds up to 120 mph and generate at least some electricity in winds as slow as 7.5 mph. The unit costs about $1,500 plus tower and installation. A bigger version (a nearly 15-foot rotor) can produce 3.2 kW at an initial cost of about $5,500 plus tower (another $500 to $1,500) and installation (the cost varies). To generate some serious electricity, like 10 kW, a 23-foot diameter rotor can do the job.

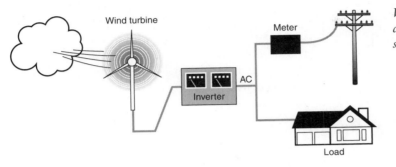

Wind turbine power can be connected to a grid just as solar power systems are.

When shopping for a wind turbine system, make sure you know the unit's power curve. For most of them you'll notice that there is an optimum range, usually between 20 and 30 mph, that offers the greatest electric output. That's important. If your site will produce an average wind of only 10 to 15 mph, look for a turbine with a power curve in this range.

Towers can be relatively inexpensive. Depending on the type, figure about $10 to $15 a foot for guyed towers. Standalone towers with no guy supports cost more. If your budget is tight, consider a roof mounting for your tower. Yes, the structure moderates the wind speed, but it can save you the cost of 20 or more feet of tower.

Using Water Power

More than two millennia ago, folks harnessed the power of water to grind wheat and do other work. Even today, many remote places throughout the world depend on hydro-power systems to generate electricity so they can perform vital tasks. If your home is in a subdivision, you're probably not going to be able to harness the power from everyone's leaky garden faucets to run your entertainment center. However, if you now live or plan to live in the country where your property has water rights, hydropower can help.

What's really cool is that like wind, hydropower is a renewable energy. Water isn't used up because energy is derived from its movement. Yes, there are other ecological issues (such as dam construction and flooding), but these have minimal impact when building a small hydropower system for your home.

Only about 10 percent of U.S. electricity comes from hydropower. In the realm of renewable energy sources, hydropower ranks at the top, well above solar power. That is, we're getting much more of our utility electricity from water than from the sun. So, fortunately, if your home is near a moving creek, stream, or river for which you have water rights, you may be able to install a small, efficient hydropower system known as a *microhydro system.* Let's see how.

Harnessing Water Power

Hydropower systems use the energy in flowing water to produce electricity or mechanical energy. Although there are many ways to harness moving water to produce energy, run-of-the-river systems are the most popular because they don't require large storage reservoirs. Of course, if your water source freezes in winter or dries up in summer, don't plan on year-round electricity from this single source. Look to solar or another more consistent power source.

What's a run-of-the-river hydro project and how does it work? I'm glad you asked. A portion of a river's water is diverted to a channel, pipeline, or pressurized pipeline (called a penstock) that delivers the water to a waterwheel or a turbine. The moving water rotates the wheel or turbine, turning a shaft. The shaft's motion can be used to pump water or to power an electric generator.

Is a microhydropower system right for you? The absolute answer is: maybe. You can easily measure how much sunlight is reaching your home on a given day or season, but how do you measure water flow? Actually, you must measure both flow, the quantity of water, and head, the speed at which it's flowing. No, you don't borrow a trooper's radar gun and point it at the river. You calculate head based on charts and instruments.

Head is based on the vertical distance that the water falls. It's usually measured in feet or units of pressure. Head also depends on the channel or pipe through which it flows. Lots of water channeled into a smaller pipe makes the water move faster, but limits how many gallons per minute you can use without suffering a pressure drop due to pipe friction. Too much pipe friction gives you a lower dynamic head. The system acts like it has a lower head when running.

If the water falls less than 20 feet in elevation, it's called low head. Anything more than 50 feet is referred to as high head. It makes sense that you want high head because it has more energy, but not all water sources drop that much in elevation—naturally. So you can enhance it by forcing the water to drop farther.

So how can you tell how much of a drop a water flow has? Rather than buy loads of equipment, purchase 30 feet or more of half-inch garden hose or other flexible tubing and a funnel. Have someone hold one end of the hose at the point where you will capture water from the source. Then stretch the hose out along the stream to the point where you expect to install the water turbine. Have your partner seal the funnel tightly in the upstream end of the tubing and submerse it until stream water begins to flow into the funnel and runs from the downstream end. Run it until all the bubbles are expelled. Now lift the downstream end to the point where water doesn't flow from it anymore. Finally, measure the vertical distance between your end of the tube and the water surface. To be safe, subtract a couple of inches to compensate for the water's upstream force that shoves water down the tube.

Of course, you and your assistant can test the waters in various locations to find the one with the highest head. Your turbine doesn't have to be as close to the house as possible, but located in the optimum spot for generating electricity. You can always run a few more feet of electric wire to your house.

What about flow? What's the quantity of water you can expect to be delivered to the downstream hydro turbine? Flow is measured in gallons per minute (gpm) or in cubic feet per second (cfps). Before going to the expense of getting flow measurement equipment or hiring someone, check with the local office of the U.S. Geological Survey, the Army Corps of Engineers, the Department of Agriculture, or your county engineer, who may have maps and data on the flow for the water you're borrowing energy from. To find these resources, try the "Government" section of the local phone book.

Sun Spots
How much water head is needed to generate hydro electricity? Experts say that the minimum is typically about 2 feet of vertical drop or head, depending on other conditions and your budget. However, new technologies such as submersible turbines can generate electricity with a head of just over 1 foot! Ask your hydropower equipment supplier to see the latest gadgets.

If you can't find data, you can do it yourself. Try the bucket method! First, temporarily dam the stream with logs or boards so that all the water is diverted to a foot-wide opening. Then use a 5-gallon bucket to capture and measure the flow, checking your watch to see how long it takes to fill the bucket. If the stream's full flow takes 1 minute to fill a 5-gallon bucket the flow is 5 gallons a minute. Divide 5 gallons by your fill time in seconds, and then multiply by 60 to get gallons per minute. If your dam isn't totally efficient and is leaking slightly, visually estimate the loss and add it to the total. If it's very much, pile on some more logs or boards.

If you can't or don't want to dam the stream, you can estimate flow by first measuring the width and depth of the stream at its straightest and most uniform point. Draw these dimensions on a graph paper to look like a cross section of your stream. Next, measure off a point 20 feet upstream from your cross section and have an assistant release a float while you time its progress to your cross-section point. If it takes 10 seconds to arrive, the flow rate is 2 feet per second. If 5 seconds, the calculation comes out to 4 feet per second. You get the picture. Repeating this test many times will give you a good average.

Now what? Multiply the average flow rate by the cross-sectional area of the stream to know the total flow. What you're trying to answer is: How much water passes a specific point in a given time? You can now answer it with reasonable accuracy.

Of course, there are many variables. The stream may be low or even dry for parts of the year. Large rocks at the bottom of the stream may significantly slow down the flow when the water level is low. In addition, you may be limited as to how much water you can divert from a stream. Water rights in agricultural areas, especially, are specifically defined. Your property's deed will tell you more.

Estimating Hydropower Output

You now know about how much water flow you have to work with. Here's how you can calculate the approximate power output to expect from a microhydropower system:

> (Net head [feet] × flow [gpm]) ÷ 10

Net head is the total or gross head less any loss from friction of the pipe or channel bed. Hard to figure, but a hydropower system provider can give you a good estimate. For now, figure that net head is 80 percent of gross flow.

So a typical calculation goes like this:

> (8 × 2,000) ÷ 10 = 1,600 watts = 1.6 kW

As you can see, increasing the drop (head) or the flow can make a significant difference in the system's output.

Here are typical hydropower system components:

 ◆ Water delivery system (channel, pipeline, or penstock)

 ◆ Turbine or waterwheel that transforms flow energy into rotational energy

 ◆ Alternator or generator that converts rotational energy into electricity

- ◆ Regulator that regulates or controls the generator

- ◆ Wiring that delivers the electricity to your home

How much does a small hydropower system cost? A hydroelectric turbine runs $1,000 to $1,500 and can produce electricity from as small a flow as 3 gpm up to 100 gpm. It produces from 30 to 1,500 watts of power depending on flow and head. Other types and sizes are available. You'll also need pipes, system controls, and wiring. Controllers will add a couple of hundred dollars to the cost. Labor (yours or someone else's) is extra.

So for just $1,500 to $4,000 you can install and benefit from a small hydropower system. It does require a steady flow of water, but, unlike solar power systems, it works day *and* night. You can even sell excess hydropower to your local utility to increase the return on your investment, as I'll discuss in Chapter 25.

Amazing, isn't it?! You can combine wind and hydropower with solar power to dramatically increase your home's energy efficiency. What else does the future hold? Chapter 13 describes some other power sources that you should consider in addition to solar, wind, and water.

Bright Idea

In determining whether a micro-hydropower system is a good economic investment for you, remember that once the system is installed, the only operating cost is periodic maintenance. Most small systems are virtually trouble free. It's the initial investment that hurts.

The Least You Need to Know

- ◆ Even an average wind of less than 10 mph is enough to generate electricity with an efficient turbine system.

- ◆ A wind power system includes a turbine, tower, and wiring.

- ◆ You can measure your own water source to find out if it has enough power to generate electricity—or you can hire someone to do it.

- ◆ A hydropower system needs a channel, a turbine or waterwheel, an alternator or generator, a regulator, and some wiring.

- ◆ Both wind and hydropower systems can tie into a solar power system for greater efficiency.

Chapter 13

Future Power Sources

In This Chapter

- How fuel cells replace combustion
- When fuel cells will be available
- Inside the fuel cell
- Energy technology of the future

It's crystal ball time! You've seen what solar and other technologies have done to bring us power. Now let's gaze into the crystal ball and see what the future might bring.

This chapter offers ideas on what may be coming: fuel cells and other energy breakthroughs. No, you're not going to be able to pick one up at Home Depot this weekend. Or for many weekends to come. But knowing what's on the horizon can help you in planning your current system to keep it cost-effective.

The Next Best Thing: Fuel Cells

Fuel cells really aren't a new idea. The first fuel cell was built in 1839 by an amateur scientist, Sir William Grove. However, it wasn't until the 1960s that fuel cells were given serious consideration as an alternative fuel source. That's when the U.S. space program chose fuel cells over riskier nuclear energy and more expensive solar energy. Fuel cells furnished power for the Gemini and Apollo spacecraft. They continue to provide electricity and water for the space shuttles.

Sun-Day School

A **fuel cell** uses a chemical process instead of combustion to release energy from fuels. It combines hydrogen and oxygen extracted from other fuels to produce electricity through an electrochemical reaction. That means fuel cells give off few emissions and, because there are no moving parts, they are quiet. In addition to electricity, fuel cells produce water and heat that can be recycled.

Technically a fuel cell is not an energy resource. It's a device that converts hydrogen, itself an energy carrier, to useful energy. Hydrogen has to be produced from some other resource such as water, natural gas, or coal. Instead of burning a fuel source to get at the energy, fuel cells use chemistry.

Fuel cells are *not* the final solution to our power needs. They are one option. Right now, they are too expensive for most applications. The raw materials aren't that expensive—it's the technology. So, as folks figure out how to mass-produce fuel cells and bring the price down, more and more homes will be using them to generate electricity or to heat water. Experts think that cost-effective fuel cells may be available within about five years.

Hydrogen made from renewable energy resources provides a clean and abundant energy solution. But fuel cells themselves are *not* a renewable energy resource. What's renewable is the type of energy source used as input to the fuel cell: fossil fuels (not renewable) or solar and others (renewable). Even the byproduct from fuel cells, water, can be reused to make even more power.

The most abundant element on Earth is hydrogen. Fuel cells can run on hydrogen— or, if set up with the proper equipment, ethanol, methanol, natural gas, fossil fuels, or even biomass.

Fuel cells are ideal for power generation, either connected to the electric grid to provide supplemental power, or set up to provide off-grid power where power lines can't reach. Because fuel cells operate silently, they reduce noise pollution as well as air pollution. In addition, the waste heat from a fuel cell can heat water and air. Pretty handy gadgets!

Fuel cells are relatively expensive compared to other energy resources. A residential fuel cell power plant costs about $3,000 per kilowatt right now. That's higher than any other energy resource considered here. However, expanded interest and lowered manufacturing cost could soon cut that number in half and make a fuel cell power system comparable in price to solar or other renewable energy systems. It will be many more years before fuel cells can complete with fossil fuel combustion systems.

In fact, your future car may be powered by a fuel cell! Fortunately, fuel cells are much more energy efficient than gas burners. Current estimates suggest that a typical fuel cell car of the near future will go up to 80 miles on a gas-equivalent gallon of fuel cell power. A prototype Volkswagen hydrogen fuel cell car went over the Swiss Alps between Switzerland and Italy in early 2002. It was part of the first long-range test drive of the newly designed vehicle. It used lightweight compressed hydrogen cylinders developed by Canadian company Dynetek Industries Ltd.

Parts of a Fuel Cell System

Let's get back to how fuel cells might someday be used in the home. There are three main parts of a residential fuel cell system:

- ◆ Hydrogen fuel reformer
- ◆ Fuel cell stack
- ◆ Power conditioner

Here's how they work together. The hydrogen fuel reformer extracts hydrogen from propane, natural gas, or other fuels. The fuel cell stack then adds oxygen from the air and converts the combination into electricity, heat, and water vapor. Finally, the power conditioner converts DC into AC electricity for appliances and such.

Solar Eclipse

Wait a minute! Hydrogen? Wasn't the Hindenburg filled with hydrogen—just before it burned up in a flash? A NASA scientist recently figured out that the Hindenburg didn't burn because of the hydrogen that kept it airborne, but because of the paint used to cover the large dirigible. It contained cellulose acetate or nitrate. (Yes, gunpowder! What were they thinking?) Of the 33 people who died when the Hindenburg burned, 30 died of injuries caused from jumping from the burning dirigible. Only three people died of burns. It was panic that killed most of the rest. The tragic accident virtually stopped the production of dirigibles as aircraft.

How does solar power play in the future of fuel cells? The key to the technology is stripping hydrogen from the fuel or feedstock. The three best ways of doing this use reforming, enzymes, or solar and wind power. Reforming and enzymes use heat and chemistry to get at the hydrogen. Solar and wind power are used to electrolyze or separate water into hydrogen and oxygen.

That's a simplified look at fuel cells. Fortunately, a number of developers and manufacturers are now duking it out to see who can offer a cost-effective fuel cell system. We, the consumers, typically win the fight.

The federal government is trying to get into the act as well. Bills have been proposed in the House and Senate offering a tax credit for installing fuel cells. If passed, the law will give a $1,000-per-kW credit toward the purchase of fuel cell systems. Many of the state credits that apply to renewable energy systems also apply to fuel cell systems. Check with your state's energy office (listed in Appendix B) for the latest and greatest information. Chances are, you can sell fuel-cell electricity back to the local utility with net metering (as discussed in Chapter 25).

Understanding How Fuel Cells Work

A fuel cell is an electrochemical energy conversion device. And it's very efficient—two to three times more efficient than a car's engine in converting fuel to power!

A fuel cell takes in hydrogen and oxygen and puts out electricity, water, and heat. That's a pretty good deal. How does it actually work? The following figure shows how the chemical process works within the typical hydrogen fuel cell.

Cross section of a typical fuel cell.

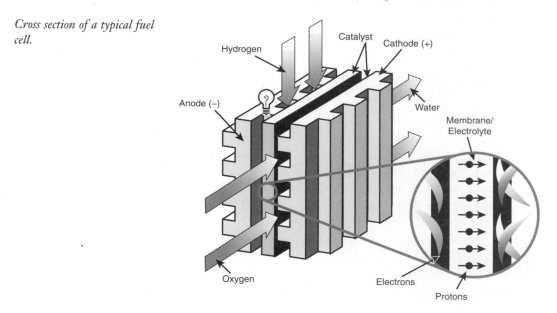

As shown in the following figure, hydrogen and oxygen are combined to make water (water is H_2O, two parts hydrogen and one part oxygen). Making water produces more energy than the process requires, so there's some left over in the form of electricity.

It's not much electricity. In fact, a single cell produces just 0.7 volts—it would take a dozen of them to equal a 9-volt battery. But modern manufacturing can stack such fuel cells into modules (just as solar cells are produced as modules). Together, a bunch of fuel cells can produce enough electricity to be useable.

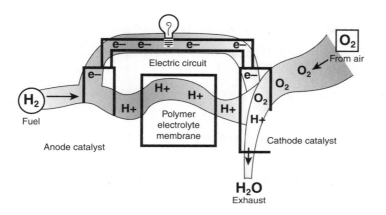

The chemical process inside a hydrogen fuel cell.

(©Gaiam Real Goods)

That's the future: figuring out how to make fuel cells more productive yet less expensive. If you don't think it can be done, consider that just over 15 years ago PCs ran at speeds one-thousandth of today's. And hard drives today are now more than a thousand times larger. Technology can do this! But don't look for fuel cells at the hardware store in the next few months. They're coming, but not quite that quickly. Instead, think of fuel cells as an emerging option for your solar-powered home.

Sun Spots

In a recent University of Massachusetts test, microbes in an aquarium transformed organic matter in mud to enough electrical current to activate a simple timer. Really! The current was small, but may be useful in powering underwater experiments.

Technology Marches On

What other new energy sources will we and our children use to power our homes and lives? Frankly, we don't know. Experts agree that all known resources are now being scrutinized. They don't expect that missions to Mars will bring back any new energy sources that will fuel tomorrow.

So the energy experts are focusing on doing more with what we have: sun, wind, water, nuclear, and fossil fuels. They are using technology (applied science) to concentrate on getting *more* out of what we have. That means …

◆ Designing larger, lower-cost PV modules.

◆ Using thin-film technology to get more power output from PV cells in the future.

◆ Using special reflective materials to concentrate solar energy for higher PV cell output.

◆ Improving manufacturing methods to lower the cost of producing PV modules.

◆ Designing more efficient inverters that can better manage electric input and output with fewer and less expensive parts.

◆ Using composite materials to develop wind machines that can work more efficiently and offer higher output.

◆ Developing new batteries that require less harmful chemicals while extending their functional life.

◆ Building more efficient fossil-fuel-powered electric generation and distribution systems.

◆ Developing buying networks that can help consumers purchase energy-efficient residential power systems at lower initial cost.

◆ Learning how to cut power costs with more energy-efficient appliances to reduce total power needs.

The future of power technology is bright indeed!

You've learned how to generate electricity from many renewable resources: solar, water, wind. You've also been tipped off to the opportunities of net metering. Now it's time to pull it all together. Chapter 14 gets specific on how to store and distribute power.

The Least You Need to Know

◆ Fuel cells use a chemical process instead of combustion to release energy from fuels.

◆ Fuel cells are not, themselves, a renewable energy; they offer a more efficient way to turn hydrogen from fuels into electricity.

◆ Fuel cell technology is here, but expensive; however, costs are coming down and fuel cells might be a practical energy source of the future.

◆ Solar, wind, hydro, and other renewable energy resources will continue to advance with technology, offering improved and more cost-effective power options in the future.

14

Storing and Distributing Power

In This Chapter

◆ Selecting the right inverter for your solar power system

◆ Figuring out which batteries to use

◆ Following the National Electric Code

◆ Learning about the other stuff your solar power system needs

In Chapter 9, I introduced the parts of a typical solar power system. They include the inverter and power panel, PV modules, batteries, cables, and some related hardware. We then got more specific on PV modules, leaving the storage and distribution system for "later."

Well, it's later! This chapter offers more specifics on the systems that support power generation. These systems don't much care if the power was generated from solar energy, wind, water, fuel cells, or squirrels on a treadmill. Their job is to convert DC to AC, store it if needed, and get the power to awaiting appliances and lights. Power to the people!

Selecting Batteries

Batteries are a necessity for many home power systems. Batteries store electricity for use at night or for meeting demand during the day when the power source isn't keeping up with demand. Without batteries, you're not going to be able to turn on a light when it's dark outside.

You could use just about any type of 12-volt car battery to store DC electricity. However, it isn't going to last long. To provide electricity over long periods, your home power system needs deep-cycle batteries. These batteries, usually lead-acid, are designed to gradually discharge and recharge 80 percent of their capacity hundreds of times. Car batteries are shallow-cycle batteries that discharge only about 20 percent of their capacity. Drawing lower will very often damage the battery.

Of course, deep-cycle batteries cost more. Think of them as an investment. Deep-cycle batteries cost from about $75 to more than $1,000 each. The cost depends on the type, capacity (in ampere-hours), the operating climate (cold, hot, dry, wet), proper maintenance, and the chemicals inside.

The batteries you choose should have a combined capacity greater than the need. The smartest approach is to get advice from your power equipment and/or battery provider on batteries that will supply your long-term needs.

CAUTION

Solar Eclipse

Most batteries contain toxic materials that can pose serious health and safety problems. Most PV and other home power system designers recommend lead-acid and wet-cell batteries, which give off explosive hydrogen gas when recharging. Make sure that the batteries are located in a well-ventilated space away from other system components—and people and pets. Read and follow the manufacturer's instructions.

Charge controllers regulate the flow of electricity within the battery system. They are either combined with the inverter or are standalone charge controllers. These standalone units typically cost between $25 and $400, depending on your system's ampere capacity and what features you want. When the load is drawing power, the controller allows the charge to flow from the power source into the battery, the load, or both. When the controller senses that the battery is fully charged, it stops the flow of charge from the power system. Better controllers will also sense when loads have taken too much electricity from batteries and will stop the outbound flow until the charge is restored to the batteries, extending the battery's lifetime.

Selecting Inverters

Inverters are devices that change direct current (DC) electricity into alternating current (AC) electricity. As mentioned, the DC could be coming from one of a variety of power sources. It can also come from batteries because they store electricity as DC. Your car's battery, for example, stores 12 volts DC—unless you're driving a 50-year-old classic with a 6-volt system.

Inverters sound like simple devices, and they are. However, technology has really enhanced them over the past 20 years to where they do much more, and they do it more efficiently. Most inverters made for the United States convert 12-, 24-, or 48-volt DC and produce 120-volt 60-*hertz* AC. Other countries prefer an AC output of 220 volts at 50 hertz.

Small inverters can power individual appliances. However, solar and other power systems that want to power many appliances need a larger inverter. Fortunately, commonly available inverters can provide up to 5,000 watts of AC electricity. The quality and type of AC current that an inverter produces depends on the waveform, frequency, and voltage.

> **Sun-Day School**
>
> A **hertz** (Hz) indicates the number of times that AC alternates in a second. DC can be stored, but can't travel very far on a wire without loss. AC can travel much farther, such as from a power plant to your home, so most appliances are AC. The two standards, 50 Hz and 60 Hz, were established long ago, and neither is really better, just different.

Waveform

A waveform is the form or shape of the wave that the electric current looks like. Backing up a bit, AC alternates around a single point, first positive, then negative. The reference line is 0 volts. If drawn, the waveform line would go above the reference line for awhile, then back and down below the reference line in a shape that looks like an "S" sleeping (see the following illustration). The line goes as far above the reference line as below it.

The height of the waveform above and below the reference line is called its amplitude. The amount of time it takes to go from the line up, then down, then back to the line is called the frequency. Those are the basics of a waveform.

Components of a waveform.

(©author)

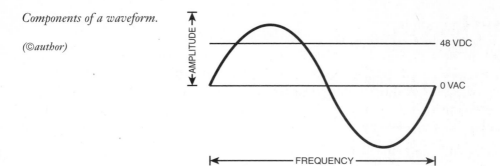

The input is direct current, or DC, that could be drawn as a straight line somewhere above the 0-volt reference point. Obviously, a 48-volt DC line would be drawn higher above the reference point than a 12-volt DC line. So the inverter's job is to get that DC input to alternate above and below (positive and negative) the 0-volt reference point. And it must do so at the amplitude and frequency needed for your appliances—twelve volts DC in, to 120 volts at 60 Hz AC out, for example.

In the ideal world, the output waveform should be a sine wave, the sleeping S. That's what appliances prefer. But, as you can imagine, turning a straight line into an S takes some work. It's more expensive than converting the straight line into a square wave.

What's a square wave, you ask? In the previous drawing, it looks like two adjacent squares, one above and one below the reference line. A square wave is the intermediate step between DC and sine-wave AC. It's cheaper to produce. There are some appliances that can run nearly as well on square-wave AC as on sine-wave AC. Heating appliances can do this. But many appliances such as stereos and color TVs really need the good stuff—sine-wave AC—to work properly.

Confused yet? I hope not! We're going to take another step and introduce a waveform that's halfway between a square wave and a sine wave. It's called a modified or quasi sine wave. Most appliances can run on AC from a quasi sine-wave AC inverter. The advantage here is that these inverters are simpler—meaning cheaper—than pure sine wave inverters. Actually, square-wave inverters just don't exist on the market anymore. Virtually all the smaller and/or lower cost inverters available now are modified-sine wave.

Here's the bottom line: Buy the least expensive power inverter that will do the job of delivering the right type of electricity to your home's appliances. Ask questions. This short explanation of waveforms will help you decipher the answers.

Frequency

I mentioned AC frequency a moment ago. U.S. appliances are built to run on a frequency of 60 Hz or cycles per second. Most other countries prefer 50 Hz. Who cares?

Your clocks care! Anything with a timing device in it relies on the frequency of incoming AC to keep track of the time. It counts 60 Hz then advances the clock by one second. Just remember that unless you're in Asia or Europe, you want your inverter to produce an output frequency of 60 Hz.

Voltage

I also mentioned voltage in talking about waveforms. Most inverters manufactured for the U.S. market supply 120 volts at the output. Some can be connected in series to produce 240 volts for things like submersible well pumps.

Alternately, a step-up transformer can be installed on those appliances to turn 120 VAC into modest amounts of 240 VAC. Chapter 2 covered inventorying your home's appliances to figure out whether you have any that require 240 VAC.

Power Rating

One final question to ask when buying an inverter: Is the power output continuous or surge? The answer is important because electric motors in your home (fans, blowers, blenders, refrigerator) that go on and off during the day need as much as six times normal operating power to get started. Much like getting out of bed on a Monday morning. The inverter you select must be rated to handle the extra load. Otherwise, some of your appliances may not start up.

So make sure that the inverter you select is able to run every device you plan to connect to it—and then some. Certainly you'll be adding electric tools and appliances in the future.

Solar Eclipse

Be careful of plugging battery chargers into a system with a modified-sine wave inverter. Many chargers, such as those for a battery-operated drill, use a temperature sensor to tell when the battery is charged. The modified-sine wave confuses the temperature sensor, and the charger won't turn off. Batteries have been known to melt! Your charger or inverter Owner's Manual may not mention this problem. If you must charge with modified-sine wave power, check your charger carefully to make sure it turns off by itself after an hour or so. If it doesn't, you have a *manually controlled* battery charger. If you don't turn it off, you, too, will melt batteries.

Inverter Types

As you begin shopping for an inverter you'll discover various types. Which one is the best? The answer depends on the application. A rotary inverter uses DC electricity to power a DC motor that turns an AC generator. Rotary inverters produce a pure sine-wave output and automatically deliver electrical load based on demand. The downside is that they have very low efficiency, don't handle surges well, and they can't adjust to changes in frequency.

More popular are electronic inverters. Two types are available. High frequency switching units use all solid-state components for lighter weight and lower cost. However, they have limited surge capacity, and generally see shorter life expectancies. Transformer-based units are larger, heavier, more surge capable, and generally have longer life expectancies, but they are more expensive initially.

Bright Idea

Get as smart an inverter as you can afford. Besides managing the power load for efficiency, some inverters have a load-sensing feature that puts the inverter in standby mode if not needed. Otherwise, the inverter can itself drain power from an otherwise sleeping system.

There's also what's called an intertie inverter. These are used on systems that intertie to the utility grid. It synchronizes power between the grid and what's produced by the home system, so it's also called a synchronous inverter. If the generated power is more than the house needs, the unit sends excess power to the utility grid. If the solar or other house power system can't keep up with demand, the synchronous inverter pulls power from the utility line, like water seeking its own level. (Chapter 25 offers more information on selling excess power.)

If you're buying a power distribution system, make sure that the inverter included in the package matches your home's power needs and will intertie with the utility grid.

Battery-Charging Inverters

We'll cover batteries for your power system in the next section of this chapter. Meantime, know that there are inverters available that include a DC source battery charge controller. This type of unit manages not only power between the utility grid and your home power system, but also the electric charge stored in batteries.

It works like a traffic cop. It watches what power is needed by the house and what's available from the house's power system, storage batteries, and the utility grid. It then manages the flow of power as needed to meet demands. If the house power system can't keep the batteries charged, it gets electricity from the utility to charge them. Pretty nifty!

Intertie Inverters

If you're planning on tying your home power-generation system into the public utility grid, you'll need to install an inverter that is approved by the utility for intertie systems. There are two types: direct and battery.

A direct intertie inverter feeds electricity directly to and from the incoming utility line. Batteries not included. There's less equipment to control, so the cost is less. A typical nonbattery intertie inverter will cost $1,500 to $2,500. An intertie inverter that must also control a battery system will, obviously, cost more—about $4,000 for the typical unit.

Building to Code

The National Electric Code (NEC) has one job: to ensure safety in all systems that generate, store, transport, and use electricity. That's a big job. It includes codes that are specific to solar and other home power systems. That's good. Whoever installs your home power system (you or a dealer or contractor) must follow NEC equipment requirements so that the system will be approved by local electric code officials. (Some states require that any electrical system be installed by a licensed electrician.)

However, many local code officials aren't familiar with PV and other home-generation systems. The solution is to start early in the building permit process finding out who will do the inspection and whether he or she is up-to-date on your type of system. If not, begin the education process. Invite the inspector to watch what you or the dealer is doing before the system is closed up in the wall or roof system. Most will be open to learning.

Bright Idea

As I mentioned in Chapter 4, a plain English translation of the NEC codes for photovoltaic power systems is reprinted in the latest edition of *Solar Living Sourcebook* published by Gaiam Real Goods (1-800-919-2400).

What Else Will You Need?

In addition to the inverter, batteries, and controller, your home power system will need cables, some fuses, and some protection. Let's take a look.

Fortunately, wire for solar, wind, hydro, and fuel-cell power systems looks like wire for utility power—because it's exactly the same wire. Electricity doesn't care what it travels on. What's important is that the wire is rated for the load and the application for which you're using it. The amount of current it can safely carry depends on its size; the larger the wire the more it can carry. To confuse things a little, larger wire has a smaller gauge number than smaller wire. That is, a 10-gauge wire is bigger, and is designed to carry more current than a 16-gauge wire.

Where you plan to run the wire also dictates the type of wire you should use. The NEC code will get specific. In the meantime, know that some wire is intended to be run through walls, other wire through the ground, and still other to lie in the sun all day.

AC systems require AC outlets. If you're planning to use DC appliances and lights, you'll need DC outlets and adapters. It's best to use an electrician to install or at least to plan and oversee the installation of any new wiring.

Fuses and circuit breakers are important to the safety of electrical systems—and to the folks who plug things in to them. Dr. Doug, Gaiam Real Goods's power guru, suggests that "Any wire that attaches to a battery must be fused!" Good advice—and it's code! Basically, any wire attached to a power source must be protected from over-current. There are numerous fuses, disconnects, ground-fault protection, and lighting protectors available. Whoever designs your power system should be following code, including fuses and other protections.

You've pulled the whole system together, from power to storage and distribution. Want an easier way to do it? The next chapter describes ready-made solar power systems that nearly anyone can install.

The Least You Need to Know

- ◆ An inverter changes direct current into alternating current as required by your appliances.

- ◆ Choose an inverter by its waveform, frequency, voltage, and power rating—and your budget.

- ◆ Some inverters also serve as system controllers, battery chargers, and as intertie with the utility grid.

- ◆ The National Electric Code (NEC) includes specific codes for installing solar and other home power systems.

- ◆ You'll also need wiring, fuses, protectors, and some other hardware depending on the system you're installing.

Part 3

Solar Systems

See how it works? The sun shines energy on to Earth and a bunch of man-made gadgets turn it into electricity. Nifty!

This part shows you how all those solar components go together into solar power systems. There's one that's right for you. Availabilities include solar power systems to power the entire home, to act as a supplemental or emergency power source, or to power your microwave on a camping trip. We'll cover everything from solar cookers to big systems that will be the envy of your local utility.

Now that you've learned how the components of a solar power system work you're ready to see how they work as a system—and power your life.

Chapter 15

Complete Power Systems

In This Chapter

◆ Considering a complete solar power system for your home

◆ What's included in a standalone system?

◆ About direct intertie systems

◆ Getting an off-grid system

◆ Monitoring your solar power system

As you've seen in the previous 14 chapters, there's much to know about solar and other renewable power systems. Lots of questions to answer. Lots of components to size and buy. Take one from column A and two from column B.

Fortunately, there's an easier way: buying a packaged system. That's what we'll cover in this chapter; we'll find and buy the right plug-and-play solar power system for your home's needs.

Maybe you saw the system approach coming and jumped to this chapter first. Good idea, but you missed out on the specifics of how solar power systems work and, especially, how you can cut solar power costs (see Chapters 3 and 4). No matter. Keep reading, but use the Table of Contents and the index to check anything that isn't clear.

What's a System?

A solar power system is one or more solar electric components that are engineered and sized to work together. Most are built around the basic component of a solar power system, the single PV module. One or more PV panels electrically connected together is a PV module. Next comes the kit of one or more PV modules plus related hardware, such as mountings and connectors.

A PV system typically includes PV modules, optional batteries, and an inverter, all serving customer loads and/or the utility grid.

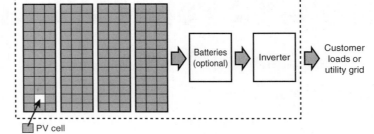

The next bigger system is typically called the standalone system and includes the PV modules, their support structure, inverter, controller, connectors, and, if planned, batteries. The standalone system is designed to produce and distribute solar power to your home. It's often called an off-grid system because the house isn't otherwise connected to the local electric utility. It is also popular for remote cabins and RVs. The standalone system is covered in Chapters 16 and 18.

The standalone solar power DC system includes few components. An AC system adds an inverter.

(courtesy of AEE Solar)

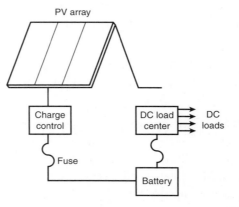

Some solar power systems must rely on a generator to keep sufficient power in the house. The generator offers a backup source for when the sun doesn't shine enough. Alternately, installing a generator in the solar power system means you don't have to size the PV modules for worst-case conditions. You'll learn more about them in Chapter 17.

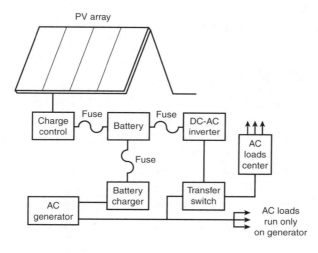

The PV-generator system adds a backup generator, inverter, and a transfer switch.

(courtesy of AEE Solar)

One step up is the intertie system. It does what the standalone system does *plus* takes electric power with the local utility as needed. Additionally, some intertie systems can deliver excess solar power from your home *to* the local utility, using the same power lines that bring utility power to you. It's called net metering. As you'll recall from Chapter 4, net metering allows your electricity meter to spin forward when electricity flows from the utility into your home, and backward when your power system delivers unused power to the utility. We'll revisit this subject in Chapter 25.

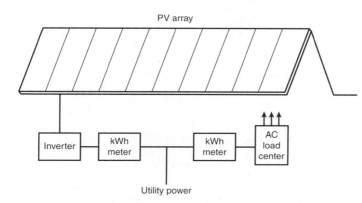

The intertie system supplements house solar power with utility power and sends surplus solar power to the utility.

(courtesy of AEE Solar)

There are other types of systems. What they have in common is that they make system selection easier. If you want a solar power system that delivers 3 kW of electricity and depends on the utility grid for anything above that, there's a system out there that matches those specs. It has the most efficient inverter, fuse system, PV module mounts, and other components. It's like buying a car rather than a bunch of parts that require assembly to become a car.

Let's take a look at some of the more popular solar power systems.

Direct Intertie System

The grid-connected, or direct intertie, system develops and delivers PV power to a home's AC electric system without using batteries. The PV array acts like a central generating plant, supplying power to the grid. DC power from the solar modules enters the inverter/controller and exits to the house's main utility breaker panel as AC power. The panel distributes it to the house through installed wiring. If there is an excess of PV-generated power, it goes through the AC utility meter and back up the line to the utility pole wires for distribution. Your meter runs backwards, reducing your monthly obligation to the power company!

The inverter/controller includes disconnection apparatus required by the National Electric Code (NEC). The typical unit also includes DC and AC circuit breakers, a lightning arrestor, and a metering system that displays system status and cumulative production.

Components of a typical direct intertie system.

(©Gaiam Real Goods)

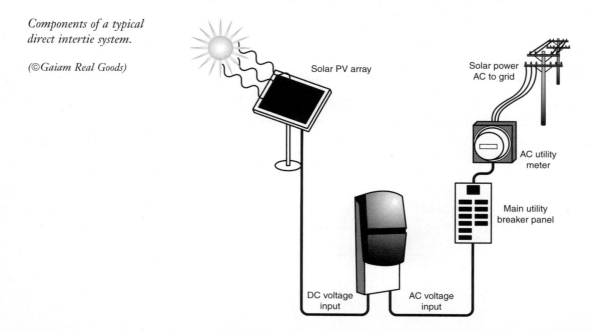

Solar PV array

Solar power AC to grid

AC utility meter

Main utility breaker panel

DC voltage input

AC voltage input

Direct intertie systems are available in various models depending on the system's power production. For example, one manufacturer offers models that develop and distribute 1 kW, 1.5 kW, 2 kW, and 2.5 kW. Larger systems can be built by wiring smaller systems in parallel to increase the total system size.

A typical 2.5 kW direct intertie system will include the inverter/controller and 24 120-watt PV modules with rooftop mounts. Your house already has the main panel and meter. If your home's location averages 5 and a half hours of sunlight a day (the U.S. average), it will deliver about 13.3 kWh per day. For the average home, that's about 85 percent of its power needs.

PV module efficiency *(percent)	PV capacity rating (watts)							
	100	250	500	1000	2000	4000	10000	100000
	Roof area needed in square feet							
4	30	75	150	300	600	1200	3000	30000
8	15	38	75	150	300	600	1500	15000
12	10	25	50	100	200	400	1000	10000
16	8	20	40	80	160	320	800	8000

Amount of roof area typically needed for PV modules based on module efficiency and capacity.

The price for this typical 2.5 kW direct inter-tie system is under $20,000 plus wiring and installation, probably $1,000 to $2,000 more, depending on who does the work. Some states offer rebates equal to as much as *half* the cost, cutting it to around $10,000. Depending on how much your local utility charges for power—and how much it pays you for your excess power—the payback time can be 5 to 10 years.

There are, of course, many variables such as manufacturer costs, system quality, dealer markup, installation charges, and what rebates and tax incentives are available. It's a ballpark estimate.

Solar Eclipse

Safety first! Make sure your solar power system includes appropriate bypass switches. For example, install an inverter bypass switch between your inverter, generator, and load center for use if the inverter fails. Also include a main shutoff to your solar power system so you can safely turn off electric power to work on your system as needed.

Systems with Batteries

Many direct intertie systems benefit from having a battery system within. The batteries can keep you from buying utility power when the sky is dark.

Unfortunately, a lead-acid *battery* isn't environmentally friendly, and it needs periodic maintenance. The best lead-acid batteries are only about 80 percent efficient, and they contain toxic substances. However, they are the best we can afford right now. Maybe tomorrow's technology will replace them.

Sun-Day School

A **battery** is a device in which stored chemical energy is converted directly into electrical energy. It can be either rechargeable or nonrechargeable.

Direct intertie systems that use batteries can be purchased as full systems, needing only local wiring and installation to be put to work. They include PV modules, inverter/controller, mounts, interconnection cables, and related hardware. The inverter for a direct intertie system is a special model that can both handle intertie to the utility grid and manage the battery system.

A mid-size system includes 20 PV modules with mounting hardware, all cables and fuses, the inverter unit, and batteries. How many batteries you need depends on how you're planning to use the battery system. A mid-size system may use a bank of six batteries at an additional cost of $2,000 to $3,000 installed. If the home gets "average" solar radiation (5 and a half hours a day year-round) it will deliver about 11.6 kWh a day. That's about 75 percent of the typical house's power needs. The package price is around $21,000 plus batteries, installation, and finish wiring.

A larger system with 30 PV modules, the inverter, and everything else (including eight batteries) will run up a bill of about $30,000 to $40,000. Take off any rebates or incentives you can get. Add $3,000 to $5,000 for a larger battery bank—even more if you want to go with top-of-the-line batteries that can last over 20 years with proper maintenance.

Bright Idea

I've mentioned average battery banks here, but the best battery arrangement depends on whether they are for emergency use only or you're trying to sell excess power to the utility. In addition, if your home is off-grid you may have selected DC lighting and appliances that will rely heavily on batteries for juice when the sun isn't cooperating. The best tip is to work with your solar power system supplier on sizing and buying the most cost-effective battery and charging system that fits your home's needs.

Off-Grid System

You can capture enough solar power with a half-dozen PV modules to fully power a small house that has no other electrical connection. Of course, output depends on how much sun the home is getting.

For example, a standalone system with four PV modules of about 50 watts each that get five hours of direct sunlight a day can, theoretically, provide about 1 kWh of power a day. Actually, the modules and system may not be 100 percent efficient. Use the module efficiency factor from the manufacturer to calculate net output. Add in batteries as needed and you have a basic system.

Another system that can provide 1 kWh/day will include a 240-watt solar electric ray, a 1.5 kW inverter with battery charger, enough batteries for a five-day reserve, a controller, and related wiring and safety equipment. Approximate cost (before rebates) is about $5,000.

You can get a system that's four times the size for about three times the money. Included is a 4 kWh/day system with 960 peak-watt modules, 16 batteries, a charger, and a controller, with wiring.

These are examples and guidelines. There are *so many* variables when selecting and installing a solar power system that you really need advice that's specific to your conditions, budget, and economic opportunities. Check Appendix B as well as your local telephone book under "Solar Products—Dealers & Services" for more information.

Monitoring Power Production

Technology is amazing! Not only are you about to gather energy from the sun, wind, and water, and convert it into electricity, but you can also use technology to manage it. The latest inverter/controllers manage the process of making and storing power. They can also monitor your system. For example, many solid state inverter/controllers have monitoring systems that can tell you how much power is currently being produced, how much has been produced over a specific period, and how much has been delivered to the utility and/or stored in batteries.

You can also watch it all on your computer! Software is available that monitors and displays system information on PV modules, inverters, battery status, and other data, both current and historical. With it you can see how efficiently your solar power system is working and determine whether there's anything you can do to increase productivity. Maybe you can shut down part of the system when not needed. Or you can decide whether more PV modules would be a good investment.

In addition, a monitoring system can manage solar tracking motors on the mounts so that the PV modules follow the sun across the sky. Don't expect this technology to be cheap, but it can help you manage a larger home power plant.

Fortunately, you don't have to spend big bucks on a solar power monitoring system. Simpler systems that include voltmeters and ammeters can be installed and mounted in your system for less than $100. Keeping track of your power system can save you money. I'll cover system tracking and maintenance in Chapter 22.

Next, let's consider supplemental power systems in Chapter 16.

The Least You Need to Know

- A solar power system is one or more solar electric components that are engineered and sized to work together.

- Some solar power systems are plug-and-play, while many need additional sizing of battery banks to match home needs.

- Generators and even local utility lines can supplement a solar home's power requirements.

- Intertie systems connect to utility lines and can even deliver solar-generated electricity to the utility grid.

- Monitoring your solar power system can help you make it run more efficiently.

Chapter 16

Supplemental Power Systems

In This Chapter

- Using solar and other energy sources for supplemental power
- How generator-inverter systems work
- Using the sun to power outdoor lighting
- Using the sun to power DC appliances and lights
- Solar power for remote needs

Not every home needs—nor might you want—a complete solar power system. The total cost may be too high for your budget. Perhaps there isn't enough local sunlight to energize a full system. Or your home may already have a primary renewable power source. There are several good reasons.

This chapter offers ideas and specifics on how to select a supplemental solar power system. It also covers other power systems that can work with your solar power system to power your home.

Using Supplemental Power

One alternative to investing in a complete solar power system is to use solar energy as a supplemental power system. Let it power your outdoor lighting, supplement power from your local utility grid, or add solar power to your wind or hydropower system.

Typical hybrid utility intertie system with solar PVs, wind turbine, and fossil-fuel generator.

(©Gaiam Real Goods)

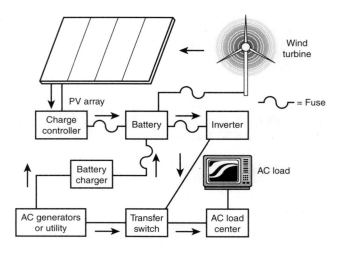

Genverter Systems

Some homes just don't get enough sunlight for a full solar power system. Yet they are off-grid and can't depend on the local utility company. Nor are wind and hydro systems an option. What to do?

Unfortunately, the best option is to install a fossil-fuel burning generator. Fortunately, there are some relatively efficient units out there that can supplement solar power and make life a little easier off-grid.

The most common power source for homes off the utility line is a gas or diesel generator. A generator is a mechanical device used to produce DC electricity. Power is produced by coils of wire passing through magnetic fields inside the generator. Solar power is the second most common power source. Combining the two is a better, more environmentally friendly source than a generator alone.

Some generator power systems operate on demand only. That is, in the evening when lights are needed or throughout the day as a refrigerator's compressor needs power, the generator is turned on to furnish power. For some houses this can mean that the

Solar Eclipse _____

Thinking about adding a generator to your power system? Make sure it's portable—or at least can mount on a portable trailer. If your generator needs service, it's cheaper to take it to a mechanic than to have the mechanic make a house call.

generator is on up to 16 hours a day producing kilowatts of power when only watts are needed. Not very efficient! Alternately, a generator system can be on just a few hours a day to charge a bank of batteries that power the home throughout the day and night. It's a smarter option.

Ultimately, an even better system relies on solar power to charge the batteries and the generator supplements solar to keep battery power at needed levels. A control system can even run the generator in the evening when power demands are highest. Appliances will get power directly from the generator, and excess power will go to charge the batteries.

The system described is called a generator-inverter-charger-battery, or "genverter" system. It can supplement a solar-inverter-charger-battery or solar power system. Using a battery bank and including solar energy can dramatically reduce the generator size required to help power your home.

Switching between generator, solar, and battery power can be manual or automatic. The most efficient system uses a single controller that not only manages the power sources but also serves as the system's inverter changing DC to AC. Some power control units can even manage loads for DC as well as AC appliances.

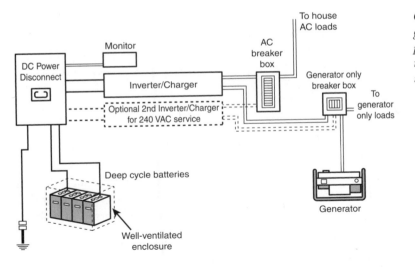

Components of a typical genverter system. A solar power system can be linked to the primary or a second inverter.

Components

What components will you need for a genverter system? The inverter/controller is the most important—and expensive—component. You'll want one that can handle the power resources you've selected including generator, solar, wind, hydro, grid, or whatever. It must be sized to handle the highest anticipated load in kilowatts. Make sure it can manage anticipated DC as well as AC loads.

You'll also need a bank of batteries with cables. How many depends on your system requirements, so refer to Chapter 14 on storing and distributing power for more info.

Other components you'll need include a monitor and an AC distribution panel. The AC panel is probably already in place because it's your home's main panel. The monitor reads voltage and amperage from the battery charger and to the inverter. It also stores and reports cumulative data so you can check operating history and manage the system better.

Sun Spots

Greg Dunbar, one of the technical reviewers on this book, tells of moving to the country a couple of decades ago and installing a generator system to supplement solar power. Alas, so did a half-dozen other pioneers. Although all the homes in the valley to which they moved were spaced thousands of feet apart, the sound of generators carries well. During winters when solar power was unavailable, everyone started a generator to power the home. Soon, all were wondering why they had moved to the noisy country instead of the relatively quiet city!

Cost

What's a genverter system going to cost? If you're simply adding a generator to your existing solar power system, probably not much more than the cost of the generator and wiring. Of course, if you have to resize the system with a new inverter/controller, the cost goes up. A small battery bank (four 24-volt batteries), 2.4 kW inverter, AC panel, monitor, and a fused disconnect will set you back about $3,000. Add to that the cost of the generator.

Electric generators range from small 3 kW units to all-you-need 15 kW generators. The rating is the *maximum* power output. Manufacturers suggest that you double your required wattage to come up with the maximum unit you need. Of course, they're in the business of selling generators. You may not have to double your needs, but the unit should provide at least 150 percent of your requirements. The "rated" or watts is typically 10 to 20 percent less than the maximum watts.

You can purchase a small portable generator for less than $500. However, one that will help power your house will cost much more. A 10 kW stationary generator, for example, will cost about $3,000 plus shipping and wiring. Diesel generators of 15 to 20 kW start at about $8,000. Most households need at least 5 kW in order to charge batteries and run the washing machine or well pump simultaneously. Generators over 10 kW are expensive to run. Don't go bigger than you really need or can use. Generators run most efficiently at about 70 to 80 percent of full load.

How can you choose the right generator for the job? Here are some questions to consider:

◆ What is the total wattage of appliances and equipment that I need to operate?

◆ Will the generator be used in conjunction with a solar or other power system?

◆ Should the generator be stationary or portable?

◆ Should the generator have a manual or automatic starter system? (Automatic is best unless the generator isn't used often.)

◆ What's the best fuel for this generator: gasoline, diesel, natural gas, or propane?

◆ How will fuel be delivered and stored for lowest cost and optimum running time between refills?

◆ Do I need more than one power outlet on the generator itself?

In adding up the total wattage of equipment you need to power, double the wattage of anything that has a motor or compressor that turns on. Remember to plan for the future. It will get here very soon!

Bright Idea

If you're not sure of an appliances wattage, use this formula: Volts × Amps = Wattage. Check the manufacturer's plate on the appliance (typically on the back or bottom) for the amps. Most household appliances are 110V, but manufacturers figure wattage based on the top limit, 120V. So a 7.5 A toaster is 900 W (120 × 7.5 = 900). Most small appliances draw 1 kW or less of electric power. A water heater is typically 3 kW to 4 kW.

Outdoor Solar Lighting

One popular method of using solar power at home is outdoor lighting. In fact, it's the first place many people start when looking at solar power. Outdoor lighting offers both security and beauty, so it's an important use of electricity. Because it is outside, it's the perfect application for solar electricity. And it's an inexpensive way to try solar power.

Outdoor PV lighting systems use small PV modules that convert sunlight into electricity. The electricity is stored in batteries for use at night. They can be cost effective relative to installing power cables or step-down transformers for relatively small lighting loads.

Several companies now market units for marking or decorating driveways, walkways, and patios. Most of these devices are totally self-contained units that need only to be staked into the ground in a sunny location. Others have the lights separate from the PV module so that it can be placed in a sunny location. Units vary in size and function from small ⅛-inch red glowing pathway markers to pole-mounted patio and high-beam security lights.

Outdoor solar lighting is also being used by governments to add lighting where it's more expensive to run electrical wiring. For example, many roadside emergency phone systems are powered by PV modules mounted atop the telephone post. Solar lighting is used at municipal parks, campgrounds, rest areas, highway signs, and even on billboards.

Home outdoor PV lighting systems are available in hardware, lighting, and even discount stores. You can also buy them through environmental companies that sell from catalogs and online. Most parts of the country have sufficient sunlight to power outdoor home lighting. Even so, make sure the spots you plan to install the lights aren't too shaded to capture enough sunlight. If so, consider a system where the PV module is separate from the light.

Most outdoor solar light units will list a specific number of hours of sunlight needed to charge the batteries for overnight lighting. Some only require four hours of direct sunlight while others need eight hours to recharge. A short charge means that the lights won't be on early in the morning when it's still dark outside. In addition, completely draining the batteries each night will dramatically shorten the life of the batteries.

Remember that outdoor solar lights aren't intended to turn night into day. To keep PV modules small (and costs down), most outdoor solar lights use very small bulbs and refracting lenses to maximize output. Typical units are intended for lighting pathways. If you're trying to light up a driveway or doorway for security you'll need larger PV modules.

Solar Eclipse

Winter in many locations means less daytime sunlight. Clouds get in the way. That means outdoor solar lighting won't get as much solar energy to recharge batteries. The total charge may be cut by 30 to 50 percent. It's a good idea to select outdoor solar lighting based on how much sunlight is expected during winter months.

Batteries inside outdoor solar lighting units are nickel cadmium, sealed lead acid, or lead acid. Most batteries can be removed and replaced as needed. However, some lighting units use built-in batteries that can't be replaced. Low batteries mean a new lighting unit. Make sure the solar lighting units you purchase have removable batteries.

Outdoor solar lighting is like anything else: You get approximately what you pay for. Small driveway marker lights can be purchased at large hardware stores for $10 to $20 per light. Standalone porch lights will range from $25 to $50. Better quality solar-powered garden path lights will cost $50 to $100 each. A solar-sensor porch light that is motion activated to turn on when someone comes near will run around $100. Beyond that, a PV module can be installed to supply power to a wired string of solar outdoor lights.

DC Appliances and Lighting

As you learned in Chapter 9, direct current (DC) is electric current that flows in one direction only. Solar, wind, and water power systems develop DC; batteries store DC. Alternating current (AC) is electric current that alternates in direction. AC can travel farther over wires than DC, but cannot be stored. An inverter converts DC into AC. Your supplemental power system budget can stretch farther if it doesn't need an inverter to convert DC solar power into AC for your home. How can this happen? By installing appliances and lighting that run on direct rather than alternating current.

Many home appliances that are available for AC circuits are also available in DC models. Due to fewer models being available, prices are typically higher. Even among manufacturers that make both an AC and a DC model, the DC version is usually higher in price.

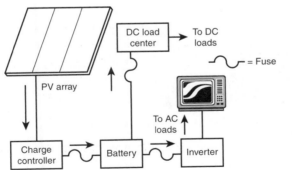

Small standalone DC/AC solar power system.

(courtesy of AEE Solar)

For example, an energy-efficient 16 cubic foot (c.f.) DC or AC refrigerator can cost about $2,500—more than twice that of the typical refrigerator. It is designed and manufactured to be highly efficient, drawing less power than comparable units sold at major appliance stores. All you need is two 75-watt PV modules to power the DC refrigerator. Higher initial cost, lower operating cost. Of course, prices will come down as more people buy these more energy-efficient appliances.

Sun Spots

Because fluorescent lighting needs only a quarter of the electricity of incandescent lighting, most DC lights are fluorescent. They give more light (measured in lumens) than standard lights.

DC freezers are available, too. Chest models are more popular than upright freezers because they are typically more efficient. One super-efficient model claims that operating costs are just 5 cents a day. In addition, it doesn't use freon or other chlorofluro-carbon (CFC) refrigerants that damage Earth's ozone layer.

DC can power your home lighting as well. Unfortunately, DC lighting is much more expensive than AC lighting. A good quality 12-volt DC light "bulb" can cost $25 or more. It also lasts longer. DC lights are more popular for recreational vehicles and other low-use applications. They can also be used for emergency lighting systems.

Remote Power

Another practical application of solar technology is powering remote equipment such as pumps. These units are especially popular on large ranches where livestock water pumps are located far away from electrical service. A submersible pump is powered by a PV module installed above ground level. Solar pumps are rapidly replacing the wind pumpers on the plains because they cost one-third as much and are far easier to install.

Solar-powered pumps can also move water from a spring or pond to a stream or a tank. In most cases, the pumps use DC electricity so the DC from the PV module can be applied without an inverter.

Farmers also use remote solar power systems to power fan blades that keep birds off of their crops. Others use large field fans to minimize the effects of freezing temperatures on delicate crops. PV modules are also put to work at remote greenhouses, saving the cost of running wiring for greenhouse lights or fans.

You may not be a farmer, but there are many applications for remote power that PV modules and solar technology can solve for you. Think about it.

What's next? Many people who want solar or other power systems use them as emergency backup. That's the topic of our next chapter.

The Least You Need to Know

- ◆ Gasoline and diesel generators are a popular source of supplemental power for off-grid homes.

- ◆ A genverter system can cost-effectively supplement your home's solar power system.

- ◆ Many homeowners start their solar experience with outdoor lighting systems.

- ◆ DC appliances and lighting are available, but can be costly to purchase.

- ◆ Solar power systems are ideal resources for remote equipment such as well pumps and other powered devices that are too far from electrical service.

Chapter 17

Emergency Power Systems

In This Chapter

- ◆ What's an emergency—and what's an annoyance?
- ◆ Planning your power system for an emergency
- ◆ Finding alternatives to more electric power
- ◆ Selecting and installing backup power systems

Y2K! It's a term that reminds us of emergencies that don't arrive. There was much talk about the beginning of the year 2000, everything from inoperable computers to the end of civilization. Didn't happen.

For those of us who remember it, there were the bomb shelters of the 1950s and 1960s leading up to the Cuban Missile Crisis of 1962. Some U.S. cities saw near panic as people emptied store shelves and headed for safety. Fortunately, that emergency didn't happen either.

What about the next one? Or what about the time when the local utility has a major blackout or brownout and your home is without power? That's when an emergency power system can come in real handy. This chapter offers ideas to help you plan for "what if." It will help you decide how much, if anything, you need to invest in getting through power emergencies.

Planning for the Worst

If the sun falls out of the sky, your solar power system won't work any longer. However, that won't be the *worst* of the subsequent problems! So, let's list some of the things that could go wrong, things we can all agree are emergencies:

◆ The utility company goes bankrupt and there's no one willing to take over power generation. (Hey, it could happen!)

◆ Local utility services are disrupted due to inclement weather, natural disaster, sabotage, excessive use, or mismanagement.

◆ Your solar power, wind power, or hydropower system is broken and can't supply you with electricity.

On the other hand, here are some *non*emergencies that fit on a nuisance list:

◆ Your home's power goes off during the final episode of *24*.

◆ Power goes out overnight and the breakfast milk isn't cold.

◆ The lights flicker and your computer needs to be restarted.

◆ Someone hits a nearby power pole and you are without electricity for a few hours.

You get the picture. There are power emergencies and there are annoyances. Fortunately, it's easy and not all that expensive to prepare for annoyances. It's the emergencies that threaten life, health, and economy that require more planning—and more money.

What's an Emergency?

The first step in emergency preparation is defining your version of an emergency. Maybe winters can offer emergencies. If power goes out during a Miami winter, no one will freeze to death. But if it goes out during a Minneapolis winter, you could have a *real* emergency. What are the chances?

If the local power service is frequently interrupted, a backup system may be a good investment as a long-term outage could become an emergency. For example, if you're 12 miles from the closest power pole, you may want a backup power generator for bad weather protection.

If you live in areas where clouds can move in for months at a time (like Seattle or Portland), your solar power system may need an emergency backup system. At least, you may want to stay connected to the public power grid.

Of course, the duration of the power outage is important. A closed refrigerator can keep foods from spoiling for 6 to 24 hours or more, depending on its insulation. Much longer than that and you'd better start eating stuff. An evening without electricity can be cozy—once a year. But once a week can cut into your lifestyle and become a real inconvenience. Still not an emergency, but possibly a health or economic hazard.

Solar Eclipse

If your business is in your home, you should especially consider what sources you have for emergency power. Phones will probably work, but you won't be able to send or receive faxes nor check e-mail.

Then there's the cost. How much will an emergency power system cost to plan, install, and operate? There are lots of variables here. If you're simply adding batteries to your solar power system, the cost may be minimal. But if you need to install a full solar power, wind power, or hydropower system as emergency backup, the cost could be many thousands of dollars.

So the first step in developing your home's definition of an emergency is to consider these questions: What can you not do without and for how long? When does a nuisance become an emergency? Think about it for awhile and ask others in your living group to come up with what would constitute a true emergency in your home.

What Do You Need?

How much power must your emergency system provide—and for how long? Finding the most accurate answer can save you money. Because refrigerators and freezers use more power than most home appliances, they are a prime consideration when designing an emergency power system. A standard refrigerator can use up 3 kWh to 5 kWh of power a day. A generator that can keep the fridge operating may cost as much as the appliance. So it's wise to invest in the most efficient refrigerator and/or freezer you can. It will mean your emergency power system doesn't need to be as powerful.

Alternately, you can have a small, backup refrigerator that can run on propane or some other power source that isn't so interruptible. It should be large enough for the necessities. Or you may prefer a propane freezer to keep your investment in TV dinners from spoiling during an outage.

Next comes heat. If you're living in Buffalo, New York, and there's a winter power outage, heat will be high on the list of things you don't want to do without for more than a couple of hours. In Tucson, Arizona, the reverse is true if the outage occurs during the summer months; having no air conditioning in August may be a major problem. You can size your emergency power system for such events. Or you can plan on alternatives, such as using a wood stove or propane heater for heating or battery-powered fans for cooling.

The same is true for lighting. Rather than buy a generator or install batteries to keep the home lights burning, consider candles, propane cylinder lights, battery lanterns, or other resources. Having several powerful flashlights on hand is a good idea, too. They may save buying an oversized generator or battery bank.

Cooking, of course, is also an issue when the power goes out. There's always going out to eat, but that's going to get old fast—not to mention expensive. Rather, if you need to plan for emergency cooking, consider a small propane cylinder cook stove or even a solar oven. Both are relatively inexpensive—compared to a generator—and will serve your basic needs during an emergency.

So, what else can go wrong? You can lose communications. Fortunately, standard telephones have their own built-in power, which means they work even when your home power is out. Cordless phones may not work without battery backup. However, if you depend on them for your health or livelihood, backups are available. Consider a cell phone if you live where even telephone service goes out during an emergency, such as an ice storm.

If you're in the country and power goes out, you may not get water from your well. Water pumps usually run on electricity. Backup can be a solar-powered water pump, a UPS (which we'll talk about in a moment), or even a hand pump just in case the water delivery system stops.

A PV module can power a remote water pump, saving wiring.

(©Gaiam Real Goods)

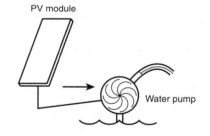

PV module

Water pump

Once you know what your emergency power system needs are, you can better select from the many options that are available. Check catalogs such as those listed in Appendix B for additional ideas and products for emergency preparedness. You can get everything from a water filtering system to a portable solar oven!

Calling for Backup

Your emergency power options depend on your needs, your primary power source, and your budget. Fortunately, you can select and install a backup power system for just a few hundred to a few thousand dollars.

UPS

Let's start small. If you're most concerned about a computer going down, get an *uninterruptible power supply (UPS)*. These are battery systems installed between the power plug and your PC. When everything is going along well, the power is serving your PC *and* charging the UPS. When the power goes out, the UPS takes over and the PC never knows the difference.

A UPS has a time limit, however. You may get 6 hours, 12 hours, or even 72 hours of battery life, depending on which you buy. The longer the life, the higher the cost. The life also depends on how much juice your PC needs. Also, turning off the printer or other connected hardware (such as a scanner or fax) when the UPS is needed will increase the number of hours you can run your PC.

Sun-Day School

An **uninterruptible power supply (UPS)** is a power supply capable of providing continuous uninterruptible service; it normally contains batteries to provide energy storage.

A UPS can be used for other important household appliances. If you have frequent outages—or think you might—and don't want to lose that freezer full of prime steaks, consider a UPS for it. Get the appliance's power requirements from the manufacturer's plate (typically on the back) and shop for a UPS that will exceed requirements for whatever period you think you'll need it.

UPS units are also popular with those who have home health equipment that cannot be without power, such as an oxygen system or a dialysis machine. Some of these units have built-in backup batteries, but their lifespan may be shorter than the outage. At just a hundred dollars or so for smaller units, a UPS is good insurance. Get them at larger hardware or computer equipment stores. Be aware that the batteries in all UPS units will need periodic replacement. Three years is about average; five years is maximum. Don't expect your 10-year-old UPS to function without routine maintenance.

Generators

Many folks install generators to increase the available power because their solar or other power source just doesn't deliver enough juice. Others install generators as backup for emergency use only. The difference between the two is function and size.

A backup generator can be purchased and installed for less than $1,000. The keys to buying the best backup generator for the situation are your emergency power requirements and the generator's fuel source. A light-duty generator is about 6.5 kW or less in power at 3,600 revolutions per minute (RPM). Large commercial generators and quieter models run at half the speed (1,800 RPM).

You estimated your home's energy needs in Chapter 3, and subsequent chapters guided you in sizing solar and other renewable power systems. So by now you have a pretty good idea of what power you really *need* if something bad happens to your primary power source. You may decide that an "emergency" is more than 24 hours without electricity at which time you'll need 1.2 kW of power for at least 5 days. In this case, a backup generator may be your best choice.

You can purchase a small 2 kW pull-start gas-operated backup generator for about $500. If power goes out you fill the tank, start it up, turn off any unnecessary circuit breakers, and plug it into the main power panel. If you're powering only a couple of vital appliances you can run a power cord from the generator to the appliances. Of course, you want to keep the noisy, smelly generator outside the house.

A few words of warning: A fossil-fuel generator is powered by an internal combustion engine. That means thousands of explosions are going off inside it every minute! Make sure the generator you select has an automatic shutoff in case of overheating. Also, be sure that there are no fuel leaks or faulty wiring that can start an *external* combustion!

A larger 5 kW or 10 kW backup generator will nick your wallet for $1,500 to $4,000 installed, depending on whether it's auto start (requires a battery), has lots of outlets, has a large fuel tank, and how quiet you want it. The quieter generators typically are more expensive.

What fuel should you use? Again, it depends on how much power you need and for how long. If you're buying a small, once-a-year backup generator, gasoline is the most popular fuel source. If you need more power or for longer running time, diesel fuel is less expensive than gas, though not quite as easy to get. The preferred fuel for long-running generators is propane gas. It burns cleaner than other fossil fuels and can be less expensive if delivered in bulk. Check around; prices will vary.

Additionally, your fuel choices may be limited. Natural gas may not be available in your area. Or a fossil-fuel generator may make too much noise for quiet neighborhoods.

Legally, your local building code may not allow you to wire your generator system into the main power panel in your home. You probably need a licensed electrician for this job. However, you can save some money by getting the generator in place and ready for the electrician.

Battery Banks

Generators are great workers—when they work hard. They're happiest when they deliver about 80 percent of their capacity. A 2 kW generator prefers to deliver about 1.6 kW. It's not very efficient to use a generator to deliver 1 kW or less of backup power. Batteries, however, aren't as picky.

We've talked about batteries before. However, selecting and sizing a *battery bank* is different for a backup power system than for selling excess power back to the local utility.

If you're installing a solar or other renewable power system, a battery bank makes sense as a backup. Even if you're not ready to invest in a battery bank for your solar power system, spend a few extra bucks on an inverter that includes a battery charger and controller for the day when you do add batteries. You probably will.

Sun-Day School

A **battery bank** is a group of batteries wired together to store power in a solar electric system. A battery bank allows you to use the stored power at night, on cloudy days, or to run more power than the array can produce at one time.

How many batteries? Again, know what load you'll need the batteries to cover and buy enough to at least meet that power goal. It's better if batteries exceed your power needs so they don't run low and damage the cells. Also, you'll probably want to increase the load someday. But don't install 24 batteries when 12 will do the job just fine. It's a waste of money. Your solar power system provider and/or your local utility can help you select the most cost-effective backup battery bank.

Should you choose 12V or 24V? The nominal voltage of your system depends on the system size. Small to medium systems with mostly DC loads can use 12V system output. However, the PV modules and loads can't be far from the battery bank because

Bright Idea

Batteries are available as 2V, 6V, and 12V. Prices typically are based on how much electric current (amps) a battery can store. Check with local hospitals and others who must have backup batteries; they sometimes sell used (but still good) batteries for a fraction of the new cost.

of high line loss. Medium to large systems typically require 24V output to cut line loss. For big systems, consider 48V system output.

Whether your system voltage output is 12V or 24V, you'll probably use either 12V or 6V batteries. Smaller systems can use 12V batteries; as battery capacity (and weight) goes up the batteries tend to be sliced into 6V sizes, so they're still manageable physically. Connecting batteries in series (positive to negative) increases the output voltage. Connecting them in parallel (positive to positive, negative to negative) increases the output current.

Connecting 6V and 12V batteries for 12V and 24V output.

(courtesy of AEE Solar)

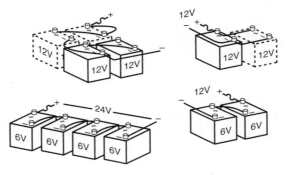

Other Renewable Backup Systems

If you're thinking about a backup source for your home's solar power system, consider other renewable resources. Chapters 12 and 13 offered more information about wind power, hydropower, and fuel cells. Deciding which option is right for you will take some knowledge of what other renewable resources are available in your piece of the world. For example, observation may tell you that, even if the sun doesn't shine on a specific day, there's always wind on a nearby high spot. Or your property may get lots of stream water during the winter when the sun isn't as efficient for you. So consider a wind turbine generator or a small hydroelectric power system. These can provide emergency power "when the sun don't shine."

If you have other renewable backup power systems available, combine them with a battery bank for greatest efficiency. Then the wind or water can help keep the solar power's battery bank charged. It can give you enough juice to get through any emergency. If not, there's always a backup-backup generator!

Want to use solar power for your *other* home? Chapter 18, coming up next, offers dozens of ideas for adding solar and other renewable power sources to your recreation vehicle, cabin, or other residence. It also offers ideas for apartment dwellers who want to take their solar power system with them from place to place.

The Least You Need to Know

- An emergency is an event that can cause health or safety problems if electric power is interrupted.
- It's important to first define what constitutes a power emergency for *your* home.
- Consider lower-cost power sources to meet potential emergencies.
- Size your emergency system based on current and future needs.
- Select the most cost-effective (and ecologically friendly) emergency power system for your home.

Chapter 18

Portable Power Systems

In This Chapter

- ◆ Let's go RVing: taking solar power on the road
- ◆ Solar power for boaters
- ◆ Solar power for apartment dwellers
- ◆ Get cooking with solar energy
- ◆ Designing a portable PV system for use in remote locations

Solar power on the go! Nope, you don't have to have a stationary site for your solar electricity system. It can be mounted on a travel trailer or motor home, or it can be one that you pack up and move with you from apartment to apartment. It can even be small enough to carry wherever you go!

This chapter offers information and ideas to help you become even more independent. Imagine taking many of the comforts of home with you yet being miles from the nearest electric plug. You can make it happen—with portable solar power systems.

Taking to the Road: Solar RV Systems

I've owned a number of recreation vehicles (commonly known as RVs) over the years, shunning RV parking lots for remote sites were no one but tenters usually camp. I've used generators and batteries to make living more independent, but many people today are replacing fuel burners with solar power systems.

Most folks who RV are looking for a way to have dependable electricity while enjoying nature where trees don't have power receptacles. Solar power systems offer the nearly perfect solution. RVs already run on DC. Most don't need much power compared to the typical house. They usually have enough roof space to mount PV modules. And they are less expensive—and quieter—than a generator.

Bright Idea

Going on a camping trip with your solar-powered RV? Remember to ask campground hosts if solar sites are available that offer unobstructed solar access for your PV modules.

Since batteries are charged when traveling, RVs depend mostly on the vehicle's alternator as the primary power source. Power to charge the battery bank is also provided through a converter when plugged into the utility at home or in a campground. However, for those of us who like to spend days, weeks, or even months without driving or plugging in, photovoltaics can mean freedom.

PV modules can be mounted atop recreation vehicles for portable power.

Fortunately, a PV array can put as much power into your batteries during a day as a small gas or propane generator. Of course, generators can run at night when PVs can't. By sizing and monitoring your solar power system you don't have to return to "civilization" until you want to. Nor do you have to put up with the noise of a generator.

Most RVs can get sufficient power from one to three PV modules. Of course, the exact number and power rating depends on how much electricity your home-on-wheels needs. As with estimating home power needs, you need to total up the wattage of all appliances and lights you use each day as well as the average number of hours used. You want watt-hours (Wh) or kilowatt-hours (kWh).

Unfortunately, RV air conditioner systems take lots of power. If you need to run them, you'll probably have to start an on-board generator to supply large amounts of AC power. Microwaves don't take as much power to operate, but they need AC from an inverter or an AC power utility plug. Most RV refrigerators can run on AC, DC, or propane.

Another part of your power calculation is estimating how much solar radiation you'll be able to collect on the road. That is, if you winter in Arizona's desert, you may get eight or more hours of quality solar radiation. If you're planning a winter trip across Canada, however, available sunlight will be less. If you don't really *know* where you'll be (you nomad, you!), plan for a worst-case scenario. Your system can always turn itself off if you get too much solar power for the day.

One good thing about mounting PV modules on an RV roof is that the RV can be turned to capture the best solar radiation. Alternately, you can install moveable mounts or even trackers (see Chapter 9). If you prefer to park under the trees but still want solar power, consider a portable ground-mounted PV array and enough cable or extension cord to get the power to your RV.

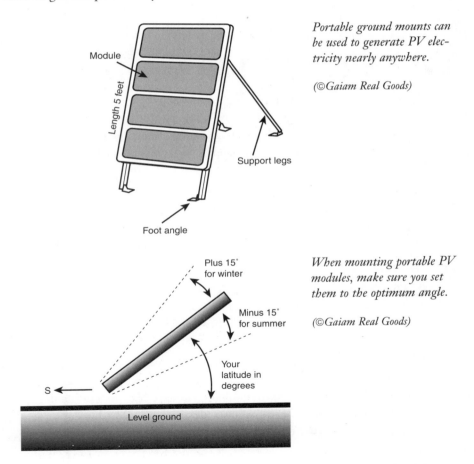

Portable ground mounts can be used to generate PV electricity nearly anywhere.

(©Gaiam Real Goods)

When mounting portable PV modules, make sure you set them to the optimum angle.

(©Gaiam Real Goods)

Of course, you want to plan your entire electrical system—not just the solar part—if you plan to travel the boondocks very much. That is, your battery bank should be sized for long-term visits to the world without utilities. The same goes for your fresh- and wastewater systems. Most RVs are built for a weekend or up to a week away from services. If you're planning longer, make sure your RV power and services are up to it. Fortunately, an RV without a generator under a rear bed has room for more tanks or equipment.

Also look at alternatives for any electrical equipment in your RV that takes lots of power. Consider fans instead of an air conditioner. Try a solar oven or do your cooking over an outdoor campfire. Planning ahead can help you stay on vacation longer.

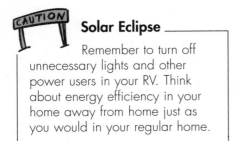

Solar Eclipse

Remember to turn off unnecessary lights and other power users in your RV. Think about energy efficiency in your home away from home just as you would in your regular home.

Taking to the Water: Solar Power for Boaters

Another popular recreation vehicle is, of course, the boat. It's used for sailing, water skiing, cruising, fishing, and just relaxing on the water. *Outdoor* activities. That means the sun is shining—you hope—and you can take advantage of it! Many boaters rely on small portable solar power systems to furnish electricity and to recharge batteries. They're just like the ones that land-bound RVs use.

Boaters and RVers also use solar showers. A specially designed bag is hung where the sunlight can heat up the water inside. Once ready, open the spigot and enjoy warm water that doesn't need fossil fuel. Of course, follow directions on the unit to make sure you don't get scalded. Larger solar shower units can be built in to boats and land RVs.

Cooking with Solar Power

The sun gets hot! Hot enough to fry an egg? Yes, and then some. In fact, a solar cooker can reach 600°F!

If you're looking for ways to cook away from home, leave the portable grill in the garage and try a solar cooker (also called a solar oven). A simple solar cooker is available for less than $40 and folds flat to a 13-inch square for portability. The kit also includes a 3-quart cooking pot. It was originally designed for distribution to developing countries where fuel shortages are an ongoing problem.

Sun Spots

For those who depend on fuel wood, it takes about 2 pounds of wood per person each day to cook one's food. For a family of five, that's 3,650 pounds of wood a year! In 40 of the world's poorest countries, over 70 percent of the country's fuel comes from dwindling supplies of fuel wood. The good news is that with sunshine, there is a simple alternative to fire for cooking. In many developing countries, solar cookers can be used 200 to 300 days a year. In addition, they can be used to pasteurize contaminated water for drinking. They are being distributed in Kenyan refugee camps and other places around the world. Part of the purchase price of a Solar Cookit (www.solarcooking. org; 916-455-4499) goes toward supporting low-cost distribution in Third World countries. Solar cookers can make a difference!

Prices go up from there. A rugged solar cooker with oven and built-in thermometer can cook most anything. Cooking temperatures range from 350° to 400°F. Once preheated, the unit can cook a cup of rice in less than 45 minutes. The cost is under $250 and solar cookers are available through renewable resource catalogs (see Appendix B for a list).

Want to know more? Check out the many books and solar equipment catalogs available on cooking with the sun.

Portable PV Systems for Remote and Apartment Living

Small portable solar power systems are available for powering your remote cabin, your RV, a boat, or any other location away from power plugs. One such system can produce and deliver up to 12 amps of DC electricity. An inverter can be added to power AC equipment. Add a battery and you have a full system. The final cost depends on how many PV modules are needed, but a portable solar power system can be built for less than $1,000. Most solar power catalogs have a system like this.

Another system includes a 10-watt PV module, battery, inverter, and carrying case for less than $600. It doesn't provide much electricity, but can power a laptop computer, video, GPS unit, sound recording equipment, or communication equipment from the top of any mountain—or anywhere the sun shines. A larger system costs about $800 with PV modules and weighs less than 100 pounds—more "transportable" than "portable."

There are also PV modules specifically designed to power a laptop computer. The cost is about $100. Or you can add a solar charger to your car's battery for less than $40. Lots of neat things are coming on the solar market every month.

A portable solar power system can be used to bring backup or emergency power to your home or temporary housing such as an apartment, campsite, or remote location. If your power needs are frugal you can use a solar power system to power communications equipment from the top of Mt. Everest—it's been done! Or you can use it to cut power costs in your apartment. Solar power offers many options.

In addition, portable PV systems are useful for those who want solar power, but don't own their dwelling. Perhaps their landlord doesn't want tenants installing PV modules on the roof and rewiring the electrical system. For these nomads, PV systems must be portable as well as efficient.

Solar Eclipse

Before installing any portable solar power system, make sure your landlord, local zoning board, or neighbors don't object to your portable ecology. Include your solar power equipment in

Smaller systems can be used to power some appliances to reduce the need for utility power without permanent wiring. Larger PV modules can be installed on frames on the ground to feed an inverter, battery bank, or both. Within a few hours the units can be disconnected and loaded up for the move—leaving the apartment or rental house undamaged.

Designing Your Portable Solar Power System

Let's take a closer look at plans for typical portable solar power systems. They will give you an idea of what you'll want in your own portable system.

One popular application is a weekend cabin. If it's built in a remote location, electric utilities may not be available or may be prohibitively expensive. So the first question to ask is: AC or DC? If your cabin has or requires only minimal electrical lighting and only a small appliance or two, a DC system may be the best. It's the least expensive because, as you've learned, solar PV cells provide DC electricity. No conversion is needed.

A DC-only weekend cabin system would require a couple of 12-volt PV solar panels wired in parallel (positive to positive, negative to negative), a fused disconnection, a couple of 6-volt batteries wired in series (negative to positive), and a 12-volt circuit breaker panel. The system could power a 12-volt DC refrigerator, radio, and lights.

An AC weekend cabin system requires the addition of an inverter that converts DC into AC. The circuit breaker also needs to distribute both DC and AC electricity safely. And you'll need twice as many batteries. Then you'll be able to plug in an AC TV or radio, maybe a low-watt microwave, a small refrigerator, and possibly a computer. Size the system for the largest expected load. Use the following worksheet to help figure out what you'll need.

Electrical device	Device watts	X	Hours of daily use	X	Days of use per week	÷	7	=	Average watt-hours per day
		x		x		÷		=	
		x		x		÷		=	
		x		x		÷		=	
		x		x		÷		=	
		x		x		÷		=	
		x		x		÷		=	
		x		x		÷		=	
		x		x		÷		=	
		x		x		÷		=	
		x		x		÷		=	
		x		x		÷		=	
		x		x		÷		=	
		x		x		÷		=	
		x		x		÷		=	
		x		x		÷		=	
		x		x		÷		=	
		x		x		÷		=	
		x		x		÷		=	
		x		x		÷		=	
		x		x		÷		=	
		x		x		÷		=	
		x		x		÷		=	
		x		x		÷		=	
		x		x		÷		=	
		x		x		÷		=	
		x		x		÷		=	
		x		x		÷		=	
		x		x		÷		=	
		x		x		÷		=	
		x		x		÷		=	
		x		x		÷		=	

Make sure you calculate all electric devices when planning a portable PV power system.

(©Gaiam Real Goods)

If you need more power than a PV system can furnish to your cabin's site, consider a generator or other backup system as covered in Chapters 16 and 17.

What's next on the agenda? Save some money and get the best equipment you can afford by learning how to buy solar components and systems in Chapter 19.

The Least You Need to Know

◆ Because RVs already have a DC power system, they are a good application of solar PV modules and electric power.

◆ Boaters can use solar power to charge batteries, power appliances, and even take warm showers.

◆ One of the lowest cost applications of solar energy is cooking—and it's being done around the world.

◆ Portable solar power systems can be built to move from apartment to apartment.

◆ A weekend cabin can be powered by a DC or inverted-AC solar power system that brings home to the woods.

Part 4

Getting It Done

So many options! And there's more. Now you need to figure out whether you will install your solar power system yourself or hire someone else to do it.

Don't be intimidated. Solar power systems are not that difficult to install—once you have a plan. Fortunately, manufacturers and suppliers know how it's done and can share their knowledge with you.

This part lets you in on how to buy solar power systems and components, and either hire a qualified contractor or figure out whether you can install some or all of the system yourself. Once it's working, you'll learn tips and techniques for maintaining your solar power system for many years.

Buying Systems and Components

In This Chapter

- Figuring out what components you need
- Finding lots of sources for solar equipment
- Hiring the best equipment supplier
- Taking delivery of your solar equipment

So you're going to take the solar plunge, eh? You've decided to buy solar power components or a full system. Now what?

Good question. This chapter reviews the various components in a solar power system and guides you toward finding the right supplier—and the right price. Following chapters will show you how to install or hire someone to install your solar power system.

Solar Power Sans Batteries

What's included in a solar power system? As you've learned, it depends on what type and size solar power system you've selected. Systems vary

greatly due to variation in size and run times of loads. The heart—the PV module—
can be as small as a single 5-watt or as large as a 40-plus module array. And all the
interconnections with your existing system add to its complexity.

*Make sure you know exactly
what components you'll need
for your solar or hybrid
power system.*

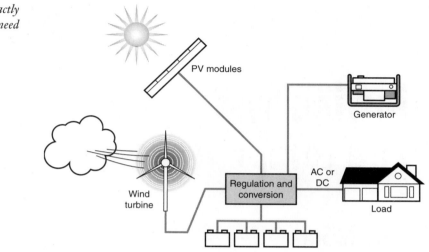

If you're buying a pre-designed solar package or hiring a contractor or supplier to
design the right system, your job is easier. All you need to do is ask questions like "Do
I really need an oversized inverter if I don't expect to add to my array?" Those kind of
questions can save you bucks. And now that you've learned how solar power systems
work, you know what to ask!

There's no such thing as a typical photovoltaic system, which is a complete set of
components for converting sunlight into electricity by the photovoltaic process,
including the array and balance of system components. However, most PV systems
have common components. Only the largest systems have them all. Here they are:

- ◆ PV modules: Generate electricity from sunlight.

- ◆ Mounting: Supports and aims PV modules toward the sun.

- ◆ Combiner/Fusing: Combines and protects module output wiring.

- ◆ Inverter: Changes low-voltage DC to high-voltage AC.

- ◆ Batteries: Store DC electricity.

- ◆ Controller: Regulates power to and from the batteries.

- ◆ Monitor/Metering: Reports the system status (current and cumulative) and
  power flows.

- Generator: Provides backup to AC power.

- Power center: Combines the controller, overcurrent protection, and monitors in one enclosure.

- Wiring: Connects the components so electricity can flow.

- Fuses/breakers: Protect the system against electrical overload. (A fuse is a device used to protect electrical equipment from short circuits. It's made with metals that are designed to melt when the current passing through the fuse is high enough. When the fuse melts, the electrical connection is broken, interrupting power to the circuit or device.)

Bright Idea

Wire is selected by size and insulation. AWG (American Wire Gauge) is the standard measure of wire in the United States. Wire sizes range from 0000 (thumb size) to 60 (human hair size). *Larger* numbers indicate *smaller* wire size. The wire is insulated or wrapped with plastic.

That's the gist of it. You may hear some of these components called by other names, but their functions are the same. Remember to keep notes in your Solar Book on what components your system needs and where to get them.

Sun Spots

PV cells can be made from several processes or technologies. Types of PV cells you'll hear about include crystalline silicon, poly-crystalline silicon, amorphous silicon, cadmium telluride, copper indium gallium, and diselenide. They all do the same job: produce electricity from sunlight. As you shop for PV modules, ask manufacturers and suppliers why one type should be selected over others. Some use more environmentally friendly manufacturing processes, some are less expensive per watt, others are easier to manufacture, and still others are expected to last longer.

Solar Equipment Resources

In some locations, finding a PV provider can be as simple as picking up the telephone book. Make sure the supplier or contractor has *solar electricity* experience. Some providers you may hear about have furnished or installed solar water heating systems, but may not have a clue about solar electricity. Or they are electrical contractors who have read about PV, but have yet to install a solar electric system.

If you're online, check the *Directory of the U.S. Photovoltaics Industry* at www.eren.doe.gov/pv/pvdirectory.html. You can also call the Solar Energy Industries Association (202-383-2600) for a list of solar service providers.

Bright Idea

Want to save even more on buying your solar power system? Find some other folks interested in buying approximately the same system at the same time and try to get a volume discount. The group could be a neighborhood or a solar power club you form for the explicit purposes of sharing information and savings.

Another potential resource for solar power equipment and experience is your local utility company. Those who encourage residential solar power systems (most of them) have developed contacts within the local solar industry. These contacts can be useful to you as you buy and install your system.

Where can you buy components for your solar power system? Most places are listed in the yellow pages of your local or regional telephone book. Typical headings include "Solar Products—Dealers and Services" and "Solar Products—Mfrs and Whsle." In addition, some large hardware stores have solar power equipment and packages. Many have at least the mounting, wiring, fuses, and other materials.

If you can't find a dependable local source for solar power equipment, consider making some telephone calls and going online for regional and national suppliers. You'll find many resources in Appendix B. In addition, here are some dealers and distributors that offer solar power and renewable energy catalogs:

- *Backwoods Solar Electric Systems, Planning Guide and Catalog*, 1395 Rolling Thunder Ridge, Sandpoint, ID 83864; Phone: 208-263-4290; Fax: 208-265-4788; E-mail: info@backwoodssolar.com; Website: www.backwoodssolar.com.

- *Energy Saver's Catalog*, Solar Components Corporation, 121 Valley Street, Manchester, NH 03103; Phone: 603-668-8186; Fax: 603-668-1783; E-mail: solarcomponents@yahoo.com; Website: www.solar-components.com.

- *Kansas Wind Power Catalog*, 13569 214th Road, Holton, KS 66436; Phone: 785-364-4407; Fax: 785-364 5123.

- *New England Solar Electric Inc. Products Catalog*, 401 Huntington Road, P.O. Box 435, Worthington, MA 01098; Phone: 413-238-5974; Fax: 413-238-0203; E-mail: nesolar@newenglandsolar.com; Website: www.newenglandsolar.com.

- *Off Line Catalog*, Off Line Independent Energy Systems, P.O. Box 231, North Fork, CA 93643; Phone: 559-877-7080; Fax: 559-877 2980; E-mail: ofln@aol.com; Website: www.psnw.com/~ofln.

- *Photovoltaic Power System Catalog*, SunAmp Power Company, 2020 West Pinnacle Peak Road, Scottsdale, AZ 85207; Phone: 1-800-677-6527 or 623-580-7700; Fax: 623-587-5714; E-mail: sunamp@sunamp.com; Website: www.sunamp.com.

◆ *Positive Energy Conservation Products' Green Builder Catalog*, Positive Energy Conservation Products, P.O. Box 7568, Boulder, CO 80306; Phone: 1-800-488-4340 or 303-444-4340; E-mail: info@positive-energy.com; Website: www.positive-energy.com.

◆ *Sierra Sun Catalog*, Sierra Solar Systems, 563 C Idaho Maryland Road, Grass Valley, CA 95945; Phone: 1-888-667-6527; Fax: 530-273-1760; E-mail: solarjon@sierrasolar.com; Website: www.sierrasolar.com.

◆ *Solar Components Corporation's Product Catalog*, 121 Valley Street, Manchester, NH 03103; Phone: 603-668-8186; Fax 603-668-1783; E-mail: solarcomponents@yahoo.com; Website: www.solar-components.com.

◆ *Solar Depot 2000*, 61 Paul Drive, San Rafael, CA 94903; Phone: 415-499-1333, for orders 1-800-822-4041; Fax: 415-499-0316; E-mail: staff@solardepot.com; Website: www.solardepot.com. Annual, 60 pp.

◆ *Solar Design Catalog*, AAA Solar Service and Supply, Inc., 2021 Zearing Avenue NW, Albuquerque, NM 87104; Phone: 1-800-245-0311 or 505-243-4900; Fax: 505-243-0885; E-mail: info@aaasolar.com; Website: www.aaasolar.com.

◆ *SolarElectric.Com Catalog and Design Guide*, SolarElectric.Com, P.O. Box 339, Redway, CA 95560; Phone: 1-800-777-6609 or 707-923-2277; Fax: 707-923-3009; E-mail: info@solarelectric.com; Website: www.solarelectric.com.

◆ *Solar Living Sourcebook* (11th Edition), Real Goods Trading Corporation, 360 Interlocken Blvd, Suite 300, Broomfield, CO 80021; Phone: 1-800-919-2400; Fax: 1-800-508-2342; E-mail: techs@realgoods.com; Website: www.realgoods.com/renew or www.gaiam.com.

◆ *Sunelco Inc. Planning Guide and Product Catalog*, 100 Skeels Street, P.O. Box 787, Hamilton, MT 59840; Phone: 1-800-338-6844; Fax: 406-363-6046; E-mail: info@sunelco.com; Website: www.sunelco.com.

As mentioned, there are scads more solar resources listed in Appendix B of this book.

Finding Good Suppliers

In general, the most cost-effective way to find and hire good equipment suppliers is to …

1. Find a large pool of potential suppliers.

2. Choose the most qualified from that pool.

3. Negotiate the best terms you can.

4. Hire the most qualified suppliers for the fairest terms.

Common sense, right?

However, finding a large pool of qualified suppliers and asking the most telling questions can be easier said than done. You'll need a variety of components and materials for your solar (or other) power system. They include PV modules, inverter, batteries, controllers, monitors, wiring, safety equipment, and structural support. Where are you going to get all this stuff when you need it and at the lowest price?

Start calling solar power system suppliers you found in your local phone book and from the catalog list in this chapter. Then select the three or four best suppliers for your primary materials (modules, controllers). If your system is large or you have numerous potential suppliers, contact each supplier about bidding on your project. Suppliers will need specs and plans for your power system.

You will probably have more than one supplier. The PV modules, for example, may come from one supplier and installation from another. The best rule is: Know what you're buying and get fair prices from the best available suppliers.

Before selecting your primary system supplier, interview one of the salespeople who may handle your account. You want to know about quality, pricing, discounts, delivery, terms, and advice. Be sure to ask the following questions:

- Are preferred brands (if any) readily available? If not, can they be easily ordered?

- What are your prices on (list a few specific products such as a 60 W PV module or a 6V golf cart deep-cycle battery)?

- What discounts and terms are available?

- What discounts are available cash-and-carry?

- How can I set up an account with you and what are the terms?

- How soon can you typically deliver materials?

- Will I have a specific salesperson assigned to my account (preferred)?

- Who would I talk to if I can't come to an agreement with a salesperson?

You may *like* a specific supplier—or you may not. And it can be mutual. As long as you *trust* the supplier to do what is promised, that's really all you need. Trust is an important part of all business relationships. In fact, it may be at the top of your requirements list as you look for solar power system suppliers. Do I trust this person to do what she or he says? How can you keep your trustworthy suppliers working hard for you? Feed them! And what do suppliers eat? Money! So remember the Golden Rule: Those with the gold, rule. Meaning you can use gold (money) to rule (manage) your suppliers. How?

- Make sure all agreements keep work ahead of the money; that is, appropriate payment is made *after* work is done.

- Use financial incentives as needed to keep installation moving.

- Make sure work contracts say that that delays cost suppliers and contractors more than they cost you.

- Spend a dime to save a dollar whenever possible.

- Treat all suppliers as people who really want to do the best job they can.

Solar Eclipse

What can you do if you find out your supplier isn't as honest as you thought? Even well-recommended suppliers can have a bad day—or a bad employee. First, contact the supplier directly and try to work out the problem. If that doesn't work, contact any trade associations the contractor belongs to and ask for arbitration. If you're working through a state solar program, get them involved. All most suppliers need is a nudge to do the right thing. Just show them how it will be easier for them to solve your problem than take on another.

It's important that you and your suppliers keep good records. When were items ordered? When did they arrive? Were they what was ordered and the correct quantity? Who received and inspected them? Who needs them and when? Lots of details.

If you are installing a large solar power system yourself, consider using a computer and spreadsheet to keep track of materials and work. It can help you track the money and the time so you can get the best use of both.

Asking the Right Questions

A major key to getting a fair deal from a knowledgeable supplier is asking the right questions. It doesn't matter whether you're buying a new solar intertie power system or a used car. Here are some good questions to ask once you've chosen a supplier:

- Do you have solar components in stock?

- What experience do you have sizing and selling solar electric systems and components?

- How long have you been in business? (An especially important question for components with a 20-year guarantee!)

- ◆ Can you recommend installation contractors in my area?

- ◆ May I talk with some of your current and prior customers?

- ◆ Do you belong to any solar equipment trade organizations?

- ◆ Can you help me estimate my solar power system needs or do you just sell equipment?

- ◆ How long will it take for my equipment to arrive at my site?

- ◆ What credit terms are available through you on solar equipment purchases?

- ◆ Are there any discounts available?

- ◆ Who manufactures the equipment you sell and what is their product warranty?

- ◆ Will I have a specific account manager for my purchase or do I place orders with the next available salesperson?

- ◆ Why should I purchase through your company?

These are good questions to ask a supplier because the answers tell you about the people you're dealing with. Price is only one component of cost. If you have to replace a defective system in three years, will the dealer and the manufacturer be there—or in Cancun?

Fortunately, because solar components are manufactured by only a few companies, you can sometimes compare pricing for the best deal. For example, many suppliers sell a Siemens SP130 PV module. That means you can find a qualified supplier that will stand behind the product and offer a competitive (not necessarily the lowest) price. However, don't expect Wal-Mart pricing. There aren't *that many* suppliers yet.

Sun Spots

Home Depot and other large hardware chains are testing the solar market. Currently, Home Depot sells PV systems only through their stores in the San Diego, California, area. If successful (and it looks like it will be), stores in other areas will begin offering solar power systems in stock—or at least available through a catalog. That means other building supply chains will be doing so, helping to bring commodity pricing to residential solar power.

Taking Delivery

You've found the best supplier and paid a fair price for your solar power system. In fact, it's on its way to you. Now what?

Depending on the size of your system and whether it is for new construction or retro-fit, you'll probably need a safe and dry place to keep materials until they are installed. For an existing home, a garage or dry storage building is a good choice. For new construction, a lockable structure is good. Remember, your system costs many thousands of dollars. It's an investment—one you don't want to lose to theft or damage.

Alternately, your supplier may be coaxed into holding your order for delivery just prior to the day the electrician will arrive. Or you may be able to have the equipment shipped to and stored at your electrician's shop.

Make sure you inspect the equipment for obvious shipping damage as it arrives and note problems on the shipping documents. You can also sign the documents as "Received subject to inspection." You want to retain the right to make a full inspection and submit a claim if there is any damage in shipping.

If you're using an electrical or general contractor to install your solar power system, Chapter 20 offers more specifics. If you're planning to install the system yourself, with an electrician as needed, Chapter 21 will show you the way.

The Least You Need to Know

- ◆ Use your Solar Book to list the components needed for your system.

- ◆ Start contacting local solar equipment suppliers and calling for catalogs to begin the shopping process.

- ◆ Plan what questions you'll ask of each of your equipment suppliers to make sure they are qualified and trustworthy.

- ◆ Have a secure location for delivery and storage of your valuable solar equipment.

Chapter 20

Hiring the Right Contractor

In This Chapter

- ◆ Deciding whether you need a solar contractor
- ◆ Finding the best contractor
- ◆ The bidding process
- ◆ How to work with your contractor
- ◆ Following code and understanding solar equipment standards

Imagine yourself up on the roof erecting a PV module frame and wiring the units into your main electrical system. Can you see this image? Or do you see yourself in a hospital emergency room after trying it?

The better question is: Do you need a contractor to install your solar power system? Maybe. Maybe not. This chapter helps you decide if and who. A contractor can make the job easier—for a price.

Considering Contractors

First, let's figure out whether you even need a contractor for your solar power system. You can, of course, save money if you don't need a contractor and are comfortable doing the work yourself.

A contractor can be a construction manager, called a general contractor or GC, or a specialist such as an electrical or solar contractor. For most solar electrical components you'll need an electrician or electrical contractor to do the actual wiring. In most locations, you'll need a building or remodeling permit from the city or county as well. If you're having a solar power system installed in your home as it is being built, you'll probably have a general contractor in charge of the building process.

Building Permits

Let's look at the permit process. Not every community welcomes solar power systems. That's because they don't understand them or the advantages to the community. Their response is likely to be: "Absolutely not! Er, what's your question?" Fortunately, other folks have already gone through the permit process, maybe not in your area but elsewhere. You're not the first. An experienced supplier and/or solar contractor can take care of the permit hassle and help cut through the red tape.

Solar Eclipse

States have licensing authority to allow or disallow contractors. Some states have a stringent testing and certification process. Others don't. Most are designed to keep out the worst, but can't really protect you from dishonest ones. That's why it's important to do your homework before hiring a contractor.

Start by calling the local building department to find out who has jurisdiction and if anybody has solar power system experience. Briefly describe your system and ask about applicable code. You'll probably be referred to an electrical inspector because solar power systems are electrical.

Some of the issues you may face in getting a permit include the following:

- Exceeding roof load
- Improper wiring
- Obstructing side yards and setbacks
- Erecting unlawful PV frames
- Conforming to local covenants and restrictions
- Installing components too close to streets

Knowing what the permit process is can help you decide how much you can tackle yourself and how much you should or must have done professionally. In addition, local building permit departments may be able to tell you which local contractors have solar experience.

Licensed Contractors

A general contractor is a construction manager, keeping work flowing toward building or retrofitting a specific home as agreed. If you're having a solar home built, your general contractor will ...

◆ Supervise all aspects of the work done at the building site.

◆ Hire, supervise, pay, and fire subcontractors as needed to get the job done.

◆ Coordinate getting building permits and any variances.

◆ Buy all materials and supplies needed in construction.

◆ Make sure that the site is inspected and approved by the building department.

◆ Make sure that all subcontractors are legal and have the needed insurance (like worker's compensation insurance).

For this effort, the GC typically gets a management fee of 15 to 20 percent of the total value of the project. The GC subtotals the costs of materials and subcontractors, then adds the management fee. Alternately, the GC could be hired to manage the project for a specified hourly rate. Or a lump sum may be agreed upon. The *best* method of payment is the one that gives you the lowest cost while motivating the contractor to get the job done well.

So what does it take to be a licensed general contractor? Contractors are licensed based on knowledge, experience, and other assets. In many states a licensed general contractor must ...

◆ Be 18 years of age or older.

◆ Prove at least four full years of experience as a journeyman, foreman, supervisor, or contractor in the appropriate classification.

◆ Pass a written test.

◆ Have a specific amount of operating capital.

◆ Register a contractor's bond or cash deposit.

◆ Pay the examination fee and licensing fee, plus the renewal fee.

Sun Spots
The licensing examination typically has two sections. The first is on the specific trade, such as solar power systems, and the second is on law and business topics like project management, bookkeeping, bidding, safety, contracts, liens, insurance, and similar topics.

Alternatively, you may need only an electrical contractor who can plan, install, connect, and test a renewable power system for your home. Some states also license solar contractors, a specialty that incorporates both electrical and mechanical skills and experience. This is often your best bet—if you can find one in your area.

Can you be your own solar contractor? If you have experience wiring electrical systems—and local code allows it—you can save some money by doing the job yourself. Or you can hire a licensed contractor to let you help with the easy stuff. You have options.

Selecting Your Contractor

So how are you going to find the *best* contractor you can afford to build or retrofit your solar home? The search begins early. In fact, even before you've drawn up plans, you should already be looking for a qualified contractor.

Referrals are the best place to find contractors. Ask people you know who have had solar homes built or retrofitted in your area recently. Talk with local building material suppliers. Ask your lender and any subcontractors you know for recommendations.

What you're looking for at this point is a comprehensive list of contractor candidates. Then you're ready to weed. This process includes calling for qualifications and availability, then following up with interviews of the best candidates. Finally, you've narrowed the field down to a handful that you ask to bid on your project.

Availability is a key factor in many areas. Specialists who have solar experience may be quite busy already. In fact, if a candidate isn't busy when others are, maybe there's something you don't know about that person's work. Or it could be that the contractor is pickier about what he or she takes on. Or that the word about solar energy benefits is still not well-known in your area. You could be a pioneer!

How do you interview a contractor? Face to face if possible, over lunch or a long coffee break, in an office or on the job site. Seeing a contractor at a job site can be enlightening as long as your presence isn't distracting.

Make sure to ask candidates the following questions:

- Can you tell me about your license and construction experience?
- What type of contracting license do you have and what is the license number?
- What experience do you have with solar power systems?
- What references can you give me?

- Can you post a performance bond (guaranteeing that the contractor will complete the job)? If not, why not?

- May I see your worker's comp policy (this protects you from job-site injury claims)?

- How do you go about hiring subcontractors?

- How do you plan a solar construction or retrofit project?

- Do you typically meet your building schedules?

- What lenders do you prefer to work with? Why?

- What suppliers do you prefer to work with? Why?

- What things do you need to make a firm bid on this project?

- How do you develop an accurate bid?

- Do you have any problem with my attorney looking over your standard contract?

Of course, there are many more questions you could ask depending on your house plans and how you will participate in the building process. Remember, you want to ask open-ended questions that aren't answered by a simple "yes" or "no." You want to hear explanations and find out how well the person communicates. Write down all the questions so you can ask each candidate the same ones and make sure you keep track of the answers. The question you forget to ask may be the one you later wish you had!

Bright Idea

Knowing the contractor's license number will come in handy. States that license contractors will typically keep a file of complaints and resolutions that you can access if you know the contractor's license number. You can access the file without it, but it makes the job much easier if you know the number. The file will have information about when and where the license was issued as well as any complaints or commendations filed (keep in mind complaints against contractors are heard by a board of retired contractors). This is useful information when picking a solar partner!

Calling for Bids

You've been busy. You've found and interviewed scads of contractor candidates and selected three to six you believe you can work well with. It's time to talk money!

The bidding process is critical to you and to the contractors. You don't want them to make too much money on the project, nor do you want them to lose so much that they have to cut corners or not finish the job. Ask for bid forms from each contractor. If you can't find lots of solar contractors in your area, either look farther away or get bids from electrical contractors who haven't done their first solar job yet.

The key to accurate bids is accurate specs. That is, contractors don't have to guess (to their advantage) when working with clear specifications. They know exactly how much the materials will cost, how many hours it will take for each stage, and how long until the project is done. If your contractor is also a solar engineer or planner, he or she may develop the specs for you.

Be sure you know what's included in the bids. Building permit fees? Utility connection fees? Travel expenses? Site security? Cleanup charges? Also ask for a start and finish date in the schedule. It will make a difference because you pay interest on the construction or retrofit loan.

Get job responsibilities in writing on the bid. Who will call for inspections? Who notifies the lender to release money? How will changes be handled? These questions must be answered in the building contract, so ask the contractor to include them in the bid.

Be careful. Don't get cheap! If you've developed a working relationship with these bidders, you have an idea what it will take to get a fair bid. And that's what you want.

Hiring a Hard-Working Contractor

Found the right contractor to build or retrofit your solar house? Great! Be sure to get it in writing. A typical builder agreement will include some important specifics. Attached to it (by reference) will be the plans and probably the final bid. The agreement itself will include the following items:

- Contract date and parties
- Starting and completion dates
- Conditions (who does what, who pays for what, who approves what, how changes are made and paid for, etc.)
- Contract sum
- Progress payments (matching the lender's draw schedule, if any)
- Terms of final payment
- Contract termination terms
- Anything else agreed upon that should be in writing

Don't sign anything under pressure. If you're not comfortable with the price, terms, or conditions, stop and think it through. Will this contract take you to your goal? What's the worst that can happen? Is it covered by the contract?

If it will make you more comfortable (and it probably will), have an attorney review the contractor's agreement prior to and during final signing.

Working with Your Solar Contractor

You've signed an agreement with a professional contractor to build or retrofit a solar home on schedule and on budget. Now what?

Maintain that relationship of trust, remembering that it is based on mutual benefits. You want a solar house, the contactor wants the money. You don't want legal or financial troubles, nor does the contractor. You want someone you can recommend to others, and your contractor wants a reference.

How can you maintain and benefit from this relationship? Communication is the key. That doesn't mean you have to talk on the phone or at the site all day. But it does mean you need to know what's going on to your comfort level. For example, you may agree that, if you don't hear from the contractor between five and seven each evening, the day went as scheduled and as previously agreed. If there is a problem that you can help solve, the contractor will let you know during that call.

Bright Idea

If you're not home much, make sure you have a telephone answering system or service where the contractor and others can leave detailed messages. Or exchange cell phone numbers. In fact, you and the contractor may not speak face-to-face to each other for weeks.

The most crucial part of the working relationship is establishing how changes are approved and made. Changes *will* happen. A specific energy-efficient window is back-ordered. The wiring plans weren't correct and now the main panel must be changed. You decide to upgrade or downgrade the PV modules before installation. Who approves changes? Who designs the change? Who pays for it?

There are three periods when changes occur, especially during construction of a new solar home. When changes are made impacts who makes the change and how much it costs:

◆ During planning when simple design changes lead to more research and some redrawing

◆ During installation when some time and materials are lost

◆ After installation when more time and more materials are lost

The preference is to make all changes during design, of course. They are less expensive then. Design changes can even save you some money. You may decide that the PV modules you selected are not as efficient as a newer, less expensive model, for example, so you change the order before it's shipped.

Changing the location of PV modules or of a passive solar wall during construction will be more expensive. And changing it *after* installation can be quite costly. It can even delay other construction steps.

The moral, of course, is to review the plans carefully and have others review the plans many times looking for potential changes before finalizing the plans. The other moral is to keep good communications going with the contractor so that you can efficiently participate in needed changes.

And remember that any change you make to a new home design impacts other parts of the house. Even changes in a retrofit can cause changes elsewhere. Adding PV modules may mean upgrading the inverter, for example. It can get complicated.

Builder Beware!

Someday we may all live in an ideal world. Meantime, there are folks out there who will take advantage of other people's lack of specialized knowledge.

So what can go wrong in hiring and dealing with general and solar contractors? Here are some troubling things that can happen:

◆ Poorly written or verbal contracts allow contractors to walk away with other people's money.

◆ Verbal promises go unkept.

◆ Contractors substitute inferior materials and pocket the difference.

◆ Contractors receive hiring fees from winning subcontractors.

◆ Unscrupulous inspectors are bribed to sign inaccurate inspections.

◆ Unlicensed and unbonded contractors and subcontractors are used, increasing owner liability.

◆ Unauthorized changes are made to plans during construction (such as installing inferior materials or equipment).

- Liens are not removed after payment, increasing owner liability.

- Workers not covered by worker's compensation insurance are injured at your building site.

- Available discounts on materials are not passed on to the owner as agreed.

You get the picture. Fortunately, learning how solar homes are built or retrofitted can save you both money and frustrations. And careful selection of a building contractor greatly diminishes surprises.

If you're serious about building a home that includes solar and other renewable energies, get a copy of my companion book, *The Complete Idiot's Guide to Building Your Own Home* (Alpha Books, 2002) from your local bookstore or online through www. MulliganPress.com.

Solar Codes

Modern building codes cover new construction as well as retrofitting houses with solar power systems. Solar electricity is covered under electrical codes. Solar hot water systems are covered by plumbing and other building codes. For example, PV power systems are covered by parts of the *National Electrical Code*, adapted by most building departments. Included in the NEC code are specifics for the following items:

- PV modules

- Wiring

- Ground-fault protection

- Grounding

- Overcurrent protection

- Disconnection

- Batteries

- Generators

- Charge controllers

- Inverters

- Distribution systems

- Inspections

Sun-Day School

The U.S. **National Electrical Code** (NEC) contains guidelines for all types of electrical installations which should be followed when installing a PV system. Article 690 of the NEC specifically covers solar photovoltaic systems.

In addition, the NEC code defines and specifies installation of related wiring in your home. It's comprehensive. Your local building codes will probably incorporate all or most of the NEC code. A plain-English translation of the many official Code Articles are included in the *Solar Living Sourcebook* listed in Appendix B.

Solar Standards

Standards are set by the solar industry for comparing, rating, and installing solar equipment. Some are set by the American Society of Heating, Refrigeration, and Air-Conditioning Engineers (ASHRAE) and others by the American Society for Testing and Materials (ASTM). You may see these acronyms on solar equipment you buy.

Another important acronym is SRCC. It stands for Solar Rating and Certification Corporation (www.solar-rating.org). The SRCC administers a certification, rating, and labeling program for solar hot water collectors. It has a similar program for complete solar water and swimming pool heating systems. It's a help in comparing "apples to apples" among solar hot water energy equipment.

Additionally, the Underwriters Laboratories, Inc. (UL) tests and certifies a wide assortment of devices and equipment including those used for solar power. In fact, many building codes require that specific electrical devices be tested by UL or to the UL standard.

Are you a do-it-yourselfer? If you've decided to act as your own contractor, Chapter 21 shows you how to install solar power systems in your home.

The Least You Need to Know

◆ General contractors are actually construction managers who can handle the entire new solar home or retrofit project.

◆ Getting bids from contractors and suppliers can save you money, but remember to consider value rather than just low cost.

◆ Make sure you've read and *understand* any contracts your contractor or suppliers give you to sign.

◆ Solar equipment standards and installation codes are established to help consumers select solar power systems.

Chapter 21

Doing It Yourself

In This Chapter

◆ Finding out whether you can—and should—install your own system

◆ Looking at a typical solar power installation

◆ Selecting the right tools for the job

◆ The lowdown on building inspectors

◆ Making sure you have adequate insurance—just in case

Are you considering installing your own solar power system? Thinking you can save some money by doing it all yourself? Ready to climb up on the roof and start mounting PV modules?

Don't! Don't even pick up a hammer until you've read this chapter. Here's where you find out if you *can* install your solar power system—then consider whether you *should*. If so, we'll also cover the *how*.

Can You Install Your Solar Power System?

Hey, it's a free country, right? Well, not exactly. If you're living out in the boonies and you swear on a stack of Bibles that you'll *never* sell your house to anyone—you'll burn it down first—local authorities *may* let you build without a permit. Otherwise, fat chance.

Actually, it's not quite that bad. And there's a good reason for the hard-nosed attitude of local building departments. It's called "public health and safety." It's their job to make sure that all structures built in their jurisdictions are safe and pose no health problems to current or future habitants. They don't want anyone without experience (and probably a license or two) crawling around on a roof putting up equipment that could cause a fire.

Bright Idea _____

Are you a do-it-yourselfer? Check out www.HomePower. com. It's an online resource for those who prefer to do most of their own power system installation and maintenance. It covers solar, hydro, and wind power, and publishes an informative online magazine.

Sun-Day School _____

AWG or **American Wire Gauge** is a standard system for designating the size of electrical wire. The higher the number, the smaller the wire. Most house wiring is AWG 12 or 14. Solar power systems often use much larger wire.

So local building codes typically require that a licensed electrician install electrical systems. Many go as far as to say that *only* licensed and experienced solar contractors can install solar power systems. Hey, it's for your protection—and for the protection of anyone who buys your house in the future.

In some locations, however, an owner can wire his or her own home without a license. It will still require an inspection by the local building department, though, so it had better be right. That means either taking some electrician classes or hiring an electrician to oversee the job—or both.

Solar power systems really aren't designed for do-it-yourselfers. That means they typically don't have an instruction book on installation. If there's any paperwork, it's written in electrician-eze and includes a schematic with lines and boxes that have no relationship to the physical placement of components. A 3-inch line could indicate a 3-inch wire or a 30-foot cable. No help there. You'll also need to know the *AWG* (*American Wire Gauge*), described in Chapter 19.

Fortunately, not everything in a solar power system is electrical. There's mechanical stuff, too. So, if you're mechanically inclined, you may be able to save some money by constructing the PV module frames, building a battery bank cabinet, and helping an electrician run wire. And it's legal to do so because the licensed electrician is ultimately responsible for your work. You're working for the electrician who's working for you.

Before you run out and buy wire strippers, consider that many of the rebate and buyback programs (discussed in Chapter 4) *require* that a licensed solar or electrical contractor do the work. This is especially true of systems designed to sell excess power back to the local utility (see Chapter 25). The utility doesn't want one of their linemen electrocuted by your system. Nor do you.

In fact, solar rebate programs will probably require that the installer have solar, not just electrical, experience. That means a solar contractor specialty license, certification in PV systems by a group such as the Solar Energy Industries Association (SEIA), or at least certification from the PV system manufacturer that the installer is qualified.

Should You Install Your Solar Power System?

Okay. Maybe your locality allows unlicensed electricians to install solar power systems. But *should* you? First, find out what requirements your local building department will have for approving and passing your solar power system. Then make sure there are no problems with any rebate programs you're signing up for. Then start looking for training.

> ### Sun Spots
>
> It may be extra trouble to fulfill local requirements to install your own solar power system. The upside is that you will be a knowledgeable owner who can maintain, troubleshoot, and repair your solar power system as well as or better than anyone. And you'll be able to do it at lower cost. So consider the do-it-yourself route if you're especially handy, on a tight budget, or live where professional installers aren't readily available. If your system goes down, you'll know who to call—you!

There are training classes available on solar power systems, but most focus on selecting rather than installing. Solar hot water systems don't use electricity, so a homeowner may be able to install such a system. But electrical systems require more training. Contact a local college or trade school to find out if it offers classes that get you to your goal. That goal may be to meet state requirements for an electrical contractor's license. Or the school may have certification classes on solar power systems. Find out what's available.

Solar equipment suppliers can also be helpful because they work with agencies from many states and can tell you what the requirements are. Some have licensed electricians on staff who can answer questions and help guide you through the installation process.

If allowed, you *can* do this. So the next question is: Do you *want* to? You probably want to do at least some of the work to save money. What will you be giving up? Time. Where will you get the time? Maybe by taking off from another job or responsibility. Or from a relationship.

A solar water heating system is easier for most do-it-yourselfers to install than a PV electric system.

(©Gaiam Real Goods)

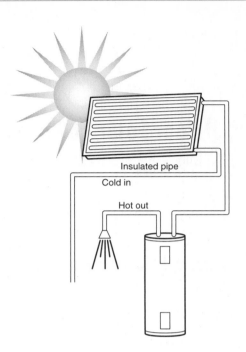

Insulated pipe

Cold in

Hot out

Actually, you're not really giving up time because you are trading it for something else. As you think about being your own solar contractor, be sure that you get a good trade.

Alternately, there are many things that you can do to improve the quality or lower the cost of solar power. What you decided to do, if anything, should depend on your skills, time, and health. For example, you can take on any of these jobs:

◆ Picking up materials and delivering them to the construction site

◆ Assembling and installing PV module framing

◆ Cleaning up after the electrician

◆ Providing site security against theft and vandalism

◆ Keeping track of expenses, deliveries, and inspections

◆ Installing fixtures or equipment as directed by the electrician or other contractor

◆ Being a gofer as needed by any of the contractors or laborers at the job site

Remember, if your contractors and craftspeople are being paid by the hour, anything you do that saves them time also saves you money!

A Typical Installation Process

To help you decide whether this is something you want to do yourself, let's go through a typical installation. Of course, there are few "typicals" in solar power systems. That's because one person may build a complete solar home with solar power and hot water systems while another may install a solar outdoor lighting system. Each one is somewhat unique.

My version of "typical" for this example is a medium-sized residential hybrid solar power system. In this case, hybrid means it also uses a generator. The system includes the following:

♦ 40 12-volt, 53-watt PV modules

♦ 4 kW inverter (85 percent efficiency)

♦ 1,000 amp-hour, 24-volt battery bank

♦ 6 kW, 240 VAC generator

The 40 PV modules are mounted on the roof in 5 sub-arrays of 8 modules each, wired in series and parallel as a 24-volt system. Output from the array is wired into a junction and fuse box on the roof then fed to the charge controller and PV power center. The power center then feeds the inverter, battery, and any direct DC loads (lights, appliances).

The PV power center contains safety and control equipment including fuses or circuit breakers, a ground-fault detector, charge controls, and related components. It is mounted somewhere convenient between the array and the inverter.

The generator is installed where it is conveniently near the fuel source. It could be powered by a gasoline, diesel, or propane fuel tank from a fuel delivery truck. The tank must be located where it can easily be filled. The 240-volt generator also needs a 5 kVA transformer that changes most or all of the voltage to 120V for use by the house during an emergency.

The inverter converts the DC electricity from the PV power center to 120 VAC for the house loads. In most cases it is wired directly into the main electrical panel for the home. In addition, the inverter includes a battery charger that makes sure the battery bank, located nearby, is fully charged for emergency use.

CAUTION

Solar Eclipse

Be aware that electrical components that have been installed, especially by a do-it-yourselfer, may not be returnable to the supplier if defective. Make sure components are tested prior to installation to make sure they work.

The balance of this typical system is the cable and wiring needed to connect everything. Your job, should you decide to accept it, is to install and electrically connect all components following the building-department approved plans. If allowed by local code, the lender, the rebate offer, and your skills, it's a job that can be done by a homeowner. Otherwise, hire a qualified solar contractor and find another way to save some money.

The Right Tools

If you do any of the work yourself, you're going to need the right tools for the various jobs. Here's a list of the basic tools needed to retrofit a house for solar power:

Sun-Day School

A **Volt-ohmmeter (VOM)** is an electrical or electronic device used to measure voltage, resistance, and current in an electric device or circuit.

- *Volt-ohmmeter (VOM)*
- Wire strippers
- Wire nuts and electrical tape
- Tape measures (25-feet and 100-feet)
- Carpenter's or combination square
- Levels (2-feet and 4-feet)

- Framing and finish hammers
- Utility knives
- Power saws
- Screwdrivers
- Power drill and bits
- Extension cords (10 or 12 gauge)
- Adjustable wrenches and pliers
- Ladders

And remember to take care of your tools. Don't leave them out in the weather, keep cutting tools sharp, and repair or replace frayed electrical cords.

Working with Inspectors

Building inspectors are both friend and foe. Their job is to make sure that your solar project is safe. They follow a written code that tells them what the standards are. Those standards are available to you. That means you can stay ahead of the inspector by knowing what's required to pass inspection.

The inspector's job is to periodically visit the construction site and make sure that the project is proceeding according to the plan approved by the building department. So inspectors become foes when they challenge your installation. Knowing electrical code will help you in the battle.

How can you make these foes your friends? As you get a building permit, ask about inspections and, if possible, meet one or more of the inspectors. Find out how much advance time you need to call for an inspection and what work, if any, you can continue doing prior to the inspection. Also find out what happens if the inspector doesn't sign off on the inspection. What must you do before calling for a re-inspection? Who do you call? What if you dispute the inspection?

You may also deal with a lender's inspector. In some cases, the lender may accept the county or city building inspector's certification. Other lenders may have their own inspectors visit the site. In many cases, draw schedules (payments for work completed) don't coincide with building inspections.

If you're serving as your own contractor, keep good records and manage your check book accurately. If you have a computer, invest in one of the checking account software programs (such as Quicken, QuickBooks, or Money) and learn how to use it. In fact, a lender may require that you do so.

Bright Idea

Many building departments prefer to hire college grads who have taken extensive coursework in building codes rather than hire from the building trades. Electrical inspectors typically require more training than other inspectors because of extensive codes. So help your inspectors by being on hand at inspection time and making sure everything is ready.

Getting Adequate Insurance Coverage

If you're doing the job yourself, your homeowner insurance may handle any claims due to injury. But if you're hiring workers or a solar contractor, make sure you or the contractor has adequate insurance coverage. You don't want someone else to own your new solar home!

Building a new solar home? An insurance policy for potential losses while you're building your home (or having it built) is called a builder's risk policy and can probably be purchased through your regular insurance agent. It covers damage and injury claims based on events that occur during construction including fire, hurricane, and theft. It *doesn't* cover the loss if a contractor takes off with your money or materials.

Once a new home is finished and an occupancy permit is issued, the builder's risk policy will probably convert to a homeowner's policy and cover additional things like all your furniture and belongings.

Your lender may require a builder's risk policy for financing. In fact, some will automatically build one into the loan package. Be careful, though, as it will probably pay only for the lender's loss, not yours. Make sure you know what it will and won't cover. If needed, add riders or additional terms to the policy to insure anything you may lose. Also, consider whether you need a rider to cover theft or vandalism at the building site.

General liability (GL) insurance covers other things that can happen during construction. Which things? That depends on what insurance is purchased. For example, a PV module flies off the roof during installation and hits a neighbor's car. Who covers the cost of fixing the car? The solar contractor? Your builder's risk policy? You? A general liability insurance policy? If you are your own solar contractor, get GL insurance before starting construction. It can save you money and worry.

If you hire workers to help with your solar project, you may need worker's compensation insurance, which covers workers while on the job. The alternative is for the injured worker to sue the contractor or you! By paying worker's comp insurance premiums, you are insuring yourself against a lawsuit for these injuries.

Your solar power system is installed by you or a contractor and the inspector says "throw the switch!" What's next? Maintaining your system for optimum efficiency and lowest cost, the subject of our next chapter.

The Least You Need to Know

- Many local building departments don't allow anyone but licensed solar or electrical contractors to install most solar power systems, although owner-builders are sometimes allowed to install solar hot water systems.

- Make sure you have the knowledge and are comfortable with the process before attempting to install your solar electric system.

- Gather the best tools for the job and know how to use them, especially electrical tools.

- Meet and work with your electrical building inspector because he or she can make installation easier or more difficult.

- Make sure you have adequate insurance before installing or hiring someone to install your solar power system.

Chapter 22

Maintaining Your System

In This Chapter

◆ Monitoring your solar power system for maximum efficiency

◆ What you should be monitoring

◆ Keeping track of maintenance issues in your Solar Book

◆ Looking for trouble: figuring out what went wrong and how to fix it

Once your solar power system is installed, there's not much to do, is there? Actually, these systems are relatively maintenance-free. There are no moving parts. They're not like generators that need a periodic tune-up and fuel refill.

So, what's this chapter about? It's about monitoring, maintaining, and troubleshooting your solar power system to *keep* it running efficiently. It's about making sure that you know what's going on in your solar power system—and what to do if things go wrong.

Monitoring Your Power

Monitoring means watching. Of course, that doesn't mean you have to stand by power system meters day and night. You can turn that job over to technology. There are three types of monitoring systems for solar power: automatic, manual, and observation.

Sun-Day School

A **charge controller** is a component that controls the flow of current to and from the battery subsystem to protect the batteries from overcharge and over discharge. Essential for ensuring that batteries obtain the maximum state of charge and longest life. The charge controller may also monitor system performance and provide system protection. Charge controllers are also sometimes called regulators.

More expensive systems include a *charge controller* that automatically diverts excess DC electricity to batteries or converts it to AC and sends it off to the local utility grid. Computerized monitors can tell you not only what's happening to the system now, but also what has happened in the past—historical data. Automatic systems typically have a method of recalling this data as a printout or meter readout so you can fine-tune your power system.

Manual systems are less expensive and rely on the operator to keep some of the historical data. For example, the operator (hey, that's *you!*) visually reads the system's meter(s) and records data on paper for future reference. Making consistent readings (same time of day, every day, throughout the year) can give you an accurate idea of what your system needs to make it more efficient.

Observation systems are suitable for simple applications such as solar outdoor lighting or other systems that aren't directly connected to your main power system. Observation is nothing more than watching the modules to make sure you are getting sufficient output. You can keep track of days when solar driveway lights don't stay on all night, for example. Historical data from this observation can tell you if the solar lights are doing the intended job, they need to be moved for more daytime sunlight collection, the batteries are ready for replacement, or they need to be replaced with more powerful modules. Remember to include observations like sunny day, cloudy day, cloudy morning, rained all day, and so on.

Think of solar power monitors as working like the gauges in your car. Computerized gauges take away most of the worry about efficiency. Indicator lights are either on or off and tell you when something's wrong. Or you can periodically poke your head "under the hood" to visually check what's going on. Which monitoring system is best? All of the above. Computerized gauges are great, but they can't always tell you what you can see for yourself. Use them, but don't totally rely on them. Observation is good backup.

What Should You Be Monitoring?

The answer to this question depends, of course, on what your solar power system is designed to do. If it's a simple system that supplements your home's power with PV module current (no batteries) you should be monitoring module output. If the system includes an inverter for converting DC into AC, you'll want a meter indicating AC output of the inverter. If batteries are included, you'll want a meter that shows battery state of charge.

In addition to monitoring output for efficiency, you'll want to know if something goes wrong. For example, you'll want to know quickly if there is a dangerous ground-fault in the system or, better, you'll want your system to shut down appropriate circuits before any damage is done—and let you know!

In fact, it's more important that your system is monitored for safety than for efficiency. It's inconvenient if you don't have enough electricity to watch Jay Leno. It's a major problem if a power system problem blows up your TV! Fortunately, National Electrical Code (NEC) and local building codes will *require* safety features to prevent this from happening *if* equipment is installed and maintained correctly.

What do you expect to see when monitoring a solar power system? Amps and volts. As you learned in Chapter 2, a volt (V) is a unit of measure of the force given the electrons in an electric circuit. An ampere (A) is a unit of measure of the flow of electrons.

PV modules and batteries will be either 12V or 24V. Most appliances and other loads in the typical home are either 220V (stove, clothes dryer) or 110V (most everything else). Monitors are meters that read and report output. Some monitors also make changes in the system based on a setpoint. For example, a monitor may shut off the 110V power line if it reads more than, say, 125V. As you learned in the previous chapter, the meter that reads voltage measurements is called a Volt-ohmmeter. (I'll get back to setpoints in just a moment.)

Bright Idea

Install your system's monitor where you live rather than where the system lives. Running some extra wiring so system meters can be installed in a laundry room or even a corner of the living room can save you many steps—and help you remember to monitor your solar power system for safety and efficiency.

The flow of electrical current is measured in amperes or amps. Many circuits in your home can handle up to 15, 20, or even 30 amps of current. However, most smaller appliances and lights don't need anywhere near this much electricity. A toaster, for example, may only use 5 amps to 7 amps. An alarm clock may need only 40 mA (milliamps; one-thousandths of an amp) to wake you in the morning.

That means ampere meters, called ammeters, in your solar power system will measure amps. An analog ammeter will use a moving needle to point to numbers on a scale. A digital ammeter will display numbers. Some meters include range switches so you can read smaller amp readings (0 amps to 5 amps) as well as larger ones (0 amps to 30 amps). A typical solar power system may include meters to measure array voltage, battery voltage, charge voltage, array amps, and load amps.

I mentioned setpoints a couple of paragraphs back. A setpoint is a preferred operating range. An alarm-point is a maximum value that the equipment or circuit should exceed. For example, a 12V battery bank's meter may have a setpoint of 11.5V to 15.0V in which batteries should normally be operating. An alarm-point may be 11.0V and 15.5V and trigger either a controller or an alarm, depending on the system.

What setpoints should you monitor for your system? Fortunately, equipment manufacturers and system designers have already figured out these setpoints for you. A PV module or array will include documentation that tells you or the system designer what normal operating ranges should be. If you're pulling your own system together, make sure you get these figures from the manufacturer.

If your system has automatic monitoring and saves historical data, your work is done for you. You'll need to learn how to read and interpret the data that your system tracks and records. Manually monitored systems require that you keep track of readings on paper. Once you've listed the components that need monitoring, their setpoints and alarm-points, you can develop a form for keeping track. To learn your system, take more readings than is recommended. Once you know how to read it and respond, you can cut back.

Keeping Track of Maintenance

As I've said, one of the great things about PV modules is that they have no moving parts! They sit there all day long soaking up the sun and converting it into electricity. It's an electro-chemical process and nothing is depleted nor needs replacement.

In fact, they are *so* maintenance-free that some folks forget to perform basic maintenance that can keep their solar power system efficient longer, such as making sure that the surface is kept relatively clean so it can do its job. The PV module's surface may be plastic film or glass. In either case, follow the manufacturer's recommendation on cleaning the surface. That may mean simply squirting water on the units through a garden hose. (Don't worry, PV modules get wet every rainy season anyway.) Or you may need to periodically clean them with a special cleaner and squeegee. That's when you'll be glad you mounted the modules on a ground mount—or wish you had.

Other components will have maintenance issues, especially batteries. Batteries require more maintenance than just about any other component in a solar power system. The best way to manage these needs is to write them down in your Solar Book (any plain, spiral-bound notebook will do) and make a plan. That plan may include cleaning modules yearly, performing battery and connection maintenance twice a year, watering battery cells four times a year, and inspecting the entire system four times a year. If you've invested in the highest quality batteries, there may be little or no maintenance required. Even so, battery connections will need to be checked for corrosion and cleaned.

Bright Idea

Your Solar Book is a good place to keep all information about your system: what's in it, when it was purchased and installed, its setpoints and normal operating range, its alarmpoints, what maintenance is needed and when it is performed, and any problems you encounter.

Troubleshooting Solar Power

Looking for trouble? You should be! Though well-designed and well-installed solar power systems are virtually trouble-free, we all know that stuff happens. A windstorm damages a module. Vermin nest in an inverter. A battery doesn't operate as long as it should. What to do?

Of course, you can *worry*—but that doesn't really fix anything. The best way to keep conditions from becoming problems is to be aware. First, be aware of how the system should be and is functioning. Maintaining and monitoring your solar power system will take care of that point. Second, know what problems mean; know how to troubleshoot your solar power system.

Let's say that you discover that DC appliances in your home aren't functioning well. Your knowledge of the system suggests that the battery bank output is lower than normal, so you check it. Sure enough. So you use a Volt-ohmmeter (VOM) to check the output of each battery in the bank and find that two of the batteries are undercharged. You see that the connection cable between the two and the battery controller is corroded. Knowing how your system works has saved the day!

What about the bigger components? Fortunately, the solar components that manage your system typically have an owner's manual that includes troubleshooting tips. For example, a controller or inverter may have a troubleshooting chart that offers both symptoms and remedies. In most cases it's something simple like "no electricity" and a solution such as "check the main circuit breaker." More expensive controllers even have built-in diagnostic tests that you can run to make sure the system is running efficiently. Even less-expensive systems may have manual diagnostics that require you to push certain buttons to get the results of tests.

Need some troubleshooting tips? Here they are:

◆ Refer to your Solar Book and maintenance logs to see if there are any probable causes that have shown up lately.

◆ If there's no AC, first check circuit breakers and fuses.

◆ Check the inverter, turning it off and then back on.

◆ Look for lights on the inverter that indicate low voltage, over current, or other problems.

◆ Read the owner's manual for troubleshooting instructions.

◆ If battery bank output is low, disconnect the bank and check and clean all connections.

◆ Check the voltage of each battery in the bank.

◆ Check the array terminal that delivers DC electricity to the inverter or other controller.

◆ If in doubt about your safety, don't do it!

Solar Eclipse

Work safely! Always disconnect the system before doing any work on it to avoid electric shock!

The best tip is to know your solar power system inside and out through careful monitoring and regular maintenance. Knowledge is power! The next best tip is be aware of what you *don't* know or can't handle by yourself—and call in an expert for help.

Wow! You've learned lots about solar power systems. Maybe you've decided along the way to let someone else do it and simply buy a finished home that uses solar energy. Good idea. That's the topic of our next chapter.

The Least You Need to Know

◆ Though solar power systems are low maintenance, they aren't no maintenance. Automatic, manual, and observation monitoring can keep your solar power system running efficiently.

◆ Make sure you know your solar power system's setpoints and alarm-points—and what to do if there's a problem.

◆ Keep track of maintenance issues by writing down a plan in your Solar Book.

◆ Troubleshooting solar equipment is relatively easy, especially if you know the system well and it comes with a troubleshooting guide.

◆ *Never* work on an electrical circuit unless you know it is safe to do so.

Part 5

Buying and Selling

Life is about buying and selling. So is solar power. This final part shows you how to buy and sell solar homes. You may have decided to buy a pre-built new or retrofitted solar home. Or you may be looking toward the day you must sell your solar palace and want top dollar.

Along the way, you can learn how thousands of solar folks sell electricity back to the local utility to reduce their monthly bill—sometimes to zero.

Finally, you'll see how to expand your solar wisdom into other parts of your life with energy-efficient gadgets and ideas. You'll feed your solar soul.

Chapter 23

Buying a Solar Home

In This Chapter

- ◆ Looking into solar housing communities
- ◆ Things to consider when buying a solar home
- ◆ How much extra will a solar home cost?
- ◆ Inspecting your solar home: making sure you get what you pay for
- ◆ What to do if you get a solar lemon

More and more homes are being built or retrofitted with solar power. That's good news. Not only are these homes reducing the nation's dependency on fossil fuel power, they are also offering options to those who don't want to design and build their own solar homes. They can now buy ready-made solar homes, powered by environmentally friendly solar energy.

This chapter describes these options and how to choose a solar home built by others. It describes solar communities as well as how to make sure the retrofitted solar home is *really* a good buy.

Solar Communities

Solar communities are planned developments across the nation that require or encourage solar construction. They may include passive solar designs as well as solar power systems. A passive solar home, you'll recall from earlier chapters, is one that utilizes part of the building as a solar collector, as opposed to active solar, such as PV or domestic hot water systems. However, a passive solar home that also uses solar electricity is called passive-active.

Buying a passive solar home can dramatically cut energy costs.

(©Gaiam Real Goods)

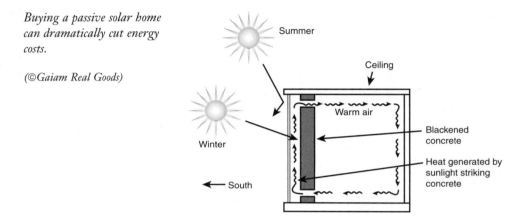

The concept of solar communities is more than a decade old and there are a few such communities that continue to quietly depend on solar energy. In addition, more communities are making it easier for solar home construction by offering local seminars, training building inspectors, and even offering special incentives and rebates to help people see the light. The future will undoubtedly offer additional solar communities.

Sun Spots

Bickford Ranch (www.BickfordRanch.com) near Sacramento, California, is planning to become the largest solar community in the United States. Developers have joined with the California Energy Commission and two PV system developers. Their goal is to construct nearly 1,000 solar power homes that rely on PV modules for electricity. Total peak energy production is projected to be as much as a 2-megawatt power plant. Larger systems will actually sell electricity to the local power grid.

Many communities in the United States and other countries use renewable energy sources including the sun, wind, water, and wood, to help supply their energy needs. Community projects include a wide range of activities, such as solar retrofits of residential and municipal buildings, solar-powered stills to purify water, programs that teach residents how to build hot water systems, and city ordinances that require new buildings to incorporate passive solar energy techniques into their design. Here are some of these communities.

Beaver Island, Michigan

After conducting an energy study on a small island in Lake Michigan, a group of students from Michigan State University and Jordan College recommended using solar energy as a power source. The island was having a problem with limited power availability from a long underwater supply cable, causing frequent brownouts from households using electric power to heat water. According to the study, solar-powered water heating systems could meet more than 50 percent of a household's hot water requirements (75 percent in the summer).

Camp Pendleton, California

The U.S. Marine Corps uses solar energy to heat domestic hot water at Camp Pendleton in San Diego. In 360 of the camp's two-bedroom housing units, thermosiphoning solar water heaters provide 71 percent of the units' domestic water heating needs.

Dallas, Texas

The Esperanza del Sol (Spanish for "Hope of the Sun") community project in downtown Dallas uses insulation, air-sealing, and passive solar measures to increase resident comfort and reduce energy bills. Passive solar space heating provides light and heat for the project's residents. Roof overhangs prevent the intense solar heat from entering the upper story windows in the summer, while allowing it in during the winter. The project's homes won the Edison Electric Institute's E-Seal award, and were showcased at an Energy Efficient Building Association Conference.

Santa Fe, New Mexico

The Eldorado passive solar community of 850 units near Santa Fe is the largest of its kind in the United States. Located in the foothills of the Sangre de Christo mountains, this community experiences cold winters and relatively cool summers. Because the sun shines 310 days a year, the area is ideal for passive solar space heating. Eldorado's house designs use the sun for heat in the winter. The homes rarely use their backup conventional heating appliances during the winter. In the summer, well-planned cross ventilation keeps the air circulating and the houses cool. Underground power lines and restrictive building covenants ensure optimal solar access for each lot.

Gardiner, Massachusetts

In Gardiner, 32 homes and 8 commercial buildings received photovoltaic (solar electric or PV) arrays from Massachusetts Electric, a subsidiary of the New England Electric

Company. Each house was equipped with a 240 square foot (22.3 square meter) array producing an average of 2,195 kilowatt hours (kWh) per year. A number of the houses in the project produce more electricity during the day than they consume. They feed this excess power back into Massachusetts Electric's power lines. Most of these power give-backs occur during the utility's daily peak demand times. The nonresidential buildings that received PV arrays are the town library, the city hall, a restaurant, a furniture store, the police station, an office building, and the community college. The commercial arrays range in capacity from 1.8 to 7.3 peak kilowatts (kWp).

Lafayette, Colorado

The Nyland CoHousing Community in Lafayette uses passive solar strategies as well as energy-efficient measures to lower its homes' overall energy use. The community, which has 42 single family homes grouped in adjoining clusters, combines an environmentally conscious and communitarian lifestyle.

Laguna del Mar, California

San Diego Gas and Electric (SDG&E) installed PV arrays on 36 townhouses in 1985. The arrays were rated at 1 kW in size and were roof-mounted. The utility sold the arrays to the homeowners, and guaranteed the components' quality.

Solar Eclipse

What are the downsides of living in a solar community? Because there are many covenants and restrictions written into your deed, individual property rights are reduced for the common good. If the homeowners association says you must (or can't) do something, you probably can't fight it. Also, folks who like four seasons may become bored by sunlight and blue skies day after day. (Really!)

Philadelphia, Pennsylvania

For over a decade, a housing development in North Philadelphia has been quietly making a statement about sustainability in American cities. The 23 row houses on the 1500 block of Thompson Street look the same as other houses, but these houses stand out because of their low energy use. These two-story, 1,280 square feet (119 square meters) homes are designed to use the sun as their main source of heating.

Phoenix, Arizona

The Solar One project in Phoenix features 24 superinsulated houses with rammed-earth walls and their own central photovoltaic power plant. The residential photovoltaic micro-utility, a 3,600-panel system with a guaranteed output of 350,000 kWh per year, was the first of its kind anywhere. Each homeowner in the development is entitled to one twenty-fourth of the system's output, or a minimum of 14,583 kWh free per year. If one of the residents needs to override his or her demand limit, he or she can do so by placing a telephone call to the system's computer. Solar One is connected to the local utility, the Salt River Project. The utility buys back excess power produced by the system, which is often when demand for power from the utility's other customers is highest.

Sacramento, California

In California's state capital, there are 500 residential rooftop solar photovoltaic systems and 20 commercial and church rooftop systems, feeding over 1.5 MW of clean electricity directly into Sacramento Municipal Utility District's (SMUD) grid. Other ground mounted-, substation-, and parking lot-sited PV systems provide nearly 5.7 MW of electricity from the sun. Under SMUD's PV Pioneer II Program, SMUD customers purchase their own PV system and own the electricity they generate.

Choosing Solar

So what should you be looking for in a new or upgraded solar home? Everything we've discussed thus far. This book offers hundreds of info bits on energy efficiency, financing, rebates, passive solar design, PV systems, water and wind power, and many other solar topics. They all apply whether you're having a solar home built or buying someone else's efforts.

You should be asking a lot of questions as you choose a solar home. Here are some for starters:

- Has an energy-efficiency audit been performed on this house? If so, what were the results?
- What solar power or other equipment has been installed?
- When was the equipment installed and by whom?
- What licenses or certifications does the installer have?
- From whom was the solar equipment purchased?
- What was the initial cost of the system and what rebates were paid?

◆ What records have been kept on system output and efficiency?

◆ What equipment is under warranty and are the warranties transferable to the new owner?

◆ Who designed the solar power system and what are his or her qualifications?

◆ What system documentation is available?

◆ Was the system designed for expansion?

◆ Has the owner considered other power sources (wind, water) and, if so, why were they not implemented?

◆ If a net-metering agreement has been signed with the local utility, what are its terms?

◆ Was the system inspected by the local building department under a permit?

◆ Is there a solar water heating system and, if so, how and by whom was it installed?

◆ Was a solar retrofit financed by a second mortgage and lien against the home?

◆ What passive solar elements were designed into the home and how effective are they?

◆ Is the home oriented and landscaped to take advantage of solar radiation?

Make sure the home you buy takes advantage of solar energy while protecting it from excess solar radiation.

(©Gaiam Real Goods)

◆ Does the home have *too many* west or southwest-facing windows that will keep the house *too hot* during the summer?

◆ What is the age and physical condition of the solar power equipment?

◆ What is the effective life of the primary components of the power system?

◆ How soon will batteries, if any, need replacement?

◆ What maintenance, repairs, or enhancements have been or should be made to the solar power system?

◆ If it's a new solar home, is the builder experienced and reputable?

◆ What homeowner warranties are available for this solar home?

Too many west and southwest-facing windows in a home can make it excessively hot and difficult to cool.

(©Gaiam Real Goods)

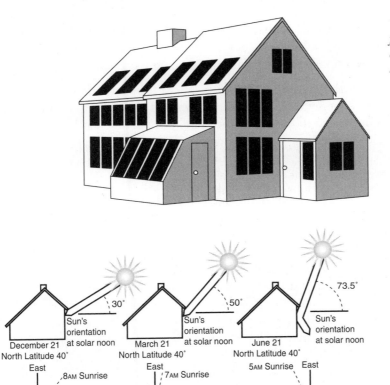

The home you buy should have been designed for optimum solar collection without excessive heat.

(©Gaiam Real Goods)

Buying a new or retrofitted solar home is like buying *any* home—*plus* buying solar. It takes more work, but the rewards are also greater. An efficiently designed and installed solar power system can actually save money on utility bills to help you buy your home.

You Get What You Pay For

Will you pay more for a solar home than for a conventional home? Definitely! How much more? Ah, there's the rub. It's difficult to determine the actual value of a solar home without some calculations and maybe an expert or two.

An appraiser is someone who determines the value of something. A qualified home appraiser can calculate the value of your home, even if it's solar. Appraisers do this by using interpolation—adding and subtracting—to figure the value of all types of homes. They may come up with a square-foot figure that helps them value a larger-than-standard home. Or they may subtract for a garage turned into a family room. Or quality landscaping may add to the value of your solar home. Fortunately, appraisers have help in figuring out a home's value. They have data books and software to help them find the value of additions and subtractions including local market conditions.

First, let's discuss value, as there are many kinds. A lender wants to know mortgage value, a price at which the lender can easily sell the home if necessary, typically a *conservative* price. The seller wants to know market value, or how much a buyer will probably pay for it based on the sale of similar homes in the area. The property tax person wants to know the tax value, a conservative ballpark number that's easy to calculate. It's usually lower than any of the other valuations.

Bright Idea

Want to save on taxes? Some states offer a moratorium on property taxes covering solar installations. It may be for only the portion of a home that is solar or for a specified number of years, but it's still savings. And any dollar you can save from the tax collector also earns valuable bragging rights.

If you're buying a solar home you want to know the fair market value or price that other buyers would pay for it. You'll probably sell it someday and want to make sure you can attract a buyer while making a reasonable profit on appreciation or increased value. But how can you or a fair market appraisal estimate the price that any home—and especially a solar home—is worth? Again, interpolation. In appraising, interpolation means taking the price of a *standard* house, then adding and subtracting elements as needed to get a value that a local buyer will probably pay for the home.

For example, the solar power home you're looking at may be similar in design, size, age, and construction to a neighboring home that just sold for $250,000. They are both of similar design, square footage, and quality. The difference is that the home you're considering has a solar power system installed two years ago at a net price (cost less rebates) of $25,000. In this example, the appraiser calculates depreciation of 5 percent a year over a 20 year system lifetime and takes 10 percent off the value (5 percent times two years). So $22,500 is the estimated value of the solar power system.

Added to the value of a similar nonsolar home, the market value of your solar home is estimated at $272,500.

That's a simplified example. An appraiser may also look at potential income from selling power to the local utility. Or the appraiser may determine that the installation was not adequate and that $5,000 in maintenance or repairs is necessary before the system can be valued as in good condition. Or there may be tax incentives that the new owner can take advantage of, adding value to the home.

You don't have to be the seller to hire an appraiser for a home you're planning to buy. You can write an offer to buy a home subject to an acceptable appraisal at your expense. That means if the appraiser comes up with a valuation that isn't acceptable to *you* (the one who hired the appraiser), you can back out of the deal. Of course, try to find a local appraiser with training and experience valuing solar power systems.

Inspecting Your Solar Home

Let's say you've made an offer on a new or retrofitted solar home. It may be passive solar design or it may have a solar electric system—or both. How can you make sure it works as advertised?

First, you need to know what's in the system. The seller should disclose to all buyers exactly what solar equipment is included in the sale. It must be in writing. If it's not clear, ask for a specific list of solar equipment from the seller or through your real estate agent. You may want to have the seller or agent show you each component included on the solar power system list. Or you may want to hire an inspector or solar expert to check out each component.

Remember that passive solar power systems are nothing more than properly placed south-facing windows with a roof overhang for summer shading, and something inside to soak up the heat, often a tile or cement floor. There aren't any "components" to passive solar power systems other than solar-conscious design.

In most states, real estate law says that if it is attached to real estate, it *is* real estate. And if it *isn't* attached, it's personal property. Personal property included in a real estate sale *must* be listed to be included. For example, a refrigerator is personal property, but an installed door is real estate. That rule suggests that any attached solar power equipment sold with the home is *probably*

Solar Eclipse

Make sure you read and understand all the fine print in the contract. Have an attorney read it over on your behalf and advise you of any potential problems. Unless you have the contract drawn up by your attorney it will be written to favor the seller and his or her real estate agent.

considered part of the home. However, to be safe, make sure that it is specifically listed in your offer to buy.

Now that you know what's included in the solar power system you're buying with the home, you can inspect it. Use the seller's list of what's included as a guide in your inspection. As needed, hire an experienced solar electrical contractor to do or help you with the inspection. If an agreement has been signed to supply power to a local utility, ask the utility to send an inspector so you can check things out together.

What should you be looking for as you inspect a solar power system?

- ◆ If the system is new, check all the building permits, owner manuals, and other system documentation to make sure it is complete.

- ◆ If retrofitted to the house, inspect all building permits to ensure that installation was completed according to local electrical codes.

- ◆ Follow the system from where it starts (PV modules or heating coils) to its end (main power panel or hot water heater), asking questions and looking at condition.

- ◆ Verify that the output is what the owner says it is; that is, check the amount of current and voltage or the hot water temperature delivered to the home.

- ◆ Make sure the system has adequate safety equipment such as ground-fault inter-rupters (GFIs), lightning arrestors, fuses, and circuit breakers.

- ◆ Look for obvious problems such as birds' nests around PV modules, damaged cable or wire, broken frames, inoperable gauges, or other conditions that can impact operation or safety.

- ◆ If the system includes other power sources (grid, wind, water, generator), care-fully inspect the equipment and interconnection.

- ◆ Make sure you are knowledgeable about the system and comfortable with its safe operation before purchasing a home with a solar power system.

Buyer's Recourse

Chances are, this is the first solar power home you've ever purchased. You'll be much smarter for the *second* one. In the meantime, there are many things you can do to take care of problems that arise *after* you've bought this home.

A new solar power home will be subject to the builder's and equipment supplier's warranties, so make sure you clearly understand them and what to do if there is a problem. In most cases, equipment manufacturers don't directly handle problems with equipment under warranty. That's handled by whomever installed the equipment. If you can't get satisfaction through the installer, the manufacturer is your next contact. If you don't know who installed it, the manufacturer may be your first contact.

The builder of a new solar home may offer a buyer's warranty program that covers all houses the builder constructs. That includes any solar equipment installed by or for the builder. So the thick package you received when you bought the new solar home may have specific warranty information. Alternately, you can call the builder to discuss any problems you're having with the solar package.

Because many states are encouraging solar power, they are more sensitive to consumer complaints about solar power systems. That means you probably have a solar consumer advocate or ombudsman who can help you get resolution on disputes with builders or suppliers. Check Appendix B for state energy offices.

As much as you've enjoyed it, there may come a day when you want or need to sell your solar home. How? How much? Those are some of the questions answered in the next chapter.

The Least You Need to Know

- For many, the easiest and smartest way to go solar is to buy a solar designed home in a solar community.

- Knowing what to ask the seller and the real estate agent can save you money and headaches when buying a solar home.

- You can interpolate standard home values and equipment costs to determine how much to pay for a solar home.

- Make sure you or an expert inspector go over every component of your new home's solar power system.

- No matter what you're buying for your solar home, make sure you get warranty information on the equipment and installation—just in case something goes wrong.

Selling Your Solar Home

In This Chapter

- ◆ Working with an agent to sell your house
- ◆ Should you try selling your home yourself?
- ◆ Pricing your solar home for a profitable sale
- ◆ The solar edge: marketing your home
- ◆ You have a buyer! Now what?
- ◆ Planning your *next* solar power home

Once you've built your new solar home—or retrofitted your home for solar power—you'll start getting knockers. "Knock, knock! Can I ask you about your house?" You may even invite them on the grand tour, selling the idea of solar-powered homes.

What about the day when someone says, "Knock, knock! I want to buy your solar home!"? What if they make you an offer you can't refuse? Or what if you must move for a job and leave your solar home behind?

This chapter offers ideas and suggestions on how to get top dollar for your solar home in any real estate market. And you'll *want* top dollar, so that you can invest in your next and even more efficient solar home.

Hiring an Agent

Most people who sell their homes actually hire a real estate agent to do so. Selling homes is a specialty that requires a knowledge of contract law, marketing, persistence, and finesse. Not everyone has these skills—not even all real estate agents.

You'll also be looking for someone who has at least a smattering of knowledge about solar power. It will help in marketing your home.

How can you find and hire the best real estate agent for your solar-powered home? By first becoming a buyer. Or at least thinking like a buyer. You can start shopping for a solar home to find out what agencies and agents have the most experience with them. Here are some tips:

- ◆ Check the local newspaper's classifieds under "Homes for Sale" looking for houses that are obviously solar.

- ◆ Look for local and regional real estate sales magazines that cover your area.

- ◆ Start calling local real estate offices asking if they have any solar home listings and, if so, who the agent is.

- ◆ Ask your solar equipment suppliers if they know of solar homes for sale or real estate agents with solar experience.

- ◆ Ask contractors and acquaintances in the building trades if they can recommend an experienced solar real estate agent.

The ideal agent for your home actually lives in a solar power home and can gush about its benefits. If your community has lots of solar homes, it may be easier to find an owner who sells real estate than vice versa. Experienced agents in larger solar communities may even openly promote their specialty. Here are some questions you can ask prospective agents to help you narrow down the field:

- ◆ How many homes have you sold and closed in the past 12 months? (An agent needs at least one closing a month to survive financially.)

- ◆ How many listings (homes for sale) do you currently represent? (If it's more than the number sold, the agent probably prefers to list homes and let other agents sell them.)

- ◆ What is your experience with solar-powered homes?

- ◆ How would you try to sell my home?

◆ How long do you think it would
take to sell my home? (Remember
that the answer is a guess and *not* a
promise.)

◆ Why should I list my solar home
with you and your office?

Bright Idea

You may determine that the
best real estate agent for your
home is someone who has
plenty of skills, but no solar
experience. In that case, you'll
need to educate her or him about
solar. Lend them this book—or,
better yet, have them buy a copy!

A good agent will be enthusiastic about learning a new aspect of the real estate market.
And you can help your agent by offering specific information about your solar power system and its benefits. Sell the seller!

Selling It Yourself

You may not be as knowledgeable about real estate law and marketing as a professional
agent—but *you* only have one client. That's why many home owners decide to sell
their own houses and save 5 to 10 percent in commissions.

Should you attempt to sell your own home? Ask yourself the following questions:

◆ What experience do I have marketing, advertising, and selling things?

◆ Can I take the time off from work or other activities to show my home when
buyers may want to see it?

◆ What do I know about the financing and title transfer of a home?

◆ Am I willing to pay a small commission to an agent who brings me a qualified
buyer?

◆ How am I at negotiation?

What about the legal issues? You can hire a real estate attorney to advise you. You can
even hire a marketing expert to help you through the process and still have money
left over.

Of course, if you've sold your own homes before, you know the process. You know
about title companies, escrow officers, mortgage payoffs, offers, and all the other
components of a sale.

However, you may not be able to sell your own home. Sure, you can legally. But
maybe it's a tight market and homes aren't selling easily. Or maybe you need to move

quickly and have someone else handle the marketing and sale. There are many reasons *not* to try selling your own home. There are just as many that suggest, "Hey, I can do this!"

Start with a copy of *The Complete Idiot's Guide to Buying and Selling a Home* by Shelley O'Hara (Alpha Books, 2000). It offers clear, step-by-step tips on getting your house ready for sale *and* getting top dollar for it. Recommended reading!

Setting Your Price

Whether you try selling it yourself or hiring a real estate agent, you'll have to set a price for your solar home. Chapter 23 introduced the idea of interpolation. That is, you find similar subject homes without solar, then add and subtract features to come up with the price of your solar home. For example, you might add for the depreciated value of the solar power system, subtract because your home isn't quite as large as the subject home, or add because yours has a solar swimming pool the subject home doesn't. That's what your real estate agent (or appraiser, if you'll be using one) will be doing when he or she develops a market analysis.

Sun Spots
A certified appraisal is typically a better indication of value than one from a real estate agent. That's because appraisals are all appraisers do. Appraisers don't market, nor do they work on commission. You pay a set fee for the appraisal.

Even if you use an agent, you should know how the agent arrived at the suggested market price. In fact, you may ask two or three agents to develop a market analysis for you. They will probably come up with slightly different numbers. That's because they will probably use different subject homes. Or they may interpolate or weigh additions and subtractions differently. Remember, you're not looking for the agent who suggests the highest starting price. You want the agent who can defend the suggested pricing to you—and to the buyer.

Setting your price also depends on the Rush Factor. If you must be out of town by sunset, you will price your house lower than if you're retiring when the house sells. Your price will also be lower if the local real estate market is soft. Of course, keep in mind your home has something most others don't: solar power.

Marketing Your Solar Home

You have a marketing advantage. *Your* home is solar powered. That means it is unique as well as energy efficient. Of course, some people look at a solar home and wonder why you plastered those black rectangles all over the roof.

You can overcome initial objections to the look of solar *and* increase the perceived value of your solar home by marketing solar. That is, gather information about your solar house and either publish a flyer or ask your real estate agent to do so.

Here's what you should include in your solar home flyer:

♦ Exterior and interior photos to show that it isn't Frankenstein's castle.

♦ Basic information on the solar power system. (You don't want to tell them *everything* because you want to encourage questions.)

♦ Data on how much money is saved by your solar, wind, hydro, or other power system.

♦ Information about open houses (every Sunday afternoon, every other Monday, and so on).

♦ Any other advantages your home has over others in the same price range.

♦ Listed price as well as probable monthly payments based on typical down payments.

♦ Information on how to contact the seller or agent including telephone, cell phone, fax, and e-mail.

Even if you've hired a real estate agent to sell your solar home, help him or her with the marketing. Suggest open houses. Pass out flyers to friends and neighbors. Post flyers on local bulletin boards. Leave the flyers on a prominent table in the home in case other agents show your home while you're away. You get the picture.

Closing on Your Home

Hey, that was fast. You recently offered your solar home for sale and you already have an offer to buy. Fantastic! Now what?

First, make sure you clearly understand what the offer is. Your real estate agent or attorney should explain every point of the offer to your satisfaction. That's what they are paid to do. There are no dumb questions.

Especially make sure that ownership to the solar equipment is clear. If it is considered part of the real estate and you have a mortgage or loan against it, make sure it will all be paid off with the proceeds of the buyer's new mortgage (if any). If some or all of the solar equipment isn't attached to the house it may be considered personal property, and so title to it may not transfer with the house. It's best to clarify these issues prior to offering your home for sale, but it's critical that it be addressed before an offer to buy is accepted.

If your home has a net-metering agreement with the local utility (see Chapter 25), be sure that the utility knows of the offering and participates in the sale. This may mean simply having the new owners sign an agreement with the utility. Or the agreement may automatically transfer with the home's title. Just make sure you *know* how the contract works when selling.

Rebates and buy downs, too, may impact the title to your solar home. To discourage investors, the state's rebate may make it tough for you to sell your solar home within a year of installation. If you or your agent don't know what impact selling will have on the rebate, contact the state energy office that first offered it. Alternately, restrictions may have been recorded with the home's deed. You can get a copy through the courthouse or a local title insurance company.

Moving Out and Moving On

Moving is never easy. I know! I've moved 45 times—and authored *The Complete Idiot's Guide to Smart Moving* (Alpha Books, 1998). It's even more challenging moving from a solar home. First, you have to remember *not* to pack anything that really should stay. That includes solar equipment owner manuals, documents, warrantees, spare parts, receipts, and operation records. Find a spot near the system control for all of these components.

Second, you need to make sure you fully instruct the new owners on how to best operate your (oh, *their*) solar power system. In fact, be good to them and videotape your instructions so they can review it later. Alternately, you can audio tape it or write it all down. Also make sure they have telephone numbers of resources for their new solar equipment.

Need more good moving tips? Here are some from *The Complete Idiot's Guide to Smart Moving*:

- ◆ Start a Moving Notebook early so you can begin organizing the move to your new house. Include a list of tasks and contacts that you can check off as they're done.

- ◆ Once you know the date you'll be moving in, send out change of address cards to family, friends, healthcare providers, and services.

- ◆ Contact utilities such as the phone company ahead of time to arrange for service before your move-in date.

- ◆ Decide a month or two in advance whether you plan to pack and move your things or to hire a service to do some or all of it. If you choose to use a moving company, begin shopping early for the best prices. If you'll be moving yourself, arrange for boxes and rolls of tape to be dropped off, and check prices for truck rentals, if necessary.

◆ To help them feel ownership in the move, ask children to pack their most precious belongings and unpack them first when they arrive.

◆ Instruct older children on packing methods to teach them new skills and independence they will need in coming years.

◆ Make sure your insurance company knows about your new house and your moving plans.

Bright Idea

Contact the Internal Revenue Service (www.irs.gov) for Publication 521 on deductible moving expenses.

◆ Start packing items early that you know you won't use, such as books and collectibles. Dust them as you pack so when you unpack them they'll be ready to put on the shelves.

◆ Label all boxes according to what room they'll go in. If the contents of a box are fragile, make sure it's clearly labeled on the box.

◆ If possible, set aside a room or the garage to store packed boxes and large unused items in preparation for moving.

◆ In advance, carefully plan out the two most important days: moving-out day and moving-in day.

◆ Set aside a special "open me first" box with cleaning supplies, paper towels, bath towels, soap, toilet paper, and other necessities.

◆ Make sure you take some time to have fun and relax to reduce the stress of moving.

Now what? You've been spoiled by solar. You're never going to be able to look at a utility bill again without wincing. Maybe you're already planning what you want different in your *next* solar home. Maybe you'll add a solar pool or a wind turbine generator for backup. Or you'll enlarge the system and sell power to the utility. Good for you!

That's our next topic: selling power to the local electrical utility. We return to the topic of net metering in the next chapter.

The Least You Need to Know

- ◆ Make sure your real estate agent has solar home experience—or is at least interested in learning how to sell one.

- ◆ Many solar home owners sell their own house with the help of a real estate attorney and an experienced appraiser.

- ◆ Pricing a solar home means adding to and subtracting from the value of comparable homes.

- ◆ As a knowledgeable solar home owner you can help your agent and buyer to understand the benefits of solar living.

- ◆ Make sure you and your buyer know exactly what's included in the sale of your solar home—and what's not.

- ◆ Start right now planning your next solar home; you're hooked!

Chapter 25

Selling Excess Power

In This Chapter

◆ Deciding whether net metering is smart for you

◆ Understanding the interconnection process

◆ Signing an agreement to sell power to a utility

◆ Installing an intertie solar power system

You've been buying electricity from the local utility for years. In this chapter I'll tell you how you can *sell* your excess solar power to the utility. Better yet, you'll learn how to deposit it into their "bank" and draw it out when you need it.

This chapter isn't for everyone. Its not for solar homeowners who live off-grid. They can't *truck* their excess power to the local utility. And it's not for those who want a small solar power system. It's about selling *excess* electrical power, meaning a bigger system and a bigger initial investment. It can also mean justifying a bigger system that can give you more power for less money.

How Net Metering Works

As you learned in Chapter 4, the 1978 Federal PURPA act says that individuals and businesses that generate excess renewable-generated power can sell it to the local utility at "avoided cost" through a program called net metering. Avoided cost is the minimum amount an electric utility is required to pay an independent power producer, equal to the costs the utility calculates it avoids in not having to produce that power. It's usually substantially less than the retail price charged by the utility for power it sells to customers. Avoided cost is essentially wholesale pricing. How would you like to get residential retail pricing for the electricity you sell to the utility? Of course you would. That's net metering, and it's good stuff.

Net metering can dramatically decrease the long-term costs of your solar power system. The Database of State Incentives for Renewable Energy (DSIRE) is a comprehensive source of information on state, local, utility, and selected federal incentives that promote renewable energy. For a good up-to-date listing of net-metering states and the particulars of those individual state programs, check DSIRE's website at www.dsireusa.org.

Bright Idea

If your state doesn't have a net metering program, contact your state energy office (listed in Appendix B) about becoming an advocate and getting laws passed in your state legislature to make it available.

Is your system eligible? As of spring 2002, nearly two thirds of U.S. states and the District of Columbia have net metering programs that allow you to sell electricity to utilities at residential power prices. Three more states have net metering programs with specific, but not all, utilities in the state. In California, for example, Public Utilities Code section 2827 says that all utilities in the state must offer the option of interconnecting on a net metering basis to residential and commercial customers with PV or small wind systems that produce 10 kW or less of power.

How does it all work? As an eligible customer, you interconnect with your utility and feed your surplus electricity to the utility grid. You can use an equivalent amount of electricity later without additional cost to you. Your system may include batteries or a generator.

Your electricity meter spins forward when electricity flows from the utility into your home. Net metering allows the meter to also spin *backwards* when your system produces surplus electricity that is not immediately used. Think of it as "banking" your excess electricity on the utility grid.

You could set up two meters, one for incoming power (from the grid) and one for outgoing power (to the grid), but it's simpler to have one meter that moves both forward and backward.

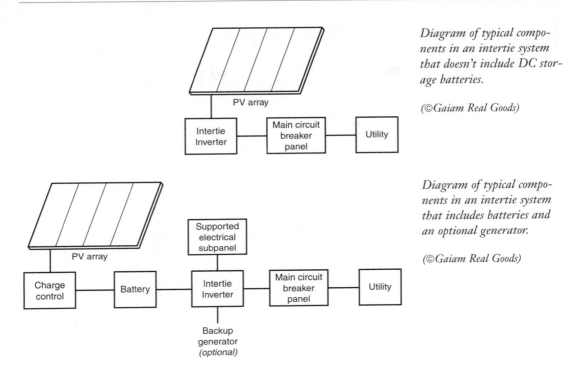

Diagram of typical components in an intertie system that doesn't include DC storage batteries.

(©Gaiam Real Goods)

Diagram of typical components in an intertie system that includes batteries and an optional generator.

(©Gaiam Real Goods)

Why would folks at the utility do this for you? First, because the law says they must. Second, because thousands of mini-generation systems like yours can save them building new power plants. Your system becomes a *Small-Scale Renewable Energy System* (*SRES*). However, don't expect them to make it easy for you.

Net metering gives you more value from your home-grown electricity by offsetting your future electricity (retail) purchases rather than selling your excess electricity at avoided cost (wholesale). For example, if you sell your excess electricity to the local utility at 3 cents per kWh, then have to buy some back later at 12 cents per kWh, you're not making much. However, if you "bank" the surplus on the grid and get it back later, you're both buying and selling at retail price.

Sun-Day School

A Small-Scale Renewable Energy System (SRES) is a system with less than 100 kW of capacity that converts renewable energy (solar, wind, water, biomass, biofuels) into electricity. A residential solar power system is an SRES. So are those installed in business and industry that fit the capacity criteria. Together, these systems can replace larger fossil-fuel power systems.

How your utility deals with billing will vary from state to state, and sometimes from one utility to another. Generally, credit from one month, like June for instance, can be rolled over to the next month, or the next. At least once a year, the utilities are required to charge you for the *net* energy consumed by your house over the previous 12 months. They are *not* required to carry over your credit past 12 months. It's gone forever.

How to calculate cost savings for net-metering systems.

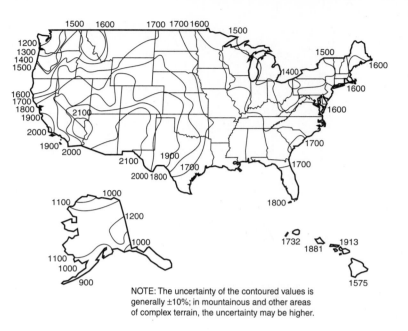

NOTE: The uncertainty of the contoured values is generally ±10%; in mountainous and other areas of complex terrain, the uncertainty may be higher.

Exactly how this all works depends on the agreement you sign with the local utility. Your home's electric generation system *must* be certified as a Qualified Facility and you *must* agree to do certain things before the utility *must* buy power from you. However, solar power system contractors and suppliers know about local requirements and can help you with the paperwork and red tape. It helps them sell more systems.

In fact, based on the interconnection agreement you sign and the state's net metering laws, you can probably afford a larger solar power system than you otherwise could. The system is not only reducing your power bill, it's actually generating some income from any surplus. That means you can size and manage the system to generate a surplus for sale. Again, make sure that your system meets the utility's requirements and doesn't exceed its production limits. The utility wants assistance meeting local power needs—it *doesn't* want competition.

The Interconnection Process

What's needed to interconnect your solar power system with the local utility grid? Many states have streamlined the process to make it easier for customers to interconnect with the least red tape. Others are still back in the stone (or fossil fuel) age. You'll find the more modern ones may even have an Internet website that guides you through the interconnection process.

A typical interconnection process will include these steps:

- ◆ Complete the application form.

- ◆ Furnish a system diagram and project details.

- ◆ Read and sign a copy of the interconnection agreement.

- ◆ Furnish proof of insurance coverage.

- ◆ Furnish a copy of the approved building permit for the system.

In some locations, the interconnection process will go quickly while in others it may take months. The interconnection process depends on who's managing it, how much pressure is put on the managing department by economic and political powers, how well the department is staffed, and how many other folks are doing what you're doing. Hope for the best, but plan for the worst.

Understanding the Interconnection Agreement

Setting up a two-way connection with your utility (previously one-way) requires that you enter into an interconnection agreement and a purchase-and-sale agreement. Many utilities have developed standardized interconnection agreements for small-scale PV systems. These agreements may be a single contract with your local utility or separate contracts with your utility and your electrical service provider.

The interconnection agreement defines the terms and conditions for connecting your system to the power grid. Included are the technical requirements your system must meet to ensure safety and power quality. The agreement also will spell out your obligation to get all necessary permits, to maintain the system, and to be responsible for the system's safe operation.

The agreement also defines the type of interconnection you and the utility will have. Residential customers usually have a net metering system in which one meter tracks both incoming and outgoing power. Commercial and industrial customers are often required to set up a dual metering system with one meter for incoming power and another for outgoing. It also spells out the utility interconnection standards.

Solar Eclipse

Call your homeowner insurance agent to make sure that there are no clauses that exempt claims from intertie systems. This is new stuff to most insurance companies and you don't want to find out too late that your system isn't covered. Ask questions now.

Utility interconnection standards or UIS tell you what you can and cannot do as you set up a two-way connection with the utility. Mostly, they ensure that the power you deliver to the utility matches requirements and won't cause a system hazard or injure utility workers. That makes sense.

The most important part of the standards covers inverters. As you remember from Chapter 9, inverters convert the DC electricity generated by PV arrays into AC electricity used by loads in your home. Modern inverters do even more, managing and conditioning power. They include protective relays, disconnects, and other components to make solar power systems safer.

The point here is to make sure that the inverter you buy meets the standards required by your utility's interconnection agreement. Two commonly used standards are from Underwriters Laboratories (UL) and the Institute of Electrical and Electronic Engineers (IEEE). Many utilities require UL 1741 certification for inverters intertied to the utility grid. They will also want a lockable disconnect switch either before or immediately after the main power panel.

Typical interconnection plan.

(©author)

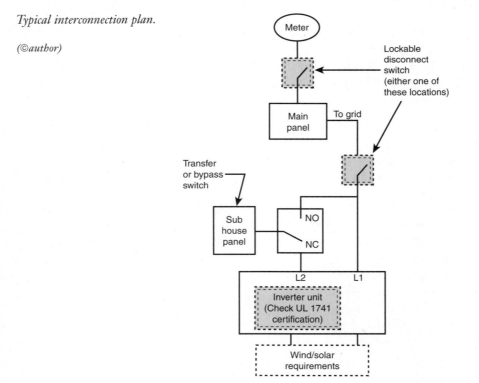

Getting Permits

In most locations, you'll need permits from the local building department before installing a PV system. That means you'll need to know—or hire someone who knows—local electrical code requirements. It probably will be based on the National Electric Code (NEC) for residential solar power installations. It's called Article 690.

Before installation, you or your contractor should find out about building permit requirements. Do so at the city or county building department that has jurisdiction for your property. The more you know before installation the more easily the permit and inspection process will go.

Local building codes may be more stringent for power systems that are being connected to the local utility grid. Inspectors may take a closer look at the installation because they don't want to get into trouble with the utility by approving something that isn't up to snuff. It's also true that your system may get a harder look if it is the first solar installation your inspector has seen. Just make sure that someone (you, your electrician, your contractor, your supplier) knows the local electrical code well and has installed equipment that meets the UIS requirements.

What you're aiming for is called a sign-off. It's a copy of your building permit with the signature of the inspector who made the final inspection and approved it for use. You can't even switch the system on until you get this sign-off. You'll also need it to get any rebates or buy downs (covered in Chapter 4) for the purchase and installation of your system.

Installation

Installing an interconnection, intertie, or net-metering system is the same as standard solar power systems. The difference is primarily in the meter itself and the inverter.

Fortunately, most homes built over the past couple of decades already have a bidirectional watt-hour meter or electrical meter so no upgrade is necessary.

The inverter is the key player. It is either designed for intertie with the local utility grid or it isn't. Even folks who don't plan to intertie soon often spend the extra money for an intertie inverter—just in case. It's cheaper and easier to upgrade now than to retrofit later.

> **Sun Spots**
>
> The inverter you buy will also depend on whether you're installing a battery bank. If you believe you *may* want battery backup in the future, consider adding the functionality to your inverter now. Your solar equipment contractor or supplier can give you the specific dollar differences and potential benefits.

That's it! You've selected, installed, and enjoyed your solar power or other renewable energy systems. You've also learned how to cut system costs by first cutting your home's dependency on *any* power. Next, I'll show you how to apply the same skills to the rest of your life.

The Least You Need to Know

◆ Offering interconnection to small-scale renewable energy systems is required of utilities by law.

◆ Net metering allows you to bank your solar power system's excess power with the utility and get it back when needed.

◆ Make sure you know the exact terms before signing an interconnection agreement with a utility company.

◆ Solar and other renewable power equipment must meet certification requirements to allow intertie with a utility grid.

◆ Start the building permit process early so you know the requirements needed for the final sign-off.

Chapter 26

The Energy-Efficient Lifestyle

In This Chapter

- Finding new ways to live more energy efficiently
- Deciding whether off-grid living works for you
- Ways we can borrow from grandpa and grandma—instead of our children
- Selecting transportation that makes long-term sense

There's so much waste in this world. Our dumpsites are nearly full. Our fossil fuels will be depleted within a blink of time. Cars are the size of trucks, and it seems every family has at least two. We may see endless resources stretching to the horizon—unaware that it's all done with mirrors.

Good solar citizens make good neighbors in other ways. Now that you've become more aware of how energy-efficient solar and other power resources are, what can you do to make our world an even better place? You can consider the energy-efficient lifestyle. You can apply other technologies— as well as simplicities—to extending the useful life of Earth. That's what this final chapter is all about.

Expanding Awareness

The biggest step you can take toward making a better world is to become more aware of our limited resources. You've already started by learning about the limits of fossil fuels and where we're headed. You're now more aware of the *long-term* costs of energy—not just the monthly electric bill. Good for you!

You can carry that awareness over into other aspects of your life. You have daily choices: how to spend your money, what to drive, whether to recycle, what efforts to support and which to discourage. Your decisions have long-term implications. You can make them with an eye on greater energy efficiency.

Want some examples?

- Take a closer look at MPG (miles per gallon) estimates when buying a new or used car, or selecting a rental car for a trip. (Or consider an electric or hybrid car—more about "green cars" later in the chapter.)

- Think about long-term fuel costs as you plan your daily or weekly errands. Run as many of your errands as you can at one time to avoid making a lot of short trips.

- Find out what recycling opportunities your solid waste (trash) service offers. (In many places, recycling your trash is required; if it's still not required in your area, why not get in the habit anyway?)

- Reuse whatever you can around the house. For example, used computer paper makes great drawing paper for kids, and kitchen scraps can be composted for the garden.

 Bright Idea

There are numerous alternative, back-to-basics magazines available through larger newsstands. They include *Mother Earth News, Home Power Magazine, Backwoods Home Magazine, Popular Science,* and others. In addition, call for harder-to-find periodicals such as *Energy and Housing Report* (301-565-2532), *Independent Energy* (612-983-6892), and *The Solar Letter* (301-565-2532).

- Read and consider the EPA label when buying major appliances.

- Rinse out and reuse plastic food bags—as long as they don't need detergent to come clean.

- When grocery shopping, ask for paper bags instead of plastic bags; paper bags are kinder to the environment. Or better yet, carry your own reusable grocery bags.

- Use natural light or less light whenever possible. Use lower-watt light bulbs and dimmer switches where possible. And don't forget to turn off the lights when you don't need them.

◆ Consider alternative transportation, such as the bus and train, for commuting. Carpool if possible. If there's no carpool available, organize one!

◆ Walk or ride your bike instead of taking the car on short trips; it saves on gas and it's good for you!

◆ Review Chapter 3 for tips on cutting your power costs.

◆ Start planning your *next* solar home right now based on what you've learned with this one.

These suggestions are just a start. By being aware of what you're using up and how it can be reduced or reused, you're helping to cut costs and our dependency on borrowing from the future. Thanks!

Living Off-Grid

The idea of living off-grid—without a connection to the electric utility grid—isn't for everyone. Living far from the power line means dramatically reducing your reliance on readily available power and other resources. But you've already seen that solar and other power systems can make it easier.

However, living off-grid probably means you'll be living off-water and off-sewer. You'll have to find a source of water and a way of getting rid of waste. Fortunately, technology has become more helpful for off-grid water users. Solar water pump systems can efficiently pull water from the ground or a stream and deliver it to your house. Who needs a water company?

At the other end of the process, waste can be recycled and removed using technology. There are composting toilets, greywater systems, and other tools for minimizing, er, waste. Let's take a look at them.

Composting Toilets

Older toilet designs use up to eight gallons of water per flush. Newer designs use fewer than four gallons per flush. Composting toilets use little or no water, depending on the design. Installing composting toilets in a home can cut total water usage by 25 percent!

Composting toilets simply furnish a chamber where waste can be composted by a friendly microbiological community, dry, and later be removed without wasting all that flushing water. Like a traditional toilet, it has a seat. Under the seat is a composting chamber where waste collects and added microcritters do their job. It then moves, via gravity, to an evaporating chamber where water evaporates. There's typically some type of slide-out drawer that allows for dried waste removal.

A composting toilet requires no plumbing.

(©Gaiam Real Goods)

Although it may sound icky, a well-designed composting toilet with a fan is relatively clean and efficient. Some models offer the composting and cleanout separate from the seat to minimize odor. The seat can be in one room of the house and the rest of the unit in the basement below. Smells, particularly bad smells from a composter, are a sign that something is wrong. Under normal operation there should be only a very slight odor from a composter.

> **Sun Spots**
>
> Because many composting toilet models use low-wattage internal heaters in the process, they need to be plugged into electricity. Keep that in mind. Nonelectric models are also available, but tend to be a bit fussier to run, and have more limits on how many people they'll support.

You can build your own composting toilet with plans from many back-to-the-woods suppliers. Or you can buy one already made. A single-unit composting toilet will cost about $900 plus any additional fans or venting. A full system that will sit in the basement and serve multiple toilets will cost $1,000 to $2,000 depending on the size and features. Check the list of catalogs in Appendix B for additional resources.

Turn your nose up if you wish, but modern composting toilets make scents, er, sense. (Sorry!)

Greywater Systems

Then there's the grey area. It's all the water used in the home that isn't from the toilet, nor is it drinkable. It's greywater. It's the water that drains out of the bathtub after your bath, the shower as you're showering, the sink after food prep and dish washing. What can you do with it if your home isn't hooked up to a sewer?

Many off-grid and other rural folks use a septic system, a tank and drain field somewhere near the house that collects, treats, and disperses human waste water and greywater. It gets the water from the bathroom, kitchen, and wherever. It all flows to a buried septic tank where microbiology takes over to break down matter.

Alternately, you can install a separate greywater system in your yard. It's similar to a septic system except that it's not set up to handle human waste. Greywater systems are like light-duty septic systems. Depending on what's in the water you dump into it, the output can be used to water trees or a garden. If so, you'll need to install a removable filter to trap detergents or other things that can harm plants.

You can buy simple plans for efficient greywater systems from many back-to-the-land catalog companies. You may even find a plan in old copies of *Mother Earth News* magazine.

Living Like Grandpa

Our dependence on fossil fuels and electricity is relatively new in the scheme of things. It's been in only the last hundred years or so that we thought we can't live without electric lights. And its been only two decades since the microwave took over our cooking.

Fortunately, many people have rediscovered grandpa's—and grandma's—lifestyle. In fact, they've applied technology to make them even better without making them fuel dependent. Here are a few of their tools:

- Manual lawn mowers
- Wood cook stoves
- Compact composters
- Solar food dehydrators
- Solar clothes dryers (clothes lines!)
- 12V appliances
- Manual grain grinders
- Solar ovens and cookers
- Evaporative (swamp) coolers

You get the picture. Just because something was invented in the past 100 years doesn't mean it's the best. There are many tools and living aids designed hundreds of years ago that can help wean us from our dependency on electricity.

Driving into the Future

Another way you can expand energy efficiency in your life is to select transportation that has less adverse environmental impact than gas-guzzling cars. Get a green car (and we aren't talking color here).

Electric vehicles are a good transportation choice for shorter commutes or running errands around town. They are often gasoline-driven cars with electric motors instead of an engine. Of course, they also need batteries to store the energy. The electricity can come from traditional sources (fossil-fuel electric plants) or from solar PV modules. Electric vehicles thrive on cold starts, stop-and-go driving, and short runs—the very things that gasoline engines are worst at. However, the power generated by solar isn't sufficient to power a very big vehicle for very long. Technology is working on a solution. In the meantime, hybrid cars are becoming more popular. These specially designed cars run on both gasoline and electric batteries. Hybrids use the best features of gas and electric motors, while avoiding the worst features of each. Mileage on a gallon of gas is greatly improved over gas-alone cars.

> **Sun Spots**
>
> The Honda Insight is a hybrid car that runs on gas and stores excess energy in batteries. It goes nearly 70 miles on a gallon of gas. Emissions are improved even more. The Toyota Prius has a Super Ultra Low Emission Vehicle (SULEV) rating that spews just one tenth the emissions of the average new vehicle sold in 2002. New models cost less than $20,000.

You have other options depending on where and how you live. Commuting by bus, train, carpool, or even bicycle is more energy-efficient than relying on a car. Besides, moving by bus or train gives you time to do other things than stare at the car in front of you. Bicycles and other human-powered vehicles offer exercise. Of course, where you live and work will dictate the available options.

Congratulations! Your life is now more energy efficient. You've learned to harness the sun's energy to power the important things in your life. And you've probably decided that other things really aren't that important. You've also discovered new ways of making life better for us and those who follow.

May the Source of all things reward you!

The Least You Need to Know

- ◆ Being aware of what resources you're using up and which are renewable is the first step into a better future.

- ◆ Technology offers many valuable tools for eliminating our dependency on fossil fuels and even utility grids.

- ◆ Composting toilets and greywater systems use technology and common sense to reduce waste.

- ◆ Cars are part of the energy problem; they can also be part of the solution.

Solar Glossary

absorbers   Dark-colored objects that soak up heat in solar collectors.

absorption coefficient   The factor by which photons are absorbed as they travel a unit distance through a material.

acceptor   A dopant material, such as boron, which has fewer outer shell electrons than required in an otherwise balanced crystal structure, providing a hole, which can accept a free electron.

activated shelf life   The time it takes for the capacity of a charged battery to fall to an unusable level when stored at a specified temperature.

activation voltage   The voltage at which the controller will operate to protect the batteries.

active solar heater   A solar water or space-heating system that moves heated air or water using pumps or fans.

air mass   The air mass relates to the path length of solar radiation through the atmosphere. An air mass of 1.0 means the sun is directly overhead and the radiation travels through one atmosphere thickness. Approximately equal to the secant of the zenith angle, i.e. the angle from directly overhead to a line to the sun.

alternating current (AC)   Electric current in which the direction of flow is reversed at frequent intervals, usually 100 or 120 times per second (50 or 60 cycles per second or 50/60 Hz).

alternator   A device for producing alternating current (AC) electricity. Usually driven by a motor, but can also be driven by other means, including water and wind power.

ambient temperature   The temperature of the surroundings.

American Wire Gauge (AWG)   A standard system for designating the size of electrical wire. The higher the number, the smaller the wire. Most house wiring is AWG 12 or 14.

ammeter   A device used for measuring current flow at any point in an electrical circuit.

amorphous silicon   A thin-film solar PV cell material that has a glassy rather than crystalline structure.

ampere or **amp (A)**   The unit for the electric current; the flow of electrons. One amp is 1 coulomb passing in one second. One amp is produced by an electric force of 1 volt acting across a resistance of 1 ohm.

amp-hour   The quantity of electrical energy corresponding to the flow of current of one ampere for one hour. The term is used to quantify the energy stored in a battery. Most batteries are rated in Ah.

anemometer   A device used to measure wind speed.

angle of incidence   The angle between horizontal and the angle of a solar panel.

annual solar savings   The energy savings of a solar building attributable to a solar feature relative to the energy requirements of a nonsolar building.

anode   The positive electrode in a battery. The positive terminal of a diode.

antireflection coating   A thin coating of a material that reduces the light reflection and increases light transmission, applied to a photovoltaic cell surface.

array   A group of solar electric modules connected together in a power system.

array current   The electrical current output of a PV array when exposed to sunlight.

array operating voltage   The voltage output of a PV array when exposed to sunlight and feeding a load.

autonomous system   A standalone PV system that has no backup generating source. May or may not include storage batteries.

availability   The quality or condition of a PV system that is available to provide power to a load. Usually measured in hours per year.

avoided cost   The minimum amount an electric utility is required to pay an independent power producer, under the PURPA regulations of 1978, equal to the costs the utility calculates it avoids in not having to produce that power (usually substantially less than the retail price charged by the utility for power it sells to customers).

azimuth   The angle (in degrees) between north and a specific location. As applied to the PV array, 180 degree azimuth means the array faces due south.

balance of system   Represents all components and costs other than the PV modules. It includes design costs, land, site preparation, system installation, support structures, power conditioning, operation and maintenance costs, indirect storage, and related costs.

ballast   A circuit used to stabilize an electric current, for example, in a fluorescent light.

base power   Power generated by a utility unit that operates at a very high capacity factor.

battery   A system in which stored chemical energy is converted directly into electrical energy. Can be either rechargeable or nonrechargeable.

battery bank   A group of batteries wired together to store power in a solar electric system. Allows you to use the stored power at night, on cloudy days, or to run more power than the array can produce at one time.

battery capacity   The total number of ampere-hours (Ah) that a fully charged battery can output.

battery cell   An individual unit of a battery that can store electrical energy and is capable of furnishing a current to an external load. For lead-acid batteries the voltage of a cell (fully charged) is about 2.2 volts DC. A battery may consist of a number of cells.

battery charger   A device used to charge a battery by converting AC voltage to a DC voltage suitable for the battery. Chargers often incorporate some form of regulator to prevent overcharging and damage to the battery.

battery cycle life   The number of times a battery can undergo a cycle of discharge and recharge before failing. Cycle Life is normally specified as a function of discharge rate and temperature.

battery self-discharge   Energy loss by a battery that is not under load.

battery state of charge (SOC)   The extent of battery charge status as a percentage of full charge. Also 100 percent minus the depth of discharge.

blocking diode   A diode used to prevent current flow in an undesirable direction (for example, from the rest of the PV array to a failed module, or from the battery to the PV array when current generation is low).

boron (B)   A chemical element, atomic number 5, semimetallic in nature, used as a dopant to make p-semiconductor layers.

British thermal unit (BTU)   The amount of heat energy required to raise one pound of water from a temperature of 60°F to 61°F at one atmosphere pressure. One watt-hour equals 3,413 BTU.

building-integrated PV (BIPV)   A term for the design and integration of PV into the building envelope, typically replacing conventional building materials. This integration may be in vertical facades, replacing view glass, spandrel glass, or other facade material; in semitransparent skylight systems; in roofing systems, replacing traditional roofing materials; in shading "eyebrows" over windows; or other building envelope systems.

bypass diode   A diode connected across one or more solar cells in a photovoltaic module such that the diode will conduct if the cell(s) change polarity.

cadmium (Cd)   A chemical element, atomic number 48, used in making certain types of solar cells and batteries.

cadmium telluride (CdTe)   A polycrystalline thin-film photovoltaic material.

capacitor   An electronic component used for the temporary storage of electricity, as well for removing unwanted noise in circuits. A capacitor will block direct current but will pass alternating current.

captive electrolyte battery   A battery with an immobilized electrolyte (gelled or absorbed in a material).

cathode   The negative electrode in an electrochemical cell. Also, the negative terminal of a diode.

cell   The basic unit of a PV module or battery. The most basic unit that contains the necessary materials, such as electrodes and electrolyte in a battery, to produce electricity.

cell barrier   A very thin region of static electric charge along the interface of the positive and negative layers in a photovoltaic cell. The barrier inhibits the movement of electrons from one layer to the other, so that higher-energy electrons from one side diffuse preferentially through it in one direction, creating a current and thus a voltage across the cell. Also called depletion zone, cell junction, or space charge.

cell efficiency   The ratio of the electrical energy produced by a photovoltaic cell (under full sun conditions or 1 kW per square meter) to the energy from sunlight falling upon the photovoltaic cell.

charge   The process of inputting electrical energy to a battery.

charge controller   A component that controls the flow of current to and from the battery subsystem to protect the batteries from overcharge and over discharge. Essential for ensuring that batteries obtain maximum state of charge and longest life. The charge controller may also monitor system performance and provide system protection. Charge controllers are also sometimes called regulators.

charge rate   A measure of the current used to charge a battery as a proportion of its capacity.

chlorofluorocarbon   A family of chemicals composed primarily of carbon, hydrogen, chlorine, and fluorine whose principal applications are that of refrigerants and industrial cleansers and whose principal drawback is the tendency to destroy Earth's protective ozone layer.

circuit   A continuous system of conductors providing a path for electricity.

circuit breaker   A circuit breaker acts like an automatic switch that can shut the power off when it senses too much current.

cloud enhancement   The increase in solar intensity due to reflected light from nearby clouds.

coal   A black, solid fossil fuel found in Earth. Coal is often burned to make electricity.

cogeneration   The process in which fuel is used to produce heat for a boiler-steam turbine or gas for a turbine. The turbine drives a generator that produces electricity, with the excess heat used to process steam.

combined collector   A photovoltaic device or module that provides useful heat energy in addition to electricity.

compact fluorescent lights   Lights that use a lot less energy than regular light bulbs. We can use compact fluorescent lights for reading lights and ceiling lights.

concentrator   A photovoltaic device that uses optical elements (such as mirrors or lenses) to increase the amount of light incident on a solar PV cell. Concentrator arrays track the sun and use only direct sunlight since the diffuse portion cannot be focused. Concentrators therefore work best in clear-sky locations. Efficiency is increased, but cell life may be reduced because operating temperatures are higher.

conductor   A material used to transfer, or conduct, electricity, often in the form of wires.

conduit   A pipe or elongated box used to house and protect electrical cables.

constant-speed wind turbines   Turbines that operate at a constant rotor revolutions per minute (RPM) and are optimized for energy capture at a given rotor diameter at a particular speed in the wind power curve.

contact resistance   The resistance between metallic contacts and the semiconductor.

controller   The controller regulates the current from solar charger to your battery bank.

conversion efficiency   The ratio of the electrical energy generated by a solar PV cell to the solar energy impacting the cell.

cross-flow turbine   A turbine where the flow of water is at right angles to the axis of rotation of the turbine.

crystalline silicon   A type of PV cell material made from a single crystal or poly-crystalline ingot of silicon.

current   The flow of electric charge in a conductor between two points having a difference in electrical potential (voltage) and is measured in amps.

current at maximum power (Imp)   The current at which maximum power is available from a module.

cutoff voltage   The voltage levels at which the charge controller (regulator) disconnects the PV array from the battery, or the load from the battery.

cycle   The discharge and recharge of a battery, one complete charge/discharge cycle of the battery.

cycle life   The number of discharge-charge cycles that a battery can tolerate under specified conditions before it fails to meet specified criteria as to performance (for example, capacity decreases to 80 percent of the nominal capacity).

days of storage   The number of days that a standalone system will power a specified load without solar energy input. A measure of system autonomy.

DC daily power budget   The number of watts your DC appliances use daily.

DC to DC converter   An electronic circuit that converts DC voltages (such as a PV module voltage) into other levels (such as load voltage). Can be part of a maximum power point tracker.

deep cycle battery   A battery designed to regularly discharge 80 percent of its capacity before recharging.

deep discharge   Discharging a battery to 20 percent or less of its full charge.

depth of discharge (DOD)   The amount of energy withdrawn from a battery or cell expressed as a percentage of its rated capacity.

diffuse insolation   Incident sunlight received indirectly because of scattering due to clouds, fog, particulates, or other obstructions in the atmosphere. The other component of sunlight is direct.

diode   An electronic device that allows current flow only in one direction.

direct current (DC)   Electrical current that flows only in one direction, although it may vary in magnitude. Contrasts with alternating current.

direct gain   In direct-gain buildings, sunlight directly enters the home through the windows and is absorbed and stored in massive floors or walls. These buildings are elongated in the east-west direction, and most of their windows are on the south side. The area devoted to south windows varies throughout the country. It could be as much as 20 percent of the floor area in sunny cold climates, where advanced glazings or moveable insulation are recommended to prevent heat loss at night. These buildings have high insulation levels and added thermal mass for heat storage.

direct insolation   Sunlight falling directly upon a collector. Opposite of diffuse insolation.

direct radiation   Light that has traveled in a straight path from the sun (also referred to as beam radiation). An object in the path of direct radiation casts a shadow on a clear day.

discharge factor   A number equivalent to the time in hours during which a battery is discharged at constant current usually expressed as a percentage of the total battery capacity; for example, C/5 indicates a discharge factor of five hours.

discharge rate   A measure of the current withdrawn from a battery over time, expressed as a percentage of battery capacity. A C/5 discharge rate indicates a current of one fifth of the rated capacity of the battery.

disconnect   A switch used to connect or disconnect components in a PV system.

distributed power   The generic term for any power supply located near the point where the power is used. Opposite of central power.

distributed systems   Systems that are installed at or near the location where the electricity is used, as opposed to central systems that supply electricity to grids. A residential photovoltaic system is a distributed system.

dopant   A chemical element (impurity) added in small amounts to an otherwise pure semiconductor material to modify the electrical properties of the material. An n-dopant introduces more electrons. A p-dopant creates electron vacancies (holes).

doping   Adding an impurity (dopant) to a material to modify its properties toward an enhanced effect.

downtime   Time when the PV system cannot provide power to the load, expressed either in hours per year or as a percentage.

dry cell battery   A battery that uses a solid paste for an electrolyte.

duty cycle   The ratio of active to total time, used to describe the operating regime of loads in PV systems.

duty rating   The amount of time an inverter can operate at full rated power. Some inverters can operate at their rated power for only a short time without overheating.

earth   Refers to physically connecting a part of an electrical system to the ground, done as a safety measure, by means of a conductor embedded in suitable soil.

efficiency   The ratio of output power or energy to input power or energy, expressed as a percentage.

electric circuit   The path followed by electrons from a power source (generator or battery) through an external line (including devices that use the electricity) and returning through another line to the source.

electric current   The flow of electrons measured in amps.

electrical grid   A network for electricity distribution across a large area.

electricity   The movement of electrons (subatomic particles), produced by a voltage, through a conductor.

electrode   An electrically conductive material, forming part of an electrical device, often used to lead current into or out of a liquid or gas. In a battery, the electrodes are also known as plates.

electrolyte   A liquid conductor of electricity.

electron volt   An energy unit equal to the energy an electron acquires when it passes through a potential difference of one volt.

energy   The ability to do work. Stored energy becomes working energy when we use it.

energy audit   A survey that shows how much energy you use in your house or apartment to help find ways to use less energy.

energy payback time   The time required for any energy-producing system or device to produce as much energy as was required in its manufacture.

environment   All the natural and living things around us. The earth, air, weather, plants, and animals all make up our environment.

ethylene vinyl acetate (EVA)   An encapsulant used between the glass cover and the solar cells in PV modules. It is durable, transparent, resistant to corrosion, and flame retardant.

extrinsic semiconductor   The product of doping a pure semiconductor.

fall   The vertical descent of water, usually measured in vertical feet. Also called "head."

fill factor   The ratio of a photovoltaic cell's actual power to its power if both current and voltage were at their maximums. A key characteristic in evaluating cell performance.

fixed tilt array   A solar PV array set at a fixed angle to the horizontal.

flat-plate PV   A solar PV array or module that does not contain concentrating devices and so responds to both direct and diffuse sunlight.

float life   The time (usually in years) a battery can maintain its stated capacity when kept at float charge.

flooded cell battery   A form of rechargeable battery with plates completely immersed in a liquid electrolyte. Most cars use flooded-cell batteries. Flooded cell batteries are the most commonly used type for independent and remote area power supplies.

flow rate   The speed at which water moves.

fluorescent light   A form of lighting that uses long thin tubes of glass which contain mercury vapor and various phosphor powders (chemicals based on phosphorus) to produce white light. Generally considered to be the most efficient form of home lighting.

fossil fuels   Fuels formed in the ground from the remains of dead plants and animals. It takes millions of years to form fossil fuels. Oil, natural gas, and coal are fossil fuels.

frequency   The number of cycles or repetitions per unit time of a complete waveform; in electrical applications usually expressed in cycles per second or hertz (Hz). Electrical equipment in the United States requires 60 Hz, in Europe 50Hz.

fresnel lens   A concentrating lens, positioned above and concave to a PV material to concentrate light on the material.

fuel   Any material that can be burned to make energy.

fuel cell   An electrochemical device that converts the energy of a fuel directly into electricity and heat and is therefore very energy efficient.

fuse   A fuse is a device used to protect electrical equipment from short circuits. Fuses are made with metals that are designed to melt when the current passing through them is high enough. When the fuse melts, the electrical connection is broken, interrupting power to the circuit or device.

gallium arsenide (GaAs)   A crystalline, III-V, high-efficiency semiconductor/photovoltaic material.

gel-type battery   Lead-acid battery in which the electrolyte is immobilized in a gel. Usually used for mobile installations and when batteries will be subject to high levels of shock or vibration.

generator   A mechanical device used to produce DC electricity. Power is produced by coils of wire passing through magnetic fields inside the generator. Most alternating current generating sets are also referred to as generators.

gigawatt (GW)   One billion watts. One million kilowatts. One thousand megawatts.

gigawatt-hour (GWh)   A measurement of energy. One gigawatt-hour is equal to one gigawatt being used for a period of one hour, or one megawatt being used for 1,000 hours.

glazings   Clear materials (such as glass or plastic) that allow sunlight to pass into solar collectors and solar buildings, trapping heat inside.

GPM   Gallons per minute.

greenhouse effect   The effect of Earth's atmosphere, due to certain gases, in trapping heat from the sun; the atmosphere acts like a greenhouse.

greenhouse gases   Gases that trap the heat of the sun in Earth's atmosphere, producing the greenhouse effect; the two major greenhouse gases are water vapor and carbon dioxide; lesser greenhouse gases include methane, ozone, chlorofluorocarbons, and nitrogen oxides.

grid   An electrical utility distribution network.

grid-connected PV system   A PV system in which the PV array acts like a central generating plant, supplying power to the grid. Also known as intertied.

ground loop   An undesirable feedback condition caused by two or more circuits sharing a common electrical line, usually a grounded conductor.

ground mount   A piece of equipment upon which solar modules are mounted.

halogen lamp   A special type of incandescent globe made of quartz glass and a tungsten filament, enabling it to run at a much higher temperature than a conventional incandescent globe. Efficiency is better than a normal incandescent, but not as good as a fluorescent light.

heat pump   Like an air conditioner or refrigerator, a heat pump moves heat from one location to another. In the cooling mode, heat pumps reduce indoor temperatures in the summer by transferring heat to the ground. Unlike an air conditioning unit, however, a heat pump's cycle is reversible. In winter, a heat pump can extract heat from the ground and transfer it inside. The energy value of the heat thus moved can be more than three times the cost of the electricity required to perform the transfer process.

hertz (HZ)   The frequency of electrical current described in cycles per second. Appliances in the United States use 60 HZ. Appliances in other countries generally use 50 HZ.

high voltage disconnect   Voltage at which the charge controller will disconnect the array to prevent overcharging the batteries.

hot spot   A phenomenon where one or more cells within a PV module or array act as a resistive load, resulting in local overheating or melting of the cells.

hybrid system   A PV system that includes other sources of electricity generation, such as wind or diesel generators.

hydroelectricity   Electricity created by water power.

hydrometer   An instrument used to measure state-of-charge (voltage) of a battery.

III-V (three-five) materials   Elemental materials that occupy groups III and V of the periodic table of the elements.

incandescent light   An electric lamp that is evacuated or filled with an inert gas and contains a filament (commonly tungsten). The filament emits visible light when heated to extreme temperatures by passage of electric current through it.

incident light   Light that shines onto the face of a solar cell or module.

independent power system   A power generation system that is independent of the electic grid.

infrared radiation   Electromagnetic radiation whose wavelengths lie in the range from 0.75 micrometer to 1,000 micrometers.

insolation   The amount of sunlight reaching an area, usually expressed in watt-hours per square meter per day.

insulation   Materials that prevent or slow down the movement of heat.

interconnect   A conductor within a module or other means of connection that provides an electrical interconnection between the solar cells.

inverter   An inverter converts DC power from the PV array/battery to AC power. Used either for standalone systems or grid-connected systems.

irradiance   The solar power incident on a surface, usually expressed in kilowatts per square meter. Irradiance multiplied by time gives insolation.

i-type semiconductor   Semiconductor material that is left intrinsic, or undoped so that the concentration of charge carriers is characteristic of the material itself rather than of added impurities.

I-V curve   A graph that plots the current versus the voltage from a PV cell as the electrical load (or resistance) is increased from short circuit (no load) to open circuit (maximum voltage). The shape of the curve characterizing cell performance. Three important points on the I-V curve are the open-circuit voltage, short-circuit current, and peak or maximum power (operating) point.

joule (J)   The energy conveyed by one watt of power for one second; a unit of energy equal to $\frac{1}{3,600}$ kilowatt-hours.

junction   A region of transition between semiconductor layers, such as a p/n junction, which goes from a region that has a high concentration of acceptors (p-type) to one that has a high concentration of donors (n-type).

junction box   A PV generator junction box is an enclosure on the module where PV strings are electrically connected and where protection devices can be located, if necessary.

junction diode   A semiconductor device with a junction and a built-in potential that passes current better in one direction than the other. All solar cells are junction diodes.

kilowatt (kW)   A unit of electrical power, one thousand watts.

kilowatt-hour (kWh)   One thousand watts acting over a period of one hour. The kWh is a unit of energy. 1 kWh = 3,600 kJ (kilo-joule).

lead-acid battery   A type of battery that consists of plates made of lead, lead-antimony, or lead-calcium and lead-oxide, surrounded by a sulfuric acid electrolyte. The most common type of battery used in RAPS (remote area power supply) systems.

life-cycle cost   The estimated cost of owning, operating, and disposing of a system over its useful life.

line loss   Voltage drop over the length of electric line wire. Line loss robs your system of power when wire is too small for the load being run through the line or when voltage is too low for the distance the power must travel.

linear current booster   An electronic circuit that matches PV output directly to a motor. Used in array direct water pumping.

liquid electrolyte battery   A battery containing a liquid solution of an electrolyte in a solvent (such as sulfuric acid in water). Also called a flooded battery because the plates are covered with the electrolyte solution.

load   Anything in an electrical circuit that, when the circuit is turned on, draws power from that circuit.

load circuit   The wiring including switches and fuses that connects the load to the power source.

load current   The current required to power the electrical device.

load resistance   The electrical resistance of the load.

low voltage disconnect (LVD)   The voltage at which the charge controller will disconnect the load from the batteries to prevent overdischarging.

maintenance-free battery   A sealed battery to which water cannot be added to maintain the level of the electrolyte solution.

maximum power point (MPP)   The point on the current-voltage (I-V) curve of a module under illumination, where the product of current and voltage is maximum. For a typical silicon cell, this is at about 0.45 V.

megawatt (MW)   One million watts; 1,000 kilowatts.

megawatt-hour (MWh)   A measurement of power with respect to time. One megawatt-hour is equal to one megawatt being used for a period of one hour, or one kilowatt being used for 1,000 hours.

micrometer   One millionth of a meter.

milliamps (mA)   One thousandth of an amp.

modified sine wave   A waveform with at least three states (positive, off, and negative) used to simulate a sine wave. It has less harmonic content than a square wave. This type of waveform is better than a square wave, but not as suitable for some appliances as a sine wave.

modularity   The use of complete subassemblies to produce a larger system. Also the use of multiple inverters connected in parallel to service different loads.

module   Modular solar electric charger; used interchangeably with solar electric panel.

monocrystalline solar cell   A form of solar cell made from a thin slice of a single large crystal of silicon.

monolithic   PV modules fabricated as a single structure.

multicrystalline   Material that is solidified at such as rate that many small crystals (crystallites) form. The atoms within a single crystallite are symmetrically arranged, whereas crystallites are jumbled together. These numerous grain boundaries reduce the device efficiency. A material composed of variously oriented, small individual crystals (sometimes referred to as polycrystalline or semicrystalline).

multijunction device   A photovoltaic device containing two or more cell junctions, each of which is optimized for a particular part of the solar spectrum to achieve greater overall efficiency.

multistage controller   A charge controller that allows different charging currents as the battery approaches full state of charge.

National Electrical Code (**NEC**)   The U.S. code specifying guidelines for all types of electrical installations, it should be followed when installing a PV system.

National Electrical Manufacturers Association (**NEMA**)   The U.S. trade association that sets standards for some nonelectronic products such as junction boxes.

net metering   The practice of exporting surplus solar power during the day to the electricity grid, which either causes the homeowner's electric meter to run backwards or simply creates a financial credit on the home owner's electricity bill.

nickel-cadmium battery (**NiCad**)   A rechargeable battery with higher storage densities than that of lead-acid batteries; it uses a mixture of nickel hydroxide and nickel oxide for the anode, and cadmium metal for the cathode. The electrolyte is potassium hydroxide.

nominal voltage   A rounded voltage value used to describe batteries, modules, or systems based on their specification (for example, a 12V, 24V or 48V battery, module, or system).

nonrenewable fuels   Fuels that cannot be easily made or renewed, meaning we can use them up. Oil, natural gas, and coal are nonrenewable fuels.

n-type silicon   Silicon doped with an element that has more electrons in its atomic structure than does silicon (phosphorus, for example).

nuclear energy   Energy that comes from splitting atoms of radioactive materials, such as uranium.

ohm   The resistance between two points of a conductor when a constant potential difference of one volt applied between these points produces in the conductor a current of one amp.

ohm's law   A simple mathematical formula that allows either voltage, current, or resistance to be calculated when the other two values are known. The formula is: $V = I \times R$, where V is the voltage, I is the current, and R is the resistance.

oil   A black liquid fossil fuel found deep in Earth. Gasoline and most plastics are made from oil.

one-axis tracking   A PV System structure that is capable of rotating on a single axis in order to track the movement of the sun.

open-circuit voltage (VOC)   The maximum possible voltage across a photovoltaic cell or module; the voltage across the cell in sunlight when no current is flowing.

operating point   Defined by the current and voltage that a module or array produces when connected to a load. It is dependent on the load or the batteries connected to the output terminals.

orientation   Position with respect to the cardinal directions, North, South, East, West.

overcharge   Applying current to a fully charged battery. This can damage the battery.

panel   Referring to photovoltaics, used interchangeably with module.

parallel connection   A way of joining two or more electricity-producing devices (PV cells or modules) by connecting positive leads together and negative leads together; such a configuration increases the current.

passive solar home   A house that utilizes part of the building as a solar collector, as opposed to active solar, such as PV.

peak load   The maximum usage of electrical power occurring in a given period of time, typically a day. The electrical supply must be able to be meet the peak load if it is to be reliable.

peak power   Power generated by a utility unit that operates at a very low capacity factor; generally used to meet short-lived and variable high-demand periods.

peak sun hours   The equivalent number of hours per day when solar irradiance averages 1,000 W per square meter.

photocurrent   An electric current induced by radiant energy.

photoelectrochemical cell   A special kind of photovoltaic cell in which the electricity produced is used immediately within the cell to produce a useful chemical product, such as hydrogen. The product material is continuously withdrawn from the cell for direct use as a fuel or as an ingredient in making other chemicals, or it may be stored and used subsequently.

photon   A particle of light that acts as an individual unit of energy.

photovoltaic (PV)   Refers to converting light into electricity. Photo means "light" voltaic means "electric." Often called PV for short. Also referred to as "solar electric."

photovoltaic array   An interconnected system of PV modules that function as a single electricity-producing unit. The modules are assembled as a discrete structure, with a common support or mounting. In smaller systems, an array can consist of a single module.

photovoltaic cell   The smallest semiconductor element within a PV module to perform the immediate conversion of light into electrical energy (DC voltage and current).

photovoltaic conversion efficiency   The ratio of the electrical power generated by a PV device to the power of the light incident on it. This is typically in the range 5 percent to 15 percent for commercially available modules.

photovoltaic effect   The effect that causes a voltage to be developed across the junction of two different materials when they are exposed to light.

photovoltaic generator   The total of all PV strings of a PV power supply system, which are electrically interconnected.

photovoltaic module   A single assembly of solar cells and ancillary parts, such as interconnections, terminals, (and protective devices such as diodes) intended to generate DC power under unconcentrated sunlight. The structural (load carrying) member of a module can be either the top layer (superstrate) or the back layer (substrate).

photovoltaic panel   Often used interchangeably with PV module (especially in one-module systems), but more accurately used to refer to a connected collection of modules (a laminate string of modules used to achieve a required voltage and current).

photovoltaic peak watt   The maximum rated output of a cell, module, or system. Typical rating conditions are 0.645 watts per square inch (1,000 watts per square meter) of sunlight.

photovoltaic system   A complete set of components for converting sunlight into electricity by the photovoltaic process, including the array and balance of system components.

photovoltaic-thermal (PV/T) system   A photovoltaic system that, in addition to converting sunlight into electricity, collects the residual heat energy and delivers both heat and electricity in usable form. Also called a total energy system.

p-i-n   A semiconductor device structure that layers an intrinsic semiconductor between a p-type semiconductor and an n-type semiconductor; this structure is most often used with amorphous silicon devices.

plates   The electrodes in a battery, usually taking the form of metal plates.

p/n   A semiconductor device structure in which the junction is formed between a p-type layer and an n-type layer.

polycrystalline silicon   A material used to make solar PV cells; it consists of many crystals, compared to single crystal silicon.

poly-vinyl chloride (PVC)   A plastic used as an insulator on electrical cables. A toxic material, which is being replaced with alternatives made from more benign chemicals

power   The rate of doing work. Expressed as watts (W). For example, a generator rated at 800 watts can provide that amount of power continuously.

power conditioning equipment   Electrical equipment, or power electronics, used to convert power from a photovoltaic array into a form suitable for subsequent use. A collective term for inverter, converter, battery charge regulator, and blocking diode.

power conversion efficiency   The ratio of output power to input power (of an inverter, for example).

primary battery   A battery that cannot be recharged.

p-type semiconductor   A semiconductor in which holes carry the current; produced by doping an intrinsic semiconductor with an electron acceptor impurity (such as adding boron to silicon).

pulse-width-modulated (PWM) wave inverter   PWM inverters are the most expensive, but produce a high quality of output signal at minimum current harmonics.

PV   Abbreviation for photovoltaic.

PV array   Two or more photovoltaic panels wired in series and/or parallel.

PV system   All the parts in combination required to generate solar electricity

quad   A measure of energy equal to 1 trillion BTUs; an energy equivalent to approximately 172 million barrels of oil.

quasi sine-wave   A description of the type of waveform produced by some inverters.

rated battery capacity (Ah)   A term used by battery manufacturers to indicate the maximum amount of energy that can be withdrawn from a battery at a specified discharge rate and temperature.

rated module current (A)   The current output of a PV module measured under standard test conditions of 1,000 W per square meter and 25°C cell temperature.

rated power   Nominal power output of an inverter; some units cannot produce rated power continuously.

rechargeable battery   A type of battery that uses a reversible chemical reaction to produce electricity, allowing it to be reused many times. The chemical reaction is reversed by forcing electricity through the battery in the direction opposite to normal discharge.

rectifier   A device that converts AC to DC, as in a battery charger or converter.

regulator   A device used to limit the current and voltage in a circuit, normally to allow the correct charging of batteries from power sources such as solar panels and wind generators.

remote area power supply (RAPS)   A power generation system used to provide electricity to remote and rural homes, usually incorporating power generated from renewable sources such as solar panels and wind generators, as well as nonrenewable sources such as petrol-powered generators.

remote systems   Systems off of the utility grid.

renewable fuels   Fuels that can be easily made or renewed and never used up. Types of renewable fuels are solar, wind, and hydropower energy.

reserve capacity   The amount of generating capacity a central power system must maintain to meet peak loads.

resistance (R)   The property of a material that resists the flow of electric current when a potential difference is applied across it, measured in ohms.

resistive voltage drop   The voltage developed across a cell by the current flow through the resistance of the cell.

resistor   An electronic component used to restrict the flow of current in a circuit. Sometimes used specifically to produce heat, such as in a water heater element.

reverse current protection   Any means of preventing current flow from the battery to the solar PV array (usually at night) that would discharge the battery.

sealed lead-acid battery   A form of lead-acid battery where the electrolyte is immobilized, either by being contained in an absorbent fiber separator or gel between the battery plates.

secondary battery   A battery that can be recharged; a rechargeable battery.

self discharge rate   The rate at which a battery will lose its charge when at open circuit (with no load connected).

semiconductor   A material that has an electrical conductivity in between that of a metal and an insulator. Transistors and other electronic devices are made from semi-conducting materials, and are often called semiconductors. Typical semiconductors for PV cells include silicon, gallium arsenide, copper indium diselenide, and cadmium telluride.

series connection   A way of joining photovoltaic cells by connecting positive leads to negative leads; such a configuration increases the voltage.

series regulator   Type of battery charge regulator where the charging current is controlled by a switch connected in series with the PV module or array.

series resistance   Resistance to current flow within a cell due to factors such as the bulk resistance of the cell materials and contact resistances.

series wiring   A system of wiring, for solar electric modules or batteries, which increases voltage. Series wiring is + to – (positive to negative).

shallow-cycle battery   A battery with small plates that cannot withstand many deep discharges (to a low state of charge).

shelf life   The amount of time a device, such as a battery, can be stored and still retain its specified performance.

shunt regulator   A type of a battery charge regulator that controls the charging current by a switch connected in parallel with the PV generator. Overcharging of the battery is prevented by shorting the PV generator.

silicon (Si)   A chemical element with atomic number 14, a dark grey semimetal. Occurs in a wide range of silicate minerals and makes up approximately 28 percent of Earth's crust (by weight). Silicon has a face-centered cubic lattice structure like a diamond. It is the most common semiconductor material used in making PV cells either traditionally in its crystalline form or more recently as an amorphous thin film.

sine wave   A waveform in which one variable is proportional to the sine of the other. The sine wave is the ideal form of electricity for running more sensitive appliances, such as radios, TVs, and computers.

sine wave inverter   An inverter that produces utility-quality, sine wave power forms.

single-crystal silicon   Silicon material with a single crystal structure. A common material for the construction of solar PV cells.

solar cell   The smallest basic solar electric device which generates electricity when exposed to light.

solar constant   The strength of sunlight; 1,353 watts per square meter in space and about 1,000 watts per square meter at sea level at the equator at solar noon.

solar electric   The preferred term used to describe something that uses sunlight to produce electricity. Photovoltaic is the more technical term.

solar energy   Energy from the sun.

solar-grade silicon   Intermediate-grade silicon used in the manufacture of solar cells; less expensive than electronic-grade silicon.

solar module   A device used to convert light from the sun directly into DC electricity by using the photovoltaic effect. Usually made of multiple solar cells bonded between glass and a backing material. A typical solar module would produce 100 watts of power output (but module powers can range from 1 watt to 300 watts) and have dimensions of 2 feet by 4 feet.

solar noon   The midpoint between sunrise and sunset; the time when the sun reaches its highest point in its daily arc across the sky.

solar power   Electricity generated by conversion of sunlight, either directly through the use of photovoltaic panels, or indirectly through solar-thermal processes.

solar resource   The amount of solar insolation received at a site, normally measured in units of kWh per square meter per day which equates to the number of peak sun hours.

solar thermal   A form of power generation using concentrated sunlight to heat water or other fluid that may then be used to drive a motor or turbine.

specific gravity   The ratio of the weight of a solution to the weight of an equal volume of water at a specified temperature; used with reference to the sulfuric acid electrolyte solution in a lead acid battery as an indicator of battery state of charge.

split-spectrum cell   A compound photovoltaic device in which sunlight is first divided into spectral regions by optical means. Each region is then directed to a different photovoltaic cell optimized for converting that portion of the spectrum into electricity. Such a device achieves significantly greater overall conversion of incident sunlight into electricity.

square wave   A train of rectangular voltage pulses that alternate between two fixed values for equal lengths of time.

square wave inverter   The simplest and the least expensive type of inverter, but which produces the lowest quality of power. The inverter uses switches that can carry a large current and withstand a high voltage that are turned on and off in the correct sequence and at a certain frequency.

standalone   A solar PV system that operates without connection to a grid or another supply of electricity.

standby current   The current used by the inverter when no load is active, corresponding to lost power.

stand-off mounting   The technique for mounting a PV array on a sloped roof, which involves mounting the modules a short distance above the pitched roof and tilting them to the optimum angle.

state of charge (SOC)   The available capacity remaining in the battery, expressed as a percentage of the rated capacity.

static head   The height of the water level above the point of free discharge of the water, normally measured when the pump is off.

storage density   The capacity of a battery, in amp-hours compared to its weight. Measured in watt-hours per kilogram.

substrate   The physical material upon which a photovoltaic cell is made.

sunspace   A room that faces south, or a small structure attached to the south side of a house.

superstrate   The covering on the sun side of a PV module, providing protection for the PV materials from impact and environmental degradation while allowing maximum transmission of the appropriate wavelengths of the solar spectrum.

surge   An excessive amount of power drawn by an appliance when it is first switched on. An unexpected flow of excessive current, usually caused by excessive voltage, that can damage appliances and other electrical equipment.

surge capacity   The ability of an inverter or generator to deliver instantaneous high currents when starting motors, for example.

system operating voltage   The output voltage of a solar PV array under load, dependent on the electrical load and size of the battery stack connected to the output terminals.

thermal electric   Electric energy derived from heat energy, usually by heating a working fluid, which drives a turbogenerator.

thermal mass   Materials that store heat within a sunspace or solar collector.

thermal storage walls   A thermal storage wall is a south-facing wall that is glazed on the outside. Solar heat strikes the glazing and is absorbed into the wall, which conducts the heat into the room over time. The walls are at least 8 inches thick. Generally, the thicker the wall, the less the indoor temperature fluctuates.

thick cells   Conventional solar cells in most types of PV modules, such as crystalline silicon cells, which are typically from 200 to 400 micrometers thick. In contrast, thin-film cells are several microns thick.

thin film   A solar PV module constructed with sequential layers of thin film semi-conductor materials usually only micrometers thick. Currently, thin-film technologies account for around 12 percent of all solar modules sold worldwide. This share is expected to increase, since thin-film technologies represent a potential route to lower costs.

tilt angle   The angle of inclination of a solar collector or solar module measured from the horizontal.

total daily power budget (TDPB)   In a DC system, the daily amount of watts your DC appliances use, plus the battery power allowance. In a DC and AC system, the daily amount of watts DC and AC appliances use, plus battery and inverter power allowances.

tracking array   A PV array that is moved to follow the path of the sun in order to maintain the maximum incident solar radiation on its surface. The two most common methods are firstly single-axis tracking in which the array tracks the sun from east to west, and secondly, two-axis tracking in which the array points directly at the sun all the time. Two-axis tracking arrays capture the maximum possible daily energy. Typically, a single axis tracker will give 15 to 25 percent more power per day, and dual axis tracking will add a further 5 percent.

transformer   Converts the generator's low-voltage electricity to higher voltage levels for transmission to the load center, such as a city or factory.

transistor   A semiconductor device used to switch or otherwise control the flow of electricity.

transmission lines   Lines that transmit high-voltage electricity from the transformer to the electric distribution system.

trickle charge   A charge at a low rate, balancing through self-discharge losses, to maintain a cell or battery in a fully charged condition.

two-axis tracking   A PV module mount system capable of rotating independently about two axes (vertical and horizontal).

uninterruptible power supply (UPS)   A power supply capable of providing continuous uninterruptible service; normally containing batteries to provide energy storage.

utility-interactive inverter   An inverter that can operate only when connected to the utility grid supply and an output voltage frequency fully synchronized with the utility power.

VAC   Volts alternating current.

VDC   Volts direct current.

VMP   The voltage at which a PV device is operating at maximum power.

VOC   Open-circuit voltage.

volt (V)   A unit of measure of the force, or pressure, given the electrons in an electric circuit. One volt produces one ampere of current when acting on a resistance of one ohm.

voltage drop   The voltage lost along a length of wire or conductor due to the resistance of that conductor. This also applies to resistors. The voltage drop is calculated by using Ohm's Law.

voltage regulator   A device that controls the operating voltage of a photovoltaic array.

Volt-ohmmeter (VOM)   An electrical or electronic device used to measure voltage, resistance, and current.

wafer   A thin sheet of crystalline semiconductor material made either by mechanically sawing it from a single-crystal boule or multicrystalline ingot or block, or by casting. The wafer is "raw material" for the solar cell.

watt (W)   The unit of electric power, or amount of work (J), done in a unit of time. One ampere of current flowing at a potential of one volt produces one watt of power.

watt-hour (Wh)   A unit of energy equal to one watt of power being used for one hour.

waveform   The shape of a wave or pattern representing a vibration. The shape characterizing an AC current or voltage output.

zenith angle   The angle between directly overhead and a line through the sun. The elevation angle of the sun above the horizon is 90 degrees minus the zenith angle.

Solar Resources

The following resources are supplied by the U.S. Department of Energy and other sources, and are current as of spring 2002.

First-Stop Solar Information

American Planning Association
1776 Massachusetts Avenue, NW
Washington, DC 20036-1904
Phone: 202-872-0611
Fax: 202-872-0643

American Solar Energy Society (ASES)
2400 Central Avenue, Suite G-1
Boulder, CO 80301
Phone: 303-443-3130
Fax: 303-443-3212
E-mail: ases@ases.org
Website: www.ases.org

Ask an Energy Expert
Energy Efficiency and Renewable Energy Clearinghouse (EREC)
P.O. Box 3048
Merrifield, VA 22116
Phone: 1-800-DOE-EREC (363-3732)
Fax: 703-893-0400
E-mail: doe.erec@nciinc.com

Center for Excellence in Sustainable Development (CESD)
U.S. Department of Energy, Denver Regional Office
1617 Cole Boulevard
Golden, CO 80401
Fax: 303-275-4830

Federal Energy Regulatory Commission (FERC)
Public Reference Room
888 First Street, NE, Room 2-A
Washington, DC 20426
Phone: 202-208-1371
Fax: 202-208-2320

National Association of Energy Service Companies (NAESCO)
1615 M Street, NW, Suite 800
Washington, DC 20036
Phone: 202-822-0950
Fax: 202-822-0955
Website: www.naesco.org

National Center for Appropriate Technology (NCAT)
3040 Continental Drive
Butte, MT 59701
Phone: 406-494-4572

National Center for Photovoltaics
National Renewable Energy Laboratory (NREL)
1617 Cole Boulevard
Golden, CO 80401
E-mail: ncpvhotline@mail.nrel.gov
Website: www.nrel.gov/ncpv

National Climatic Data Center
Federal Building
151 Patton Avenue
Asheville, NC 28801-5001
Phone: 828-271-4800
Fax: 828-271-4876
E-mail: info@ncdc.noaa.gov

National Renewable Energy Laboratory (NREL)
1617 Cole Boulevard.
Golden, CO 80401
E-mail: rredc@nrel.gov

National Technical Information Service (NTIS)
5285 Port Royal Road
Springfield, VA 22161
Phone: 1-800-553-6847 or 703-605-6000
Fax: 703-605-6900
E-mail: orders@ntis.gov
Website: www.ntis.gov

Solar Energy Industries Association (SEIA)
1616 H Street, NW, 8th Floor
Washington, DC 20006
Phone: 202-628-7745
Fax: 202-628-7779
Website: www.seia.org

Solar Energy International (SEI)
P.O. Box 715
Carbondale, CO 81623
Phone: 970-963-8855
Fax: 970-963-8866
E-mail: sei@solarenergy.org

Sustainable Buildings Industry Council (SBIC)
1331 H Street, NW, Suite 1000
Washington, DC 20005-4706
Phone: 202-628-7400
Fax: 202-393-5043
E-mail: sbic@sbicouncil.org

Urban Consortium Energy Task Force, Public Technology, Inc.
1301 Pennsylvania Avenue, NW
Washington, DC 20004-1701
Phone: 202-626-2400
Fax: 202-626-2498

U.S. Government Printing Office (GPO)
New Orders, Superintendent of Documents
P.O. Box 371954
Pittsburgh, PA 15250-7954
Phone Orders: 202-512-1800
Fax: 202-512-2250

Energy Efficiency Resources

Air Conditioning and Refrigeration Institute (ARI)
4301 North Fairfax Drive, Suite 425
Arlington, VA 22203
Phone: 703-524-8800
Fax: 703-528-3816
E-mail: ari@ari.org

American Council for an Energy-Efficient Economy (ACEEE)
1001 Connecticut Avenue, NW, Suite 801
Washington, DC 20036
Research and Conferences: 202-429-8873
Publications: 202-429-0063
E-mail: info@aceee.org

American Institute of Architects (AIA)
1735 New York Avenue, NW
Washington, DC 20006
Phone: 202-626-7300 or contact Ed Jackson 202-626-7446
E-mail: infocentral@aia.org
Website: www.aia.org

American National Standards Institute (ANSI)
25 West 43rd Street
New York, NY 10036
Phone: 212-642-4900
Fax: 212-398-0023
Website: www.ansi.org

American Nursery and Landscape Association (ANLA)
1250 I Street, NW, Suite 500
Washington, DC 20005
Phone: 202-789-2900
Fax: 202-789-1893

American Society for Testing and Materials (ASTM)
100 Barr Harbor Drive
West Conshohocken, PA 19428
Phone: 610-832-9585
Fax: 610-832-9555
E-mail: service@astm.org
Website: www.astm.org

American Society of Heating, Refrigerating, and Air Conditioning Engineers (ASHRAE)
1791 Tullie Circle, NE
Atlanta, GA 30329-2305
Phone: 404-636-8400
Fax: 404-321-5478
E-mail: ashrae@ashrae.org
Website: www.ashrae.org

American Society of Landscape Architects (ASLA)
636 Eye Street, NW
Washington, DC 20001-3736
Phone: 202-898-2444
Fax: 202-898-1185

American Society of Mechanical Engineers (ASME)
Headquarters: 3 Park Avenue, New York, NY 10016-5900
Service Center: 22 Law Drive, P.O. Box 2300, Fairfield, NJ 07007
Phone: 1-800-843-2763
E-mail: infocentral@asme.org
Website: www.asme.org

Association of Home Appliance Manufacturers (AHAM)
1111 19th Street, NW, Suite 402
Washington, DC 20036
Phone: 202-872-5955
Fax: 202-872-9354

Building America
U.S. Department of Energy
Office of Building Systems, EE-41
1000 Independence Avenue, SW
Washington, DC 20585-0121

Center for Energy Efficiency and Renewable Energy (CEERT)
1100 Eleventh Street, Suite 311
Sacramento, CA 95814
Phone: 916-442-7785
Fax: 916-447-2940
E-mail: info@ceert.org
Website: www.cleanpower.org

Efficient Windows Collaborative
Alliance to Save Energy
1200 18th Street NW, Suite 900
Washington, DC 20036
Phone: 202-857-0666
Fax: 202-331-9588
E-mail: award@ase.org

Energy Efficiency and Renewable Energy Clearinghouse (EREC)
P.O. Box 3048
Merrifield, VA 22116
1-800-DOE-EREC (363-3732)
E-mail: doe.erec@nciinc.com
Website: www.eren.doe.gov/consumerinfo/

ENERGY STAR Homes
Phone: 1-888-STAR-YES (782-7937)
E-mail: info@energystar.gov
Website: http://yosemite.epa.gov/appd/eshomes/eshaware.nsf

E SEAL Program
Edison Electric Institute
701 Pennsylvania Avenue, NW
Washington, DC 20004-2696
Phone: 202-508-5557
Website: www.eei.org/esg/e_seal/

Gas Appliance Manufacturers Association, Inc. (GAMA)
2107 Wilson Boulevard, Suite 600
Arlington, Virginia 22201
Phone: 703-525-7060
Fax: 703-525-6790
E-mail: information@gamanet.org

Institute of Electrical and Electronics Engineers (IEEE)
445 Hoes Lane, P.O. Box 1331
Piscataway, NJ 08855-1331
Phone: 732-981-0060 for inquiries; 1-800-678-IEEE (4333) for publications
E-mail: customer.service@ieee.org
Website: www.ieee.org

Lawrence Berkeley National Laboratory
Building Technologies Department
MS 90-3111
Berkeley, CA 94720
Phone: 510-486-6845
Fax: 510-486-4089

National Arbor Day Foundation (NADF)
100 Arbor Avenue
Nebraska City, NE 68410
Phone: 402-474-5655
E-mail: info@arborday.org

National Association of Home Builders (NAHB)
1201 15th Street, NW
Washington, DC 20005
Phone: 1-800-368-5242
E-mail: info@NAHB.com

National Fire Protection Association (NFPA)
1 Batterymarch Park
Quincy, MA 02269-9101
Phone: 1-800-344-3555 or 617-770-3000
Fax: 1-800-593-6372 or 508-895-8301
E-mail: custserv@nfpa.org
Website: www.nfpa.org

National Hydropower Association (NHA)
1 Massachusetts Avenue, N.W., Suite 850
Washington, DC 20001
Phone: 202-682-1700
Fax: 202-682-9478
E-mail: info@hydro.org

National Institute of Standards and Technology (NIST)
Building 226, Room 322
Gaithersburg, MD 20899
Phone: 301-975-5864
Website: www.nist.gov

National Spa and Pool Institute (NSPI)
Phone: 1-800-323-3996
Website: www.nspi.org/

Oak Ridge National Laboratory (ORNL)
Buildings Technology Center
P.O. Box 2008, MS-6070
Oak Ridge, Tennessee 37831-6070
Phone: 865-574-5206
Fax: 865-574-5227

Reducing Swimming Pool Energy Costs (RSPEC)
U.S. Department of Energy
Website: www.eren.doe.gov/rspec/

Sheet Metal and Air Conditioning Contractors National Association, Inc.
(SMACNA)
4201 Lafayette Center Drive
Chantilly, VA 20151-1209
Phone: 703-803-2980
Fax: 703-803-3732
E-mail: info@smacna.org
Website: www.smacna.org

Solar Rating and Certification Corporation (SRCC)
c/o FSEC
1679 Clearlake Road
Cocoa, FL 32922
Phone: 321-638-1537
Fax: 321-638-1010
E-mail: srcc@fsec.ucf.edu
Website: www.solar-rating.org

Sustainable Buildings Industry Council (SBIC)
1331 H Street, NW, Suite 1000
Washington, DC 20005-4706
Phone: 202-628-7400
Fax: 202-393-5043
E-mail: sbic@sbicouncil.org

Underwriters Laboratories, Inc. (UL)
Corporate Headquarters
333 Pfingsten Road
Northbrook, IL 60062-2096
Phone: 847-272-8800
Fax: 847-272-8129
E-mail: northbrook@us.ul.com
Website: www.ul.com

Volunteers in Technical Assistance (VITA)
1600 Wilson Boulevard, Suite 710
Arlington, VA 22209
Phone: 703-276-1800
Fax: 703-243-1865
E-mail: vita@vita.org

Financial Resources

Fannie Mae
3900 Wisconsin Avenue, NW
Washington, DC 20016-2892
Phone: 1-800-7FANNIE (732-6643)
Website: www.fanniemae.com/
Consumer website: www.homepath.com/

Federal Housing Authority (FHA)
U.S. Department of Housing and Urban Development (HUD)
451 7th Street SW
Washington, DC 20410
HUD's website: www.hud.gov/
EEM program website: www.hud.gov/progdesc/energy-r.html

Freddie Mac
8200 Jones Branch Drive
McLean, VA 22102-3107
Phone: 1-800-FREDDIE (373-3343)
Website: www.freddiemac.com/

Internal Revenue Service (IRS)
P.O. Box 25866
Richmond, VA 23260
Phone: 1-800-829-3676
Forms website: www.irs.ustreas.gov/forms_pubs/index.html

National Home Energy and Resources Organization (HERO)
4005 Poplar Grove Road
Midlothian, VA 23112
Phone: 1-800-373-2416
Fax: 804-560-9139
E-mail: n-hero@ix.netcom.com
Website: www.national-hero.com/

Renewable Energy Policy Project (REPP)
1612 K Street NW, Suite 202
Washington, DC 20006
Phone: 202-293-2898
Fax: 202-293-5857
Website: www.repp.org

Residential Energy Services Network (RESNET)
P.O. Box 4561
Oceanside, CA 92052-4561
Phone: 760-806-3448
Fax: 760-806-9449
E-mail: resnet@earthlink.net
Website: www.natresnet.org/

U.S. Department of Energy
Office of Energy Efficiency and Renewable Energy
Website: www.eren.doe.gov/financing/homeowners.html

U.S. Department of Veterans Affairs (VA)
Phone: 1-800-848-4904
VA Home Loan Guaranty website: www.homeloans.va.gov/

Solar Equipment Catalogs

AEE Solar
1155 Redway Drive
Box 339
Redway, CA 95560

Backwoods Solar Electric Systems
Planning Guide and Catalog
1395 Rolling Thunder Ridge
Sandpoint, ID 83864
Phone: 208-263-4290
Fax: 208-265-4788
E-mail: info@backwoodssolar.com
Website: www.backwoodssolar.com

Energy Saver's Catalog
Solar Components Corporation
121 Valley Street
Manchester, NH 03103
Phone: 603-668-8186
Fax 603-668-1783
E-mail: solarcomponents@yahoo.com
Website: www.solar-components.com

Jade Mountain Appropriate Technology News
Jade Mountain, Inc.
P.O. Box 4616
Boulder, CO 80306
Phone: 1-800-442-1972 or 303-222-3500
Fax: 303-222-3599
E-mail: info@jademountain.com
Website: www.jademountain.com

Kansas Wind Power Catalog
13569 214th Road
Holton, KS 66436
Phone: 785-364-4407
Fax 785-364 5123
Also publishes a wind-powered water pump catalog.

New England Solar Electric Inc.
Products Catalog
401 Huntington Road
P.O. Box 435
Worthington, MA 01098
Phone: 413-238-5974
Fax: 413-238-0203
E-mail: nesolar@newenglandsolar.com
Website: www.newenglandsolar.com

Off Line Catalog
Off Line Independent Energy Systems
P.O. Box 231
North Fork, CA 93643
Phone: 559-877-7080
Fax: 559-877 2980
E-mail: ofln@aol.com
Website: www.psnw.com/~ofln

Photovoltaic Power System Catalog
SunAmp Power Company
2020 West Pinnacle Peak Road
Scottsdale, AZ 85207
Phone: 1-800-677-6527 or 623-580-7700
Fax: 623-587-5714
E-mail: sunamp@sunamp.com
Website: www.sunamp.com

Positive Energy Conservation Products' Green Builder Catalog
Positive Energy Conservation Products
P.O. Box 7568
Boulder, CO 80306
Phone: 1-800-488-4340 or 303-444-4340
E-mail: info@positive-energy.com
Website: www.positive-energy.com

Sierra Sun Catalog
Sierra Solar Systems
563 C Idaho Maryland Road
Grass Valley, CA 95945
Phone: 1-888-667-6527
Fax: 530-273-1760
E-mail: solarjon@sierrasolar.com
Website: www.sierrasolar.com

Solar Components Corporation's Product Catalog
121 Valley Street
Manchester, NH 03103
Phone: 603-668-8186
Fax 603-668-1783
E-mail: solarcomponents@yahoo.com
Website: www.solar-components.com

Solar Depot Catalog
61 Paul Drive
San Rafael, CA 94903
Phone: 415-499-1333; for orders 1-800-822-4041
Fax: 415-499-0316
E-mail: staff@solardepot.com
Website: www.solardepot.com

Solar Design Catalog
AAA Solar Service and Supply, Inc.
2021 Zearing Avenue, NW
Albuquerque, NM 87104
Phone 1-800-245-0311 or 505-243-4900
Fax: 505-243-0885
E-mail: info@aaasolar.com
Website: www.aaasolar.com

Solar Electric.Com Catalog and Design Guide
Solar Electric.Com
P.O. Box 339
Redway, CA 95560
Phone: 1-800-777-6609 or 707-923-2277
Fax: 707-923-3009
E-mail: info@solarelectric.com
Website: www.solarelectric.com

Solar Living Sourcebook (11th Edition)
Real Goods Trading Corporation
360 Interlocken Boulevard, Suite 300
Broomfield, CA 95482-4004
Phone: 1-800-762-7325
Fax 1-800-508-2342
E-mail: realgood@realgoods.com
Website: www.realgoods.com or www.gaiam.com
Real Goods also publishes a quarterly newsletter that contains listings of alternative
energy products.

Sunelco Inc. Planning Guide and Product Catalog
100 Skeels Street
P.O. Box 787
Hamilton, MT 59840
Phone 1-800-338-6844
Fax: 406-363-6046
E-mail: info@sunelco.com
Website: www.sunelco.com

Regional and State Energy Resources

Arizona (ARISEIA)
2034 North 13th Street
Phoenix, AZ 85006
Phone: 602-253-8180
Fax: 602-253-3422
E-mail: Solar-Guy@msn.com

California (CAL SEIA)
P.O. Box 782
Rio Vista, CA 94571
Phone: 949-709-8043
Fax: 949-709-8044
E-mail: info@calseia.org
Website: www.calseia.org

Colorado (COSEIA)
2170 South Parker Road, Suite 255
Denver, CO 80231
Phone: 303-750-9764
Fax: 303-750-0085
E-mail: seiacolo@aol.com
Website: www.coseia.org

Federal Energy Regulatory Commission (FERC)
Public Reference Room
888 First Street, NE, Room 2-A
Washington, DC 20426
Phone: 202-208-1371
Fax: 202-208-2320
Website: www.ferc.fed.us

Florida (FlaSEIA)
145 Wekiva Springs Road, Suite 187
Longwood, FL 32779
Phone: 1-800-59-SOLAR or 407-774-9939
Fax: 407-774-9941
E-mail: flaseia@gdi.net
Website: www.flaseia.org

Florida Conservation Foundation (FCF)
1251 B Miller Avenue
Winter Park, FL 32789
Phone: 407-644-5377
E-mail: florida@sundial.net
Website: http://sundial.sundial.net/florida/

Florida Solar Energy Center (FSEC)
1679 Clearlake Road
Cocoa, FL 32922
Phone: 321-638-1000
Fax: 321-638-1010
Website: www.fsec.ucf.edu/

Great Lakes SEIA (IL, IN, MI, MN, OH, WI)
c/o Solar Works in Michigan
P.O. Box 414
Tustin, MI 49688-0414
Phone: 616-636-4995
E-mail: solarworks@wingsisp.com

Hawaii (HI-SEIA)
c/o R&R Services
P.O. Box 37070
Honolulu, HI 96837
Phone: 808-842-0011
Fax: 808-847-4938
E-mail: rolf@r7.net

Heartland SEIA (IA, KS, MO, NE)
13700 West 108th Street
Lenexa, KS 66215
Phone: 913-338-1939
Fax: 913-469-5522
E-mail: solarbeacon@E-mail.msn.com

MDV SEIA (MD, DC, VA)
1606 Lansdowne Way
Silver Spring, MD 20910
Phone: 301-920-0144
Fax: 301-920-0145
E-mail: info@mdv-seia.org
Website: www.mdv-seia.org

Mid-Atlantic SEIA (DE, NJ, PA)
c/o FIRST Inc.
66 Snydertown Road
Hopewell, NJ 08525
Phone: 609-466-4495
Fax: 609-466-8681
E-mail: lyle@solarhome.org

National Association of State Energy Officials (NASEO)
1414 Prince Street, Suite 200
Alexandria, VA 22314
Phone: 703-299-8800
Fax: 703-299-6208
E-mail: info@naseo.org

New England—Solar Energy Business Association
c/o Schott Applied Power
235 Bear Hill Road
Waltham, MA 02154
Phone: 781-684-6101
Fax: 781-890-2050
E-mail: neseia@ascensiontech.com

New Mexico (NMSEIA)
2021 Zearing Ave
Albuquerque, NM 87104
Phone: 505-243-4900
Fax: 505-243-0885
E-mail: chuck@aaasolar.com

New York (NYSEIA)
c/o ETM Solar
P.O. Box 67
Endicott, NY 13760
Phone: 607-785-6499
Fax: 607-786-3388
E-mail: etm@tier.net
Website: www.nyseia.org

Oregon SEIA
c/o The Energy Service Company
399 East 10th Avenue, Suite 207
Eugene, OR 97401
Phone: 541-302-6808
Fax: 541-302-6810
E-mail: esco@efn.org

Texas (TXSEIA)
P.O. Box 16469
Austin, TX 78761-6469
Phone: 512-345-5446
Fax: 512-345-6831
E-mail: R1346@aol.com
Website: www.treia.org

Washington (WASEIA)
6848 23rd Avenue NE
Seattle, WA 98115
Phone: 206-525-3969

Photovoltaic Periodicals

Photovoltaic Insider's Report
1011 West Colorado Boulevard
Dallas, TX 75208
Phone: 214-942-5248
This newsletter reports on developments in the PV industry in the United States
and worldwide.

PV-4 You-Connections Newsletter
Interstate Renewable Energy Council (IREC)
P.O. Box 1156
Latham, NY 12110-1156
Phone: 518-458-6059
E-mail: irec@irecusa.org
Offers consumer information on photovoltaic systems for consumers and small
businesses.

PV News, PV Energy Systems
4539 Old Auburn Road
Warrenton, VA 20187
Phone: 540-349-4497
PV News reports developments in PV technologies and applications from around the world, and includes information on markets, new technologies, policies, and projects.

Renewable Energy World
James and James Science Publishers Ltd.
35-37 William Road
London, NW1 3ER, England
This journal reports on applications of renewable energy technologies around the world.

Solar and Renewable Energy Outlook
KLA Publishing Group
7324 Bath Street
Springfield, VA 22150
Phone: 703-866-2844
Fax: 703-866-4397
E-mail: KLAGroup@aol.com
This newsletter (formerly *The Solar Letter*) is an international journal on all aspects of renewable energy.

Solar Software

aveSARC
Tait Solar Company
51 West 13th Street
Tempe, AZ 85281
Phone: 480-829-8422
Fax: 480-829-8619
E-mail: taitsolar@aol.com
Website: www.taitsolar.com
Calculates solar angles and average-day solar radiation intensities, and can estimate the relative impact of the sun on building materials, windows, and solar collectors.

AWNSHADE
Florida Solar Energy Center (FSEC)
1679 Clearlake Road
Cocoa, FL 32922-5703
Phone: 321-638-1000
Fax: 321-638-1010
E-mail: joann@fsec.ucf.edu
Website: www.fsec.ucf.edu
Calculates the unshaded fraction of diffuse sky irradiance or illuminance incident on a rectangular window for any given solar position coordinates relative to the window.

ENERGY SMART POOLS
Website: www.eren.doe.gov/rspec/software.html
Developed by the U.S. Department of Energy for swimming pool installers and/or owners to analyze pool energy consumption and project the potential savings of a variety of energy management measures and solar pool water heating systems.

ENERGY-10
Sustainable Buildings Industry Council
1331 H Street NW, Suite 1000
Washington, DC 20005
Phone: 202-628-7400
Fax: 202-393-5043
E-mail: sbic@sbicouncil.org
Website: www.sbicouncil.org
Enables building designers to optimize energy-efficient building strategies including daylighting, passive solar heating, insulation, improved windows, shading, high-efficiency mechanical systems, and other building components.

F-CHART
F-Chart Software
4406 Fox Bluff Road
Middleton, WI 53562
Phone: 608-836-8531
Fax: 608-836-8536
E-mail: info@fchart.com
Website: www.fchart.com
Assists in designing and analyzing solar space heating, domestic water heating, and swimming pool heating systems.

PVCAD
Photovoltaic Resources International
1440 West Meseto Avenue
Mesa, AZ 85202
Phone: 480-345-1686
Fax: 480-345-6698
E-mail: pvcad@primenet.com
Designs photovoltaic systems by using hourly simulations based on irradiance, temperature, and other factors. An Economic Analysis Option is available that estimates the lifecycle costs of energy from a photovoltaic system.

PV-DESIGNPRO
Maui Solar Energy Software Corporation
810 Haiku Road 113
P.O. Box 1101
Haiku, HI 96708
Phone: 808-573-6712
Fax: 808-879-5060
E-mail: sales@mauisolarsoftware.com
Website: www.mauisolarsoftware.com
Simulates photovoltaic system operation on an hourly basis for one year, based on a user-selected climate and system design.

PV F-CHART
F-Chart Software
4406 Fox Bluff Road
Middleton, WI 53562
Phone: 608-836-8531
Fax: 608-836-8536
E-mail: info@fchart.com
Website: www.fchart.com
Estimates monthly performance for photovoltaic systems with and without storage and utility feedback.

PVFORM
Photovoltaic Systems Assistance Center
Sandia National Laboratories
P.O. Box 5800
Albuquerque, NM 87185-0753
Phone: 505-844-3698
Fax: 505-844-6541
E-mail: pvsac@sandia.gov
Website: www.sandia.gov/pv/pvsys/pvsac.htm
A free photovoltaic system simulation program for standalone and grid-interactive applications. It simulates hourly performance for a one-year period.

PVWATTS
Website: http://rredc.nrel.gov/solar/codes_algs/PVWATTS/
An Internet-accessible tool developed by the National Renewable Energy Laboratory that calculates electrical energy produced by a grid-connected photovoltaic (PV) system for locations within the United States and its territories.

RETSCREEN
CANMET Energy Diversification Research Laboratory/Natural Resource's Canada
Website: http://retscreen.gc.ca
Available for free. Can be used to evaluate the energy production, life-cycle costs and greenhouse gas emissions reduction for various solar and other renewable energy technologies.

SHADOWS
Tait Solar Company
51 West 13th Street
Tempe, AZ 85281
Phone: 480-829-8422
Fax: 480-829-8619
E-mail: taitsolar@aol.com
Website: www.taitsolar.com
Predicts the length and direction of solar-related shadows cast by buildings, landscaping, or any other object. The program will handle sloped ground planes as well as horizontal.

SOLAR BENEFITS MODEL
Website: www.eren.doe.gov/solarbuildings/sbm.html.
A free spreadsheet developed with support from the U.S. Department of Energy that allows users to estimate the economic benefits of a solar water heating system.

SOLAR ENVIRONMENTAL BENEFITS CALCULATOR
U.S. Environmental Protection Agency
Website: www.epa.gov/globalwarming/tools/index.html#solarcalc.
Estimates the pollution reduction benefits of using solar photovoltaic, water heaters, and pool heating systems.

SOLAR-PRO (Version 2.0)
Maui Solar Energy Software Corporation
810 Haiku Road 113
P.O. Box 1101
Haiku, HI 96708
Phone: 808-573-6712
Fax: 808-879-5060
E-mail: sales@mauisolarsoftware.com
Website: www.mauisolarsoftware.com
For active solar water heating system design, simulation, and prediction.

SOLAR-2 AND CLIMATE CONSULTANT
Department of Architecture and Urban Design
University of California at Los Angeles
Los Angeles, CA 90095-1467
E-mail: Milne@ucla.edu
Website: www.aud.ucla.edu/energy-design-tools
Plots sunlight penetrating through a window with any combination of rectangular fins and overhangs, and can provide a printout of annual tables of percent of window in full sun, radiation on glass, etc. SOLAR-5 is a DOS-based tool that can simulate the performance of up to 40 different solar energy components in a building. It plots thermal mass, heat transfer, temperatures, daylighting, HVAC parameters, and fuel and electricity costs, and it estimates air pollution emissions.

SUN CHART
Optical Physics Technologies
P.O. Box 11276
Tucson, AZ 85734
E-mail: optics@srv.net
Website: www.srv.net/opt/sunchrt.html
Calculates the position of the sun as its apparent position changes from day to day and from latitude to latitude, and performs shading calculations and plots these shading diagrams directly onto a cylindrical sun chart.

SUN OR MOON ALTITUDE/AZIMUTH TABLE FOR ONE DAY
U.S. Naval Observatory's Astronomical Applications Department
Website: http://aa.usno.navy.mil/AA/data/docs/AltAz.html
Provides altitudes and azimuths for the sun for locations in the United States. This provides a simple way to determine if a landscape feature will shade a potential solar collector site.

SUN PATH (Version 2.0)
Florida Solar Energy Center (FSEC)
1679 Clearlake Road
Cocoa, FL 32922-5703
Phone: 321-638-1000
Fax: 321-638-1010
E-mail: joann@fsec.ucf.edu
Website: www.fsec.ucf.edu
Calculates the position of the center of the sun in the sky at locations, dates, and times specified by the user. Numerous calculation options are available.

SUNSPEC
Florida Solar Energy Center (FSEC)
1679 Clearlake Road
Cocoa, FL 32922-5703
Phone: 321-638-1000
Fax: 321-638-1010
E-mail: joann@fsec.ucf.edu
Website: www.fsec.ucf.edu
A DOS-based program that calculates the spectral distribution of solar irradiance and the integrated irradiances and illuminances for clear-sky direct beam, diffuse sky, and ground-reflected radiation incident upon an arbitrarily oriented flat surface.

WinSARC
Tait Solar Company
51 West 13th Street
Tempe, AZ 85281
Phone: 480-829-8422
Fax: 480-829-8619
E-mail: taitsolar@aol.com
Website: www.taitsolar.com
Calculates solar angles and clear-sky solar radiation intensities, and helps to estimate the impact of the sun on building materials and collectors.

Index

I-J

Q - R

S